Interreligious Friendship after *Nostra Aetate*

Interreligious Studies in Theory and Practice

Series Editors: Aimee Light, Jennifer Peace, Or Rose,
Madhuri Yadlapati, and Homayra Ziad

Palgrave's new series, *Interreligious Studies in Theory and Practice*, seeks to capture the best of the diverse contributions to the rapidly expanding field of interreligious and interfaith studies. While the series includes a diverse set of titles, they are all united by a common vision: Each volume advocates—explicitly or implicitly—for interreligious engagement, even if this involves a critique of the limits of this work as it is currently defined or embodied. Each volume provides models and resources—textual, theological, pedagogic, or practical—for interreligious dialogue, study, or action. The series models a commitment to religious pluralism by including books that begin from diverse religious perspectives. This does not preclude the publication of books dedicated to a specific religion, but the overall series reflects a balance of various faiths and perspectives.

Also in the series:
Dialogue for Interreligious Understanding: Strategies for the Transformation of Culture-Shaping Institutions
by Leonard Swidler

Interreligious Friendship after Nostra Aetate
Edited by James L. Fredericks and Tracy Sayuki Tiemeier

Interreligious Friendship after *Nostra Aetate*

Edited by

James L. Fredericks and Tracy Sayuki Tiemeier

INTERRELIGIOUS FRIENDSHIP AFTER *NOSTRA AETATE*
Copyright © James L. Fredericks and Tracy Sayuki Tiemeier, 2015.

Softcover reprint of the hardcover 1st edition 2015 978-1-137-47210-6

Fredericks, James L. "Masao Abe: A Spiritual Friendship." Spiritus 3.2
(2003), 219–230. © 2003 Johns Hopkins University Press.
Reprinted with permission of Johns Hopkins University Press.

First published in 2015 by
PALGRAVE MACMILLAN®
in the United States—a division of St. Martin's Press LLC,
175 Fifth Avenue, New York, NY 10010.

Where this book is distributed in the UK, Europe and the rest of the world,
this is by Palgrave Macmillan, a division of Macmillan Publishers Limited,
registered in England, company number 785998, of Houndmills,
Basingstoke, Hampshire RG21 6XS.

Palgrave Macmillan is the global academic imprint of the above companies
and has companies and representatives throughout the world.

Palgrave® and Macmillan® are registered trademarks in the United States,
the United Kingdom, Europe and other countries.

ISBN 978-1-349-50112-0   ISBN 978-1-137-47211-3 (eBook)
DOI 10.1057/9781137472113

Library of Congress Cataloging-in-Publication Data

Interreligious friendship after Nostra aetate / edited by James
L. Fredericks, Tracy Sayuki Tiemeier.
     pages cm.—(Interreligious studies in theory and practice)
Includes bibliographical references and index.

1. Catholic Church—Relations. 2. Christianity and other religions.
3. Friendship—Religious aspects. 4. Interpersonal relations—Religious
aspects. 5. Vatican Council (2nd : 1962–1965 : Basilica di San Pietro
in Vaticano). Declaratio de ecclesiae habitudine ad religiones
non-Christianas. I. Fredericks, James L. (James Lee), 1951– editor.
II. Sayuki Tiemeier, Tracy, 1975– editor.

BX1784.I57 2014
261.2—dc23   2014032488

A catalogue record of the book is available from the British Library.

Design by Newgen Knowledge Works (P) Ltd., Chennai, India.

First edition: February 2015

10 9 8 7 6 5 4 3 2 1

Transferred to Digital Printing in 2015

To Dana, Lauren, Olivia, and Xavier

Contents

Introduction

James L. Fredericks

Fifty years have passed since the promulgation of *Nostra Aetate* during the last session of the Second Vatican Council. We can now see that at least one measure of the greatness of the Declaration on the Relation of the Church to Non-Christian Religions is the abundance of interreligious friendships it has made possible. The present collection of essays bears witness to this happy legacy.

When it comes to behind-the-scenes intrigue, international diplomatic arm-twisting, theological fisticuffs, personal betrayals, shocking dishonesty, and downright skullduggery, *Nostra Aetate* has no equal among the documents of the Second Vatican Council. However, in the history of the declaration, one also finds friendships—often courageous and noble friendships—between Catholics and those who followed other religious paths. Without a doubt, the Declaration would never have come into being were it not for the friendships that inspired, nourished, and sustained those who labored on this council document.

On September 18, 1960, John XXIII and Cardinal Augustin Bea, SJ, met in the Apostolic Palace. The pope had made this biblical scholar the head of a Secretariat for the Promotion of Christian Unity, giving it the vague mandate to help non-Catholic Christians to "follow the work of the Council." At that meeting, Bea's mandate became considerably more complicated: he was now to facilitate reflection on the church's understanding of the Jewish people.[1]

The previous June, Pope John had spoken with Jules Isaac (1877–1963), a French Jew old enough to remember reading Émile Zola's "J'Accuse…!" on the kiosks of Paris.[2] Isaac had lost most of his family in the Holocaust. After the War, he joined with a small number of Christians and Jews in Paris to form a movement with friendship as its core: L'Amitié Judeo-Chrétienne de France—Jewish-Christian Friendship of France. Among his Catholic friends were Jean Danielou, SJ, and Jacques Maritain. Isaac was convinced that friendship (*amitié*) was the starting point from which

Jews and Christians could join together to correct "certain inexact theological conceptions, essentially opposed to the spirit of Christianity, and certain erroneous interpretations of the Gospel of Love that have led to anti-Semitism."[3] Isaac and the pope talked for only 30 minutes. During this time, he asked the pope to look on his yet-to-be-convened council as an opportunity for the church to address "the teaching of contempt (*mépris*) for the Jews."[4]

Bea began to form a subcommission within the Secretariat with expertise in Catholic-Jewish relations. Members would eventually come to include: Msgr. John Oesterreicher, of Seton Hall University, a pioneer in postwar Jewish-Christian relations; Abbot Leo Rudloff, O. S. B., founder of the Monastery of the Dormition in Jerusalem; and the Augustinian monk Gregory Baum, who was from a German Protestant family with Jewish roots. Baum escaped the Third Reich in a *Kindertransport* in 1939.[5] Many members of this group became close friends with members of the American Jewish Committee (AJC) and European groups such as L'Amitié Judeo-Chrétienne. Among their counterparts on the AJC were Rabbis Marc Tanenbaum and Zachariah Schuster. Claire Huchet-Bishop, a polymath Catholic member of L'Amitié, divided her time between New York and Paris. Among many other services, she supported Sister Rose Thering working at St. Louis University on an extensive study of supersessionist theology and offensive language in Catholic school textbooks, and coordinated Thering's work with the AJC in New York and Oesterreicher and the Secretariat in Rome. These are but a few Catholic members of the subcommission and their Jewish collaborators. In time, Bea's subcommission would include people with expertise in Islam, Buddhism, Hinduism, and other religions.

These Jews and Catholics were devoted to one another. They had to be, or the project could not have survived. Working against them were various powerful curial officials; Near Eastern bishops, fearful of their own governments; and reactionary Spanish, Italian, and Latin American prelates. Golda Meir and Gamal Abdel Nasser were both keen on influencing the work of the Secretariat. Not a few Jewish and Muslims organizations were steadfast in their opposition to the work of the Secretariat. There was even an informer working within the Secretariat, well compensated with monies laundered through a Swiss bank account, in the service of an organization that was ostensibly friendly to the Secretariat. Perhaps worst of all, during the terrible third session of the Council, when all seemed lost for *Nostra Aetate*, a prominent ally gave a reckless and self-promotional interview to a journalist that amounted to a personal betrayal of Cardinal Bea's friendship and played right into the long suit of the Declaration's worst enemies. Clearly, these Jews and Catholics had to have been more than colleagues to have survived such odds. Theirs was the steadfast commitment and personal devotion of genuine friends.

Soon, Bea needed expertise in Islam as well. For this, he turned, among others, to Georges Chehata Anawati, OP (1905–1994). Anawati was an Arab Christian, born and raised in Cairo, and a student of Louis Massignon at the Collège de France. Massignon not only trained Anawati in the most exacting historical-critical methods for interpreting classical Arabic text but also impressed upon him Islam's deep sense of hospitality, a value that he had learned firsthand during a harrowing ordeal in the Algerian desert. Even more importantly, Massignon passed on to Anawati his vision of Muslim-Christian friendship as a *hospitalité sacrée*, which seeks only to welcome and serve and not to change.

Returning to Cairo, Anawati became one of the founders of L'Institut dominicain d'études orientales in 1953. He wanted a Dominican house where he could practice Massignon's "sacred hospitality." The Institute was located a short walk from al-Azhar University, the greatest center of Islamic learning in the Muslim world. At al-Azhar, Anawati came to be deeply respected by students and faculty alike, even being awarded the title "shaikh" (master) as a facetious *sobriquet*. Anawati made the institute a house of collaboration and dialogue, but most of all, a place where Muslim and Christian scholars could come together in friendship in order to do their theological thinking in lively conversation with one another.[6]

Anawati even used the term "comparative theology." In 1948, with Louis Gardet, Anawati published a landmark study of Medieval Islamic *kalama* (philosophical thinking) in dialogue with Thomistic theology, with the subtitle, *Essai de théologie comparée*.[7] Early in their book, Gardet and Anawati state that their aim is "not to refute *kalam* in the name of a Christian theology," but "to comprehend and to compare." The book reflects, in no small measure, Anawati's conversations with his many friends at al-Azhar, some of whom he would eventually host as observers at the Council. Since interreligious friendships lie just under the surface of his experiments in comparative theology, it comes as no surprise to us that Anawati hoped to bring to this book what he said was "an attitude of profound intellectual justice, and beyond this, one might say an attitude of intellectual sympathy."[8]

The material on Islam in *Nostra Aetate* is nothing if not terse: 191 words in English, 133 words in Latin. The text mentions the oneness of God, submission to the will of God, Jesus as God's prophet, the esteem with which Muslims hold Mary, and the Day of Judgment. Bea hardly needed a distinguished scholar in the area of medieval Muslim and Thomistic theology to come up with a statement of less than two hundred words.

Bea needed someone who was known and respected among Muslims, especially Arab Muslims, and someone who could speak credibly and sympathetically for Islam at the Council.

For his part, Anawati quickly came to understand that he had been brought on staff as much for his skills in bringing people together as for his knowledge of Ibn Sīnā. Indeed, friends at al-Azhar immediately began to assist him in getting him access to Arab embassies in Rome. In November 1963, with the aim of demonstrating the theological (nonpolitical) import of the Secretariat's work, he brought together an audience of over two hundred Muslim and Catholic notables, including cardinals, curial officials, bishops, as well as an impressive number of Arab ambassadors, for a lecture at the Angelicum (the major Dominican university in Rome) titled, "L'islam à l'heure de la Concile: Prolégomènes à un dialogue islamo-chrètién."[9] Likewise, in 1965, working closely with his friends on the faculty, Anawati succeeded in arranging for Cardinal König of Vienna to give a lecture at al-Azhar itself. This was in March, before the opening of the last session of the Council. In arranging for König's historic lecture in Cairo, Anawati was already thinking well beyond the close of the Council, even before the start of the last session. The lecture was an opportunity for several prominent faculty members at al-Azhar to renew their acquaintance with his Eminence, whom they had met as observers during earlier sessions of the Council. Anawati's biographer, Jean-Jacques Pérennès, captures a good deal about this remarkable comparative theologian and his contribution to *Nostra Aetate* when he writes that Anawati's "intellectual engagement is supported and served by an extraordinary cordiality, a capacity for friendships that he valued, and in turn, loved beyond divergences of opinion."[10]

Perhaps the most affecting example of the friendships that contributed to the forging of *Nostra Aetate* has to do with a brief meeting, during the evening hours, in Rome, between a priest and a rabbi—Archbishop Johannes Willebrands was Cardinal Bea's chief secretary and Rabbi Marc Tanenbaum was one of the major representatives of the American Jewish Committee in Rome during the Council. This encounter between the two may have taken place during the dark days of the Council's third session, when the Declaration's many enemies, strange bedfellows all, were ascendant. The source materials are not clear about this.[11] During that third session, the Vatican Secretary of State, sensitive to the strident voices of Arab governments, had succeeded in significantly altering the schema. Bishops from the Middle East, fearful for their local churches, were lobbying strongly against any statement about the Jews. Theologically conservative, and in some cases, antisemitic, bishops from Latin America, Spain, and Italy were opposed to the schema in principle. Not a few observers were predicting that the Council's Coordinating Commission would have the statement on the Jews moved into the schema on revelation. Any material on other religions would be inserted into the schema on the church (the document that would eventually become *Lumen Gentium*). Others expected that the entire project would simply be given a quiet, unceremonious burial.

On a Saturday evening in Rome, after completing his preparations for liturgy for the following morning, Archbishop Johannes Willebrands was surprised by the ringing of his doorbell. Many years later, he would describe what was about to unfold as "one of the most significant and moving events of my life."[12] Waiting for him at his doorstep was his friend, Rabbi Marc Tanenbaum. The Rabbi had just finished synagogue services. Tanenbaum had not come to discuss the business of the Council. He had come to visit his friend. Willebrands led the Rabbi to his study. In silence, Tanenbaum opened up his satchel and produced his *tallith* (prayer shawl), placing it over Willebrands's head and shoulders. Then the Jew prayed words of blessing and comfort over his Roman Catholic friend. According to his diary, Willebrands could not find any words to say to Tanenbaum at that moment. Of course, as is usually the case in friendships, words are not really necessary to express one's deepest emotions.

Nostra Aetate would not have been possible were it not for interreligious friendships. The Declaration, which has been such a blessing to us for the last 50 years, takes on a greater depth of meaning when we appreciate the friendships that were present as its 41 sentences were being forged. As we reach and move beyond the fiftieth anniversary of its promulgation, let us read *Nostra Aetate* attentive not only to the friendships that made it possible but also to the friendships that it has made possible.

The pages that follow tell the stories of these interreligious friendships. There is a Muslim who has learned compassion by surviving the ravages of chemical warfare. There is a venerable Nigerian woman, ostracized by her Catholic village for following the African Traditional Religion of her youth. There is a Rabbi, cracking wise—very wise—about the Blessed Virgin. Some of our authors have joined with their friend to cowrite the story of their friendship. Other chapters tell the story of friends lost to distance and death. In no small way, *Nostra Aetate* has made all these friendships possible.

Now, all around the world, friends gather. Bread is broken. Tea is poured. Stories are told. Sometimes confidences are whispered and even tears are shed. Difficult questions find no satisfactory answer. Some questions cannot even be understood—at least not yet. Most importantly, faith is being shared among friends. Is this not the greatest legacy of *Nostra*

Aetate? We believe the essays collected in this book bear eloquent testimony to this happy truth.

As a final note, Tracy and I would like to thank Raymond Camacho, Karen Hernandez, Michael Robinson, and Eireen Ty for their hard work as our Rains research assistants. They have been invaluable throughout the process of editing this book. More importantly, they have become our colleagues and friends.

Los Angeles, 2015

Notes

1. The claim that Pope John asked Cardinal Bea to produce a document on the Jews is fanciful. The idea for a "declaration" emerged only through the conciliar process itself. For a synopsis of the drama that produced the Declaration, see Thomas Stransky, "The Genesis of Nostra Aetate," *America* 193.12 (October 24, 2005), accessed June 8, 2014, http://americamagazine .org/issue/547/article/genesis-nostra-aetate.
2. Émile Zola, "J'Accuse…!," *L'Aurore* (January 13, 1898). This open letter by Zola to the French president famously defended the innocence of Alfred Dreyfus, a French army officer and a Jew, who had been convicted of treason and who exposed the antisemitism of French society at the time.
3. Quoted from the report, coauthored by Isaac, of the historic Seelisberg meeting of August 1947. See E. Parenti, "L'Enseignement Chrétien et les Juifs, L'Antisémitisme et l'enseignement Chrétien," *Service Information Documentation Judéo-Chrétien (SIDIC) Periodical* II.1 (1969): 10–15, accessed June 8, 2014, http://www.notredamedesion.org/pt/dialogue_docs .php?a=3b&id=1281. All translations from the French are by James L. Fredericks.
4. For Isaac's own account of his meeting with John XXIII, see his unedited notes made available by C. A. Rijk and A. C. Ramselaar, "Evénements et personnes," *Service Information Documentation Judéo-Chrétien (SIDIC) Periodical* I.3 (1968): 10–14, accessed June 8, 2014, http://www.notredamede-sion.org/en/dialogue_docs.php?a=3b&id=1258.
5. John Connelly, *From Enemy to Brother: The Revolution of Catholic Teaching on the Jews, 1933–1965* (Cambridge: Harvard University Press, 2012), 241.
6. Jean-Jacques Pérennès, *Georges Anawati: Un chrétien égyptien devant le mystère de l'islam* (Paris: Cerf, 2008), 215–216.
7. Louis Gardet and Georges Anawati, *Introduction à la théologie musulmane: Essai de théologie comparée* (Paris: J. Vrin, 1948).
8. Gardet and Anawati, *Introduction*, 11.
9. Georges Anawati, "L'Islam à l'heure du Concile: prolégomènes à un dialogue islamo-chrétien," *Angelicum: Periodicum trimestre Pontificiae Studiorum Universitatis a Sancto Thoma Aquinate in Urbe* 41.2 (1964): 145–166.
10. Pérennès, *Georges Anawati*, 160.

11. See Johannes Willebrands, "Foreword: A Pioneer and Friend," in *A Prophet for our Time: An Anthology of the Writings of Rabbi Marc H. Tanenbaum*, ed. Ruth Banki and Eugene Fischer (New York: Fordham University Press, 2002), xvi. The text is ambiguous about the time of the encounter. The third session of the Council is likely.

12. Willebrands, *A Prophet for our Time*.

1

Learning in the Presence of the Other: My Friendship with Sara Lee

Mary C. Boys, SNJM

Sara Lee was my first houseguest when I moved to New York City in July 1994. About a week later, shortly after her return home to Los Angeles, she called, eager to tell me about a long conversation she had had with her seatmate on the plane. Not generally one to strike up a conversation during her frequent travels, Sara's initial exchange with the middle-aged businessman seated next to her concerned their flight status in view of an impending electrical storm. A considerable delay ensued, but once finally en route, their conversation continued, growing more personal. Having told him that she directed a graduate program in Jewish education, her companion confessed that while he was a Jesuit-educated alumnus of the College of the Holy Cross, he had long ceased to be a practicing Catholic. Realizing he knew nothing of the changes wrought by the Second Vatican Council (1962–1965), Sara reported to me that she began to tell him about some of the major shifts in the church's stances, particularly in the interreligious realm. Regaling him with stories of various Catholics she had come to know in the course of our friendship and collaboration, Sara laughed with amazement as she recounted their conversation.

We have no indication whether her testimony persuaded him to return to the Catholic Church, but her encounter bears witness to her own transformed understanding of Catholicism. Born in Boston in 1933 and raised in the largely Jewish neighborhood of Roxbury, Sara was immersed in Jewish culture; she had virtually no social contact with Catholics. Nevertheless, the church's enormous footprint in Boston raised her anxieties: "I felt on the margins, not because of the Brahmins [the wealthier White Anglo-Saxon Protestants], with whom I had no contact, but because of the pervasive Catholic culture and power Catholicism seemed to exercise."[1] Her brother Joel, in contrast, had contact with Catholics—but not the sort of encounter that makes for interreligious amity. Gangs of Irish Catholic boys from the nearby neighborhood of Hyde Park invaded Jewish neighborhoods, particularly during Jewish holidays, to beat up Jewish boys like Joel. On occasion, the Jewish gangs would reciprocate, but her brother's lifelong issues with Christianity suggest that the Irish gangs had the upper hand.

By the time Sara and I met in 1985, her initial feelings about Catholicism (and Christianity in general) had begun to change. A lonely year spent in Cleveland while her husband David spent long hours at the hospital in his surgical internship resulted in the unexpected gift of friendships with two young Catholic families. Like her, they also had a young child. This common experience initially drew them together, but it was the sharing of their own dedication as Catholics and their hospitality, especially around the Christmas holidays, that gave a face to the church and meaning to a tradition that had previously seemed so intimidating. In turn, Sara was the first knowledgeable, committed Jew whom they had known, and she had opportunities to share about her own identity.

Eventually, Sara and David settled in Los Angeles. Now the mother of three children, Sara also volunteered for Young Judea, a youth movement and camping program that had deeply shaped her own experience of Judaism. She became involved in the life of the synagogue, including teaching in congregational schools. When her husband died suddenly in 1974, Sara went to graduate school, earning degrees in education from the University of Southern California and from Hebrew Union College-Jewish Institute of Religion (HUC). Mentored by Rabbi Michael Signer, a medievalist with extensive involvement in Christian-Jewish dialogue, Sara deepened not only her knowledge of Judaica, but also the theological and historical complexities of the relationship of Judaism and Christianity.[2]

Upon graduating from the latter in 1977, she was invited to join the faculty of the Rhea Hirsch School of Education at HUC. In 1980, she became its director—a position she would hold for 27 years; she remains an adjunct faculty emerita. Collaborating with Rabbi Signer's interreligious work, she became active in the Inter-Seminary Retreat program that brought together seminarians from the various Protestant, Catholic, and Jewish seminaries and theological schools in metropolitan Los Angeles. She attributes this program with exposing her to Catholic liturgical life and developing friendships with some of the priests who served on the

faculty of St. John's Seminary in Camarillo. As an outgrowth of this program, she designed a project that placed Jewish educators in two Catholic
secondary schools to teach about Jews and Judaism, including Ramona
Convent Secondary School in Alhambra, which is sponsored by my own
religious community, the Sisters of the Holy Names.

Although she was traveling to Alhambra in order to supervise her
Jewish intern at Ramona, Cynthia Reich, Sara's initial interreligious
efforts were as yet unknown to me, then living across the country and
teaching at Boston College. That, however, would change. Rabbi Signer
had called me out of the blue in March 1985 to invite me to serve as
a guest scholar for the Inter-Seminary Faculty Retreat. Immensely persuasive and possessing a wonderful sense of humor, he was a hard man
to turn down. He coaxed this then just-tenured associate professor into
accepting a daunting invitation to lead sessions with diverse faculty,
many far senior to me. Having coaxed me into accepting, he arranged for
his colleague Sara Lee to brief me on the event, as she would be coming
to Boston to celebrate Passover with her daughter Aviva and her family
in early April.

Even at the distance of more than 28 years, I have a distinct recall of
greeting Sara in April 1985 on the porch of Boston College's Institute of
Religious Education and Pastoral Ministry. We talked so long that her
daughter, then in medical school with a small child, grew frustrated
when Sara was not ready at the time they had agreed upon for her ride
back. From the beginning, we intuited that we had two vital commonalities. Each of us was seriously immersed in our home tradition yet also
intensely interested in the other's tradition. Moreover, we spoke a common language of education, with a love of teaching and expertise in educational processes. About six weeks after our initial meeting, I flew to Los
Angeles, where Sara met me at LAX and hosted me in her home prior to
the Inter-Seminary Faculty Retreat.

At the time of our first face-to-face meeting, I had made only occasional forays into Jewish-Christian relations. One of my earliest published pieces was an essay on Elie Wiesel in 1978, but it was not until 1981
that I wandered more directly into the field with an article, "Questions
'Which Touch on the Heart of Our Faith,'" laying out seven concepts as
a "ideational scaffolding" that I believe to be "foundational to construct-
ing a more adequate understanding of Christianity's relationship with
Judaism."[3] A statement from the Catholic bishops of France in 1973 had
inspired the title, acknowledging that the continued existence and vitality
of Judaism "pose questions to us Christians which touch on the heart of
our faith."[4]

Recently revisiting that essay, I note that I had introduced it with the caveat it was an unfinished work, a "possible point of origin for a long-term project of rethinking one's understanding of Christian faith." Little did I know then that the "project" would become a lifelong quest for a way of living my Christian vocation in conversation with Jews and with determination to play a role in healing the wounds inflicted by Christianity's "tormented" history vis-à-vis the Jewish people.[5] Sara has been my vital conversation partner in this journey.

Unlike many writing for this volume, I did not focus my graduate work in the interreligious sphere; the field of comparative theology, in which I have considerable interest, but cannot claim expertise, developed after my own studies.[6] Although I wish I could have been more systematically educated for the Christian-Jewish work I have engaged in for the past 25 years or so, I am grateful that my background in New Testament has enabled me to draw upon the recent scholarship on Christian origins in light of Second Temple Judaism. And when it comes to my collaboration with Sara Lee, I prize also my learning and experience in the field of education, because ours has been a relationship forged through a partnership in the teaching-learning process. Moreover, my friendship with Sara has opened up many contacts in the Jewish world.

Sara and I stayed in touch in the years immediately following the Inter-Seminary Retreat. When our travels took us to the other's city, we took advantage of the occasion to have the other make a presentation to one of our classes or professional societies to which we belonged. We came to know one another's students and colleagues. Several of my doctoral students, for example, came to know Sara and developed great respect for her brilliance and commitment to Jewish education. When the National Association of Temple Educators met in Boston, Sara invited me to give a workshop. One summer I participated with her in the national conference of CAJE, the Conference for the Advancement of Jewish Education; I was the only non-Jew among three thousand Jewish educators on a campus in rural Georgia.[7] On another occasion, after I had led a session at the National Conference on Jewish-Christian Relations in Minneapolis, Minnesota, one of Sara's former students, Cynthia Reich (who had interned at Ramona Convent Secondary School) met with me and asked if I would encourage Sara to write. Her request spurred me to invite Sara to give papers with me at the Association of Professors and Researchers in Religious Education (APRRE), which we did in the early 1990s. We later collaborated in serving as guest editors of a journal, including writing the lead article, and ultimately in publishing a book in 2006, *Christians and Jews in Dialogue: Learning in the Presence of the Other.*

The Catholic-Jewish Colloquium

While over the years we have partnered in numerous workshops and consultations, it was particularly in imagining, planning, leading, and analyzing a three-year project, The Catholic-Jewish Colloquium, that we drew close and developed our notion of "interreligious learning" as a form of interreligious dialogue that emphasizes study in the presence of the religious other and encounter with the tradition embodied by the other. And while we have partnered in many other educational ventures since then—including serving as guest scholars at the Hong Kong International School—the colloquium was our most extensive project. Not only did it teach us a great deal about the relations between Jews and Christians, but it also served as a catalyst for a deep friendship.

In the course of our collaboration, we came to realize with new force the singular role of religious educators in forming religious identity. Religious and theological education within one's faith tradition not only offers the foundation for self-understanding as a member of that tradition, but it also influences attitudes toward the religious other. How teachers (and preachers) interpret the fundamental narratives of Judaism and Christianity has too often resulted in a reductionist or negative portrayal of the other—and contributed to a distorted and oversimplified version of the home tradition, especially in the case of Christianity.

Studies of Protestant and Catholic textbooks in the early 1960s had exposed the difficulties in each tradition in presenting the "out group." Too often the texts reinforced stereotypes or failed to foster adequate understandings of other religious, racial, or ethnic groups, with the narrowness and distortions especially evident in the treatment of Judaism.[8] Subsequent studies in the 1970s revealed that while some defects had been remedied, further work was necessary. For example, Gerald Strober's content analysis of Protestant teaching found that recent developments in Christian-Jewish relations were rarely incorporated into teaching materials and that few Protestant organizations reflected any substantial interest in out-group relations.[9] Eugene Fisher's analysis of American Catholic materials published between 1967–1975 (i.e., in the wake of the Second Vatican Council) showed that these texts were significantly more positive toward Judaism than had been earlier texts. Nevertheless, Fisher concluded, the residual prejudice was cause for concern.[10]

Such studies highlighted the importance of revising religious textbooks and teaching materials so that they provided more accurate portrayals of the religious other. While in agreement with the imperative of such revisions, Sara and I were more focused on working with the educators themselves. Reworking textbooks is only effective when the teachers who use them have transformed their own understandings. As much as we took advantage of opportunities to work with the students and professional groups, we were more interested in an opportunity for intense and extended work with religious educators, so we wrote a grant proposal for what we came to call the "Catholic-Jewish Colloquium."

In 1992, the Lilly Foundation, based in Indianapolis, granted us $142,375 for this colloquium, and we set about implementing the design we had outlined in the proposal. We hoped that both Catholic and Jewish participants would change their perspective on the other, although we anticipated that the specifics of the transformation would differ. We assumed that the challenge for Catholic participants would be to reconstruct their theology; the task for Jewish participants would be to understand the changes in church teaching that made possible a posture toward Jews that differed from previous epochs.

Our previous experiences had given rise to certain assumptions. The Catholics in our colloquium would likely be shaped by the prevalent view of Christianity as superseding Judaism, that is, that Jesus Christ and the life of the church had made Judaism obsolete. We anticipated that Jewish participants would come to the colloquium with some negative attitudes toward Christianity, shaped by their knowledge of history, including the centuries of rhetorical disparagement and physical violence. As Sara and I had already learned, whenever Jews sit down with Christians, history is always on the table. As we wrote to the colloquium participants:

> We need to look at the question of history and identity, that is, what happened to Christians and Jews on the basis of their interactions. For Jews, history has entailed constant interaction with Christians (and the church) as a minority (an often disenfranchised minority), and this has profoundly shaped self-understanding. For Christians there is less apparent shaping by its relation with Judaism, yet that relation has also been a preoccupation (witness John Chrysostom, the Crusades, blood libel charges, etc.). Perhaps this is to oversimplify, but one way of getting at the fundamental contours of our historical relationship is to say that for Jews, Christians and the church have been (and are?) the problem. For Christians, Judaism itself is the problem; Judaism's continued viability challenges supersessionism.

Although mindful of the lingering presence of historical memory, experience also taught us that transformation was more likely to happen in people who were studying in the presence of the other. So we designed our colloquium to facilitate encounter with the tradition as embodied in the other. Because we desired to transcend learning about the other in the abstract, we emphasized providing ways through which participants might encounter Judaism or Catholicism as it was lived by informed, committed Jewish and Catholic educators. Mindful that the sorts of changes in attitude and understanding we hoped for would develop over time and through interaction, we limited the size of our group to 11 professional religious educators in each tradition. Sensitive to the role played by religious symbols and the importance of hospitality, we selected a conference center in Baltimore that provided a neutral space, excellent seminar capabilities, and comfortable lodging.

In preparation for the first session in February 1993, we spent a year studying together, meeting whenever our schedules would allow. It was during that preparatory period, as well as in subsequent preparations, that our friendship deepened. Spending long periods of time in the presence of the other, talking about all manner of issues (both pertinent to the colloquium and beyond it), and sharing in one another's lives was immeasurably enriching. Because so much of Judaism is embodied in home and family life, no amount of time in the library could have replicated what I learned. I recall a remark Sara made once about how keeping a kosher kitchen was a daily reminder of her identity as a Jew. Over the years, I was privileged to share in Shabbat dinners and lunches; my role was to bake the challah, which I delight in doing. Participating in Lee family Seders meant hours of intense conversation amid a festive meal. When Sara received an honorary doctorate from the Jewish Theological Seminary of America, just across Broadway from Union, her children asked if they could use my apartment to celebrate this accomplishment, and I recall with pleasure the festive mood of the many guests who joined us that evening.

While it is certainly the case that sharing daily life together in one another's homes forged a close relationship, our collaboration in teaching formed the foundation of our friendship across religious borders. In the course of planning the six sessions of the colloquium, we resolved to confront differences as well as similarities in our traditions. Accordingly, as we planned together, it became important to explain central elements of our own life of faith to one another. Given the centrality of doctrine in Catholicism, our conversations often revolved around understandings of key teachings, such as the Incarnation and Trinity. Sara's probing questions prompted to me to read widely; as appropriate, I tried to frame my responses in terms that had resonated with Judaism. Once, after we had talked about the Holy Spirit, and I had gone about as far as possible with what I knew about analogies with the Shekinah, I returned home to read Catherine Mowery LaCugna's substantive study of the Trinity.[11] On occasion, I attended services with Sara, and she went to Mass with me. As part of our preparation for the third meeting of the colloquium in late 1993 on the topic of "Revisiting the History in the Presence of the Other," we spent a day together at the United States Holocaust Memorial Museum. Our emotional exhaustion—we had wept our way through several of the exhibits—was tempered by a bit of comic relief: the hotel in which we were staying was the site of a large bar mitzvah party, and Sara kept up a witty commentary on the excesses to which some Jews went in celebrating this life cycle event.

After the first meeting of the colloquium (February 21–23, 1993), we learned the importance of providing the occasion for what Diana Eck terms the "space and the means for the encounter of commitments."[12] We set up evening sessions in which participants had opportunity to share more deeply in small groups around their own practices and personal ways of living Judaism or Catholicism. Sara and I simply listened, and were deeply moved by what happened. One participant's testimony provides a glimpse of the power of the sessions. She had chosen to share a text from the Gospel of Luke (1:26–38) that narrates the Angel Gabriel's announcement to Mary that she will become the mother of Jesus. As she was reading the text, she later told us, "My throat closed, my eyes filled with tears and the letters blurred. I could barely continue." Looking at the faces of the two Jewish women in her group, she felt as if Mary were in the room: "Of course, I've always known that Mary of Nazareth, mother of Jesus, was a Jew. Only at that moment, however, did the fact of her Jewishness make an impact on me... To speak of Mary in the presence of devout Jews not only made her more alive in me, but also made the entire event of the Nativity more numinous.[13]

Establishing the time and atmosphere for colloquium participants to share about their own spirituality proved to be a critical element in the participants' learning, and helped to foster friendships that lasted beyond the last session in November 1995. As Michael Barnes, a Jesuit scholar of the religions of India observes, "Religion is less about what human beings actually do in worship and prayer, and much more concerned with what they take to be true."[14]

More difficult was helping participants to face the shadow side of their tradition. In particular, this meant considering how to help the Catholic participants confront a shameful aspect of the church while not paralyzing them with guilt. It also challenged us to present the Jewish experience without reinforcing Jewish victimhood and "the lachrymose conception of Jewish history," in the phrase of renowned historian Salo Baron.[15] Confronting the demands of facing the history of the Jewish-Christian encounter has been one of the constants of the conversations Sara and I have had—and this confrontation lies at the heart of relations between Jews and Christians in our time.

Moreover, the "tormented history" between Jews and Christians constitutes a significant distinction in the interreligious realm. Although tensions, ignorance, intolerance, bigotry, misunderstanding, and violence have been and remain a part of virtually every relationship between two religious traditions, these characteristics have been a constant in the Jewish-Christian relationship. Only in the past 50 or so years in the West have Christians and Jews been able to "get off the medieval battlefield," as one of our colloquium participants phrased it after we had studied history together. And facing history *together* was important. As another participant rather inelegantly put it, "You can't study history adequately with your own kind."[16]

Facing History: Auschwitz

Indeed. Thus, when I listened to my own growing desire to go to Auschwitz, I asked Sara if she would go with me. We had traveled to Israel together in 1997, including an emotionally draining day at *Yad Vashem*, the Holocaust memorial and educational center in Jerusalem. In accepting the invitation, she asked only that we also spend a few days in Prague in order to provide relief from the bleakness of the camps. That was a wise stipulation, and we were thrilled by the magnificence of that city. More memorable, however, was our day at Auschwitz, August 15, 2004.

Just as we entered the infamous gate at the entrance to Auschwitz I, with its inscription of *Arbeit macht frei* (work makes you free), Sara was drawn to a plaque in Hebrew, which she then read aloud. She had, it seemed to me, immediately and naturally identified with the Jewish victims of genocide.[17] Despite standing next to her, I felt at a distance, not so much personally, but as someone whose Aryan features and Gentile ancestry meant I would not have been sought out for elimination. As we went through the camps, I was preoccupied by the failure of the churches, not simply in the Shoah, but also in the centuries of rhetorical disparagement of Jews, as well as in the violence and persecutions of the High Middle Ages. I was acutely conscious of my membership in a church complicit in the Holocaust.[18]

Shortly after returning from Auschwitz, we spent the late afternoon and early evening talking in the bucolic atmosphere of the Planty, a park near to our hotel in Krakow. Recalling our conversation several years later, Sara wrote:

> As we talked in that sunny Krakow park, my strongest reaction was anger, not directed at my Christian colleagues or Christians in general, but

against the brutality of the Nazis who thought Jews were not worth a bullet. I felt outrage at those who had destroyed all the children, like my own, who were the Jewish future, and who deliberately created conditions that dehumanized people solely because they were Jews.[19]

Over the years, Sara and I have discussed many demanding and delicate questions—but the conversations themselves have not been difficult. To the contrary, our friendship allows us to probe in sensitive areas. We've discussed Catholic and Jewish perspectives on abortion. I have been at the dinner table when members of the Lee family have engaged in passionate debate about the State of Israel; to listen to their strong and conflicting opinions meant that I was trusted to understand the complexity of their feelings. Sara and I have talked at length about the effect of patriarchy in both our traditions; she has listened empathically as I have raged about the way Catholic Church officials demean and trivialize women, thereby alienating many and squandering our gifts. On more than one occasion when I needed to think through a topic, I've called Sara, knowing that I would gain valuable insights.

I regard our friendship as one of the great graces of my life. Not only has Sara been a terrific conversation partner and companion in many educational endeavors, she has enabled me to feel at home with Jews and to grow in my knowledge of Judaism. With her move into retirement and mine into academic administration, we will have less opportunity to teach together. Thankfully, retirement has returned her to the Boston area, and so we see each other with some frequency. She remains a source of wisdom for which I will always be grateful.

Sara, in this the year of your eightieth birthday, *ad multos annos!* And for our friendship, *Deo gratias!*

Notes

1. Mary C. Boys and Sara S. Lee, *Christians and Jews in Dialogue: Learning in the Presence of the Other* (Woodstock, VT: Skylights, 2006), 22.
2. For an appraisal of Rabbi Signer's contributions to Jewish-Christian relations, see Franklin Harkins, ed., *Transforming Relations: Essays on Jews and Christians throughout History in Honor of Michael A. Signer* (Notre Dame: University of Notre Dame Press, 2010).
3. Mary C. Boys, "Questions 'Which Touch on the Heart of our Faith,'" *Religious Education* 76.6 (1981): 636–656; citation, 638.
4. "Statement by the French Bishops' Commission for Relations with Jews, April 1973," in *Stepping Stones to Further Jewish-Christian Relations*, ed. Helga Croner (New York: Stimulus, 1977).

5. See Vatican Commission for Religious Relations with the Jews, "We
    Remember: A Reflection on the Shoah" (Vatican: March 16, 1998), accessed
    June 17, 2014, http://www.ccjr.us/dialogika-resources/documents-and-state-
    ments/roman-catholic/vatican-curia/278-we-remember. "The history of
    relations between Jews and Christians is a tormented one (III)."
6. See Francis X. Clooney, *Comparative Theology: Deep Learning across
    Religious Borders* (Malden, MA: Wiley-Blackwell, 2010). Comparative theol-
    ogy, he claims, "marks acts of faith seeking understanding which are rooted
    in a particular faith tradition but which, from that foundation, venture into
    learning from one or more other faith tradition. This learning is sought for
    the sake of fresh theological insights that are indebted to the newly encoun-
    tered tradition/s as well as the home tradition (10)."
7. Now called the NewCAJE, "Reimagining Jewish Education for the 21st
    Century," http://www.newcaje.org/about/leadership/.
8. For analysis of Protestant texts, see Bernhard E. Olson, *Faith and Prejudice*
    (New Haven, CT: Yale University Press, 1963). Catholic texts were analyzed
    in three doctoral dissertations: Sr. M. Linus Gleason, "Intergroup Relations
    as Revealed by Content Analysis of Literature Textbooks Used in Secondary
    Schools" (PhD diss., St. Louis University, 1958); Sr. M. Rita Mudd, "Intergroup
    Relations in Social Studies Curriculum" (PhD diss., St. Louis University,
    1961); and Sr. Rose Albert Thering, "Potential in Religious Textbooks for
    Developing a Realistic Self-Concept" (PhD diss., St. Louis University, 1961).
    The American Jewish Committee sponsored these studies. It also sponsored
    a study of Jewish texts by Bernard Weinryb, who found a relatively small
    sample of prejudicial portrayal of the out-group, and also found consider-
    ably less attention to it. See Bernard D. Weinryb and Daniel Garnick, *Jewish
    School Textbooks and Intergroup Relations* (New York: American Jewish
    Committee, 1972).
9. Gerald S. Strober, *Portraits of the Elder Brother: Jews and Judaism in Protestant
    Teaching Materials* (New York: American Jewish Committee, 1972).
10. See Eugene J. Fisher, *Faith and Prejudice* (New York: Paulist, 1977). Preceding
    the Fisher study, which had originated as a dissertation at New York University
    in 1976, was John Pawlikowski, *Catechetics and Prejudice* (New York: Paulist,
    1973), which made available the findings of the three St. Louis University
    dissertations. For a more recent analysis of selected American Catholic text-
    books, see Philip A. Cunningham, *Education for Shalom: Religion Textbooks
    and the Enhancement of the Catholic and Jewish Relationship* (Collegeville,
    PA: Liturgical Press, 1995).
11. See Catherine Mowery LaCugna, *God for Us: The Trinity and Christian Life*
    (San Francisco: HarperCollins, 1991).
12. Diana Eck, *Encountering God: From Bozeman to Banaras* (Boston, MA:
    Beacon, 1993), 195.
13. Julie A. Collins, "Can I Not Do To You as This Potter Has Done? Interreligious
    Learning and the Transformation of Religious Identity," *Religious Education*
    91.4 (1996): 468.

14. Michael Barnes, *Interreligious Learning: Dialogue, Spirituality and the Christian Imagination* (Cambridge: Cambridge University Press, 2012), 36.

15. See Salo Baron, *A Social and Religious History of the Jews*, vol. 10 (New York: Columbia University Press, 1983), 4. Baron's phrase has elicited a substantial literature.

16. Both participants cited in Mary C. Boys and Sara S. Lee, "The Catholic-Jewish Colloquium," *Religious Education* 91.4 (1996): 434. This entire issue, for which we were guest editors, was devoted to the colloquium. Among the authors were a number of participants; other essayists were academicians.

17. Most of the Jewish victims died at Auschwitz II (Birkenau), about a mile and a half from Auschwitz I, which housed Polish and Soviet prisoners, Sinti, gays, and lesbians.

18. The question of the complicity of the churches in the Shoah is a complex one. For my analysis, see my *Redeeming our Sacred Story: The Death of Jesus and Relations between Jews and Christians* (New York: Paulist, 2013).

19. Boys and Lee, *Christians and Jews in Dialogue*, 119.

2

Michael Signer and the Language of Friendship

John C. Cavadini

I believe there are two sorts of interreligious friendships. One is a friendship that arises from a situation of intentional interreligious dialogue. Friendship arises as a result of the dialogue, in this case. The other is a when people of different religions are friends, and discussion of religious matters arises within the context of a preexisting, or at least concurrently existing, friendship. I am not sure if this makes any ultimate difference, but it feels to me as though it does.

In the first sort of friendship, the dialogue is primary, and if the relationship goes sour, the dialogue fails. That is anything but a great outcome; still, others can carry on the dialogue. In the second sort of friendship, the friendship is primary, and if the dialogue goes sour, the friendship may fail. Unlike the dialogue, the friendship is unique and irreplaceable. Both sorts of friendships may be equally deep and satisfying, and perhaps they converge at some point in terms of the personal investments at risk, but if "all the way to heaven is heaven," as Dorothy Day loved to quote Catherine of Siena as saying,[1] then all the way to friendship is friendship, and the dialogue uniquely integrated into a personal friendship is simply one element in that friendship. It is hard to replicate outside of that friendship, and very difficult to speak about separately, though the fruits of insight gained from that friendship are more transferrable into the public domain. Nevertheless, these somewhat theoretical concerns do not diminish, but rather increase, the love and gratitude I would like to express.

My friendship with Michael was of the second sort mentioned above. It is true that he was appointed in the Department of Theology at Notre

Dame to a position that involved as its expectation participating in dialogue between Jews and Christians. And it is true that I met Michael in our common professional context and our entire friendship was conducted as colleagues. But Michael was appointed long before I became chairperson of the department and so our friendship had a few years to grow up on its own terms. It is also true that Michael was already professionally involved in interreligious dialogue, and I was not, and so, it is literally true that he taught me everything I knew about interreligious dialogue, in the context of a friendship that was not coterminous with dialogue.

The first time I saw Michael was the Spring before he had taken up residence at Notre Dame, just after he had accepted the appointment. We both happened to be speaking in the same session at the annual Medieval Studies conference at Kalamazoo. I was a junior professor; he was coming to Notre Dame to take up a chaired professorship. I felt preveniently intimidated and resigned to insignificance—until Michael started reading. His paper was conceptually lucid, well argued, and he read with a voice of ringing clarity. Michael had a very distinctive way of reading academic papers. He read loudly and earnestly, often looking up at the audience. It was slightly subversive of academic convention. Isn't he reading a little *too* loudly? But Michael was not reading, in the first instance, to establish an historical point about what Hugh of St. Victor had taught, though he accomplished that flawlessly, but rather, through that accomplishment, to communicate a spiritual truth that he had discovered through reading Hugh. The most important thing to Michael was to communicate this truth. His paper was, on that account, suffused with the warmth and solicitude for his hearers' understanding.

In retrospect, I think of a text that any medievalist would know, one Michael and I later had frequent occasions to discuss, St. Augustine's *De doctrina christiana* [On Christian Doctrine], with its insistence on the close connection between the two tasks of theology, the *modus inveniendi*, the research phase, and the *modus proferendi*, the phase of communication.[2] That afternoon Michael had performed their perfectly integrated connection. Yet I did not, that afternoon in Kalamazoo, think of the *De doctrina*, but only felt relief that my new senior colleague was not the kind of chaired professor who made a point of trying to intimidate junior colleagues. More than that, and gratefully, I recognized a great teacher speaking, someone who cared to communicate and who communicated caringly, someone with whom I knew would never be just a colleague and with whom I already felt a bond of friendship. I already loved Michael even though we had not yet spoken.

As it happened, Michael had been introduced by the session leader incorrectly. He had provided the audience with Michael's previous academic affiliation. With characteristic good humor and graciousness, Michael corrected the introduction. He pointed out that he had changed his institutional affiliation to the University of Notre Dame. Then, with a meaningful look in my direction, he added that this French expression, Notre Dame, if translated correctly according to postmodern categories of contextualization of the speaker, would technically come out as "the University of Their Lady."

I've never forgotten how funny that was at the time, but I often came back to that moment and reflected on it after one of our long conversations about texts in Origen or Augustine. I thought about it years later, when his cell phone rang and the ringtone was the Notre Dame fight song. Hmmmmm, I remember thinking. That was funny, too. But the very humor of it caused a flood of gratitude to well up in my heart. It may have been the University of "Their Lady" when talking to outsiders, but at home, with us, whom he had made his friends, at the University of Notre Dame, it was "Our Lady." Somehow, and in some way, Michael always managed to translate any technical, historical, or theological term into the language of friendship, which he spoke fluently. His whole act of coming to the University had been an act of friendship before it was an act of dialogue. Listening to the ring tone, I had been, I reflected, all the while, from the very first day, learning to speak the language of friendship with Michael, and in that context, learning to speak the language of interreligious dialogue. It was not, first and foremost, "Judaism" and "Christianity." It was, before that, Michael and John.

Can there be a real and true two-way spiritual exchange between people who disagree on fundamental religious claims? Can there be not simply an exchange of information about religious traditions, but also something else, a growth in wisdom or fundamental religious insight? And just to be clear, Michael and I did disagree on fundamental religious claims. As Michael once pointed out, in the context of explaining to me a paper he was writing on Jewish views of Jesus for a conference I was running—"Look John, I'm not sure what you are thinking, but from my point of view, as my mother put it once, Jesus absolutely never was, is not, and never will be the Messiah." "OK—Tell me what you really think!" (I remember thinking)—that seemed like a conversation stopper. But you know—it never was a conversation stopper, partly because it was just funny, the way he put it, and he had intended the humor. He was still speaking the language of friendship.

Why did I feel I could talk to Michael about these things? Not in the formal way appropriate to a public forum, but really talk to him, enthuse with him, worry with him, and yes, even argue with him? I did not feel the stiltedness of what is called "interreligious dialogue." That didn't mean, "anything goes." That is never true with a real friend, anyway. Still, I felt comfortable asking real questions, questions I really cared about, not the questions that "interreligious dialogue between Christians and Jews" are supposed to care about. I had a voice, my voice, not the abstract voice of a "dialogue partner."

Why? I felt comfortable speaking because despite a categorical rejection of my faith like the one stated above, I felt fundamentally un-rejected, or fundamentally received. And how can I explain this in a way that anyone else would understand?—I felt that this was true, not in spite of, but in a way that also included, my religious faith. I felt that that was included in the non-rejection, even though Michael did not believe it and in fact rejected it.

Isn't that what was included in the expression, said humorously but seriously, the "University of Their Lady?" "Humorously and seriously" meant "affectionately." It was an affectionate statement of disagreement. Somehow, it communicated love. Not just love of me—and indeed at that first meeting at Kalamazoo he hardly knew me—or love of what I believed just because it was me doing the believing and he loved me—there was something more—without believing the things I believed, he seemed to be able to have affection for them in themselves, nevertheless.

In other words, Michael was never patronizing. He never just tolerated the things I believed, as though they were intrinsically unbelievable and foolish and incredible, to be indulgently relegated to the realm of Lewis Carroll's Red Queen, who bragged to Alice that she could believe as many as *six* unbelievable things before breakfast. How could I put it? It wasn't *simply* that Michael loved these things as "things, however implausible, that John believes." But because he came as a friend first, with a legacy of previous friendship (and one must mention here Fr. Leonard Boyle, his doctoral advisor), he brought to the table an acquired empathy for things Catholic without being a Catholic. Michael did not send me a Christmas card, but every year he gave me a Christmas present. Michael could not only speak Latin and Hebrew and German, but he could speak Catholic. He knew the difference between a Dominican and a Jesuit; knew what a sacrament was; honestly sometimes I'd listen to him talk and think that if I didn't know Michael was Jewish, I would think he was Catholic.

Part of the reason for this is that the languages of Judaism and of Catholicism share a similar deep structure. Both are languages of liturgy, of practice, of law, of memory, of incorporation, and of the flesh, with the language of love, grace, and mercy spoken within the vocabulary of these other terms, and not overlaid on them, or ever severed from them. I learned this from listening to Michael talk. It was just as I might be waxing eloquent on this commonality in my mind—and Michael knew me well enough to see this happening—that he would say something like what I reported above about Jesus. This was not to mask or deny this shared deep structure of religious language (or "grammar" as some people might put it), but to remind me that the specific Catholic inflections of this language, involving Jesuits and Dominicans and the Incarnation and New Testament, were *not* his language even as he spoke it anyway. It reminded me that when Michael spoke this way, it wasn't simply speaking the language of Catholicism, but the language of friendship.

Michael could and did see something lovable, indeed precious, in something he did not agree with, and he wasn't afraid of feeling that or speaking out of it. You can't learn a language so well if you do not love it and the people who created it. That is why, as I thought about it, Michael could say he worked at "The University of Their Lady," or sometimes, jokingly with me, "The University of Your Lady." It wasn't his language, but he knew the language and could translate it in love. Thus, formally and materially, he spoke the language of friendship first.

Hearing the language of Catholicism spoken this way, I heard it differently. I heard it as an invitation to friendship, and therefore an invitation to think more deeply about it. If you accept an Augustinian account of signs and language, then you know that *how* a language is spoken, that is, in what spirit or "love" it is spoken, is "consubstantial" with *what* is spoken, and therefore what it means. What possibilities, across the range of its commonalities and differences with Judaism as Michael "spoke" it, can I hear within my own language that I did not hear before?

For example, in preparing for a departmental colloquium together, I had the role of working up a presentation on the homilies of Origen on Leviticus. The language of sacrifice, part of the shared deep structure of the grammar of Judaism and Catholicism, is the main subject for interpretation in these homilies. What does it mean? For Origen, Christ's sacrifice is the fulfillment of all the sacrifices prescribed by the Law, which thereby become "types" of that sacrifice. Origen's subtlety is everywhere present, resisting superficial readings of this language that would fail to leave any reader in some way uncomfortable.

Origen the preacher proclaims that he, as a man of the Church, can neither leave behind the Book of Leviticus and take the injunctions to perform sacrifice as nonbinding, nor can he follow its injunctions, as a man of the Church, literally. But no one who reads this text properly, even a man of the Church, reads without obeying the injunction of the Law to sacrifice. Reading *means* sacrificing, in this case, and this was always true of the text, because understanding the Law meant readiness to make the sacrifice required to root idolatry out of one's heart and to obey the Law. For Origen, reading itself becomes the locus, the outward occasion, for an inner sacrifice of interpretation that occurs in the heart, that always occurred in the heart, and that for him as a man of the Church, takes place over time, the more one reads in the spirit of Christ, whose whole life was the ultimate sacrifice and the fulfillment of the sacrificial law. Origen's point is that one knows neither the Book of Leviticus, essentially and interiorly, nor Christ, unless one's heart is configured, in and by reading it, to the sacrifice of Christ.

As I presented my results to Michael, a little gingerly because of the full-fledged Christian interpretation of a book so "Jewish" as Leviticus, I was surprised, even though I had now known Michael for years, at how much pleasure he took in listening to my interpretation and thinking about it. The word "supercessionism," which sometimes seems more like a conversation stopper and an unreflective formula than a positive contribution to advancing the discussion, did not come up. Michael did not engage in formulaic moralism with his friends, or at least, not with me. Here, we seemed to find what we began to call "shared access" to the truths of the text, meaning, in this case, Origen's text.

The Christian who obeyed the Law and "understood" it by reading in a way that sacrificed, in the "oven of the heart," all the fatty and fleshly parts of the soul, that offered the soul itself as a whole burnt offering, in some way really does understand the Law, which was never, and is not now, just fleshly, but always "spiritual," laden with meaning. The letter of the Law, the "body" of the text, and the sacrifices it describes, are a precious and indispensible covering for a mystery of sacrifice deeper than words in which we were both, in some way, bound, which we both, in some way, could "speak" despite its intrinsic ineffability. Christian triumphalism is Christianity that tries to escape this sacrifice even while using its language. We seemed to arrive at this conclusion together.

The world of academics is often a hard world. It seems especially disillusioning to be in a profession that speaks the language of "search for truth" and yet once "truth" is discovered it can seem to have value not so much because it is truth, but because it becomes, as soon as it is discovered, a signifier for the prestige of the discoverer. In academics we dwell on the length of our curricula vitae (CVs) and the prestige of the publishing houses our books find their way into, and we interact almost as walking CVs. "Have your CV talk to my CV."

Michael came into this world of academics not as a talking CV, but as a person. Like Moses, according to the Letter to the Hebrews as cited by Origen in the preface to *De principiis* [*On First Principles*], he chose, *rather to suffer affliction with the people of God* than to enjoy the pleasures of worldly prestige, that is, *to be called son of Pharaoh's daughter.*[3] Michael continually renounced prestige as an end, as anything but a dubious epiphenomenon of the search for empathy and insight, for understanding of the biblical language and of the Jewish and Catholic traditions of interpretation, for seeking "shared access" if not agreement. That meant many of Michael's major accomplishments were not entered into his CV. They were never lost, however, for they were emblazoned instead in the hearts of colleagues and students, almost in inverse proportion to the extent they did not get on his CV, because it was the *choice* "rather to suffer affliction with the people of God" than to enjoy the prestige "of being called the son of Pharaoh's daughter" that was the emblazoning fire.

We did not talk a lot about the phrase *people of God* and who could claim it. Michael was fond of the Augustinian metaphor, taken up into *Lumen Gentium*, of the pilgrim people, and he referred to the Church as the people of God on pilgrimage. Eventually the pilgrim people and the people of God who is Israel would meet, at the end of the pilgrimage. An interesting idea...let's talk it over...but all of a sudden I would realize, there he goes again! Speaking my Catholic language seemingly effortlessly, so effortlessly that I could and unfortunately did take it for granted, and yet it cost him. It cost him to speak it, and to speak it without drawing attention to the fact, and therefore seemingly effortlessly. He *chose rather to suffer affliction with the people of God*. Did that include me, for Michael?

Origen invokes the text from Hebrews to show that "Christ the Word of God was in Moses and the prophets." But he shows that reverse is true, too, because we do not fully understand what the spirit of Christ is unless we study Moses, who eschewed the prestige of *being called the son of Pharaoh's daughter* and preferred to *suffer affliction with the people of God*. Anyone who studied Michael, who listened carefully, watched him, walked to class with him, gradually discerned, and could come to understand, this *choice*. There is a cost to preferring the quest for truth over prestige. There is a cost, too, for allowing a new solidarity into one's heart, even as an older solidarity remains in full and loving force. If, in that way, you immerse yourself in another language, there is a kind of isolation one can feel precisely because people do not hear the "cost" of their own language being spoken by someone whose language it is not.

Michael taught me that if one can learn to absorb that cost into one's own heart, one moves beyond moralism, one moves beyond formulas, and contemplates a mystery. Christians believe this mystery has been fully revealed in the Word made flesh, but Christians also believe, as the *Catechism* points out, that this mystery is too deep ever to be fully plumbed, and only yields itself to "understanding" as the ages go forward and believers ponder different and ever deeper aspects.[4] This often occurs in conversations with friends.

Michael taught me the meaning of spiritual and intellectual generosity, which did not sacrifice frankness for sentiment, but at the same time did not confuse frankness with contempt. As I already mentioned, I felt that in his presence I could, however haltingly, have real thoughts, think my own actual thoughts, and not the thoughts that someone else expected me to think. Again, why? Because someone who pays the "cost" of solidarity, who chooses the *affliction* that this inevitably entails, by that choice creates space in which others feel permitted to be themselves. I think that is the meaning of spiritual and intellectual generosity, the willingness to pay that cost.

Michael was a very handsome man, but he had a walleye. One of his eyes listed to the side. It did not mar his looks, and to me, if I can put it this way, it was beautiful. To me, his friend, it was an expression of his spiritual substance. It was as though he were always looking at something so great you could not see it by looking at it directly, yet he looked anyway. Everything else he saw, he saw within that vision. He paid the cost of vision. By paying it, he left space for people and things to be seen as they were, recognized, not objectified, received, unmocked, and unjudged. It wasn't a vision limited to what is sometimes called, unreflectively, "unconditional love," for that implies there are no expectations contained in the love. Rather, Michael made you want to actually be as good as he "saw" you already to be.

I would like Michael to have the last word here. I would like the reader to hear his voice as I heard it. So, I will close with a message he sent to me on November 1, 2007. Guess what the subject line was? "Some Thoughts for All Saints' Day!" which is, of course, November 1. Note that he was speaking Catholic again. He did not say, "Some Thoughts for Your Holiday," or "Some Thoughts for What Catholics Call All Saints' Day." He reached out. He let it be All Saints' Day.

Could he, a Rabbi, teach me, a Catholic, about All Saints' Day? I will let the reader judge—and add here to Michael—you not only taught me something about All Saints' Day, but also about Judaism, about life, about love, and in a way I hardly expected to be so significant so soon, about how properly to remember and honor the dead:

Dear John,

Living in this world of Notre Dame often gives me pause to reflect on ways that Catholicism moves me to think more deeply about my own Judaism. The notion of living with those past and present is clearly at the heart of All Saints' Day. Within Judaism we tend to focus on our response to the divine commandments, but there is also room to reflect on those who have gone before us. One can, and indeed, does have memorial prayers on Yom

Kippur and the three pilgrimage festivals where we recall our martyrs and those in our own families whose exemplary lives stand before us. We honor them with reciting the Kaddish prayer. In one's own calendar year there is the opportunity to mark the anniversary of the death of a loved one—called "Yahrzeit"—by attending a synagogue service and reciting the Kaddish in the presence of the congregation. We are, as it were, witnesses to their lives—and on those moments we stand before God and the members of our community as testimony that their lives and their transmission of the heritage was not in vain…In moments of my isolation here at Notre Dame, I recall their names and what they did to help me enter into the Jewish community. Today, on All Saints' Day, I offer up this memory as a testimony of gratitude to them—one is never really alone, the souls of the departed need only to be named and recalled…

So, praise God for the living and the dead. Praise God for the glory of humankind acting in love and justice.

Thank you,
Michael

*   *   *

Thank YOU, Michael! You could have published something so beautiful and entered it onto your CV! But you preferred to write in friendship, *as* friendship. No matter what language you were speaking, it was always the language of friendship.

With the praise of God in mind, Michael, I now remember, and will ever remember, you.

With Love and Gratitude,
Your colleague, as always,
JC

Notes

1. See Dorothy Day, "All the Way to Heaven is Heaven," *The Catholic Worker* (June 1948), accessed June 10, 2014, http://www.catholicworker.org/dorothy-day/daytext.cfm?TextID=159.
2. Augustine, *De doctrina christiana*, 1.1.1.
3. Origen, *De Principiis*, P.1; Hebrews 11:24.
4. *Catechism of the Catholic Church*, 66, accessed June 23, 2014, http://www.vatican.va/archive/ENG0015/_INDEX.HTM.

3

The Blessing of Sitting Together*

Elena Procario-Foley

On October 28, 2015, the Roman Catholic Church will mark the fiftieth anniversary of the promulgation of the Declaration on the Church's Relation to Non-Christian Religions. Referred to more regularly by its incipit, *Nostra Aetate*, this document of the Second Vatican Council famously states in part four that "in her rejection of every persecution against any man, the Church, mindful of the patrimony she shares with the Jews and moved not by political reasons but by the Gospel's spiritual love, decries hatred, persecutions, displays of anti-Semitism, directed against Jews at any time and by anyone."[1] One wonders if the Church had awakened to its "common spiritual patrimony" with Judaism and condemned antisemitism, for instance, at Vatican I instead of in 1965 whether the Holocaust could have happened. To be sure, there were factors other than Christian anti-Judaism also driving the success of Hitler's war against the Jews, but it was at least, as Claremont philosopher John Roth has taught, a necessary if not a sufficient cause of the Holocaust.

I was interested in the Holocaust as a child, though I cannot recall what sparked my initial interest. *Night*, *The Diary of Anne Frank*, and *The Hiding Place* occupied my attention, but neither public school nor religious education addressed the Holocaust. No one told me about *Nostra Aetate*, but I knew antisemitism was wrong even though I never heard a homily at Mass or was taught in a religious education class about Christian responsibility for the Holocaust, the Shoah. Certainly, priests and religious educators never raised the question of the relationship between Judaism and Christianity in any context.

A major in theology from a Catholic university subsequently afforded me the barest of preparations for engaging in ecumenical and interreligious dialogue once I reached divinity school and, again, the Holocaust and Jewish-Christian relations were not curricular issues. As a wet-behind-the-ears graduate student, my attention was narrowly and naively focused: I thought that if I studied Christology carefully enough I would unlock the truth of Christianity and of life. At least I was smart enough to know that I did not yet know this truth, but I was ignorant enough to think that a classical study of Christology alone, whether through Roman Catholic or Protestant lenses, would suffice in itself to yield an assumed and idealized truth. By the end of graduate school, Paul Knitter's *No Other Name*, courses with an orthodox Jewish professor of biblical literature, and my dissertation that argued for a dialectical relationship between orthodoxy and orthopraxy had moved me quite a distance away from my first year's exclusive emphasis on deductive analysis. My position had shifted, but I was still missing a crucial component of a quest for religious truth: being with and for another in a radically plural religious world—walking, sitting, dwelling together as one.

Fast forward several years later, and I found myself in the position of creating a program in Jewish-Catholic studies at the college where I am employed. And it was there that the phone rang one quiet afternoon and a gentleman named William Donat inquired if he could speak with me. I met Bill over a telephone conversation just a few short years before e-mail became the de rigueur mode of self-introductions to strangers. I remain ever so glad that Bill chose to call because any other mode of communication would have elided his earnest and serious, but tentative, tone. In a traditional letter or email, I may have missed his friendly warmth conveyed by a cultured voice. In the written word, I surely would have missed the soft notes of hopefulness the conversation held for him, notes that I heard in the distance, but could not yet comprehend. Or worse, I might have placed mail from a total stranger at the bottom of the in-box and lost track of it—and that would have been a major loss.

Mr. William H. Donat, child survivor of the Shoah, called me because he read in the newspaper that my institution had established a chair in Jewish-Catholic Studies. I was still a neophyte teacher, the program was brand new, and I had not yet constructed a robust network of professional relationships. I admit that I felt somewhat shocked to be speaking to a survivor as I had no previous meaningful contact with survivors. Mr. Donat explained that he called to inquire about the new chair and to offer his assistance if the Jewish-Catholic Studies program would include education about the Holocaust. He was quick, however, to qualify his words and to assure me that he knew I needed time to assess his qualifications. If I should find him acceptable, he was ready and willing to discuss possibilities. I was, again, rather dumbfounded—*if I should find him acceptable*—who was I to find him, a Holocaust survivor, "acceptable," to judge him? He offered to come to a meeting and to submit a resume and references. I stumbled over my words assenting to his suggestion, trying my best to act my part though I felt quite inadequate to the task. We set up a meeting that turned out to be the beginning of a blessed decade of sitting and walking together.

Mr. Donat quickly became Bill, but not in that first meeting. For far from the requisite social conventions that one a generation younger should afford the older person the respect of the formal title, Bill's life and entire demeanor immediately elicited profound respect for he was a truly humble man. Despite his urging, it took me a while to be able to use the informal and personal "Bill." I revered the man and the formal appellation was one way to demonstrate my enduring respect. We talked for a very long time the first day we met in my office. Armed with resume and references, Bill was impeccably dressed for this was a business meeting and I quickly learned that there were no "casual Fridays" for Bill. He was a consummate professional. His sense of professionalism was central to his whole person; though it did not limit or completely define him, it was one of the ways by which he remained deeply connected to his parents. His professionalism also defined his approach to Holocaust education. As a survivor who could tell his family's story very well within a larger context, something not all survivors are willing or able to do, he was not solipsistic about the Donat history. Rather, his every intention was to teach to protect the futures of other children and groups of people who might be unjustly threatened.

After our first meeting, what began as a professional relationship transformed steadily into the gift of a unique friendship. If friendship requires an empathetic walking in the shoes of the friend and listening, friendship with a Shoah survivor requires such actions in exponential fashion. Paradoxically, what is required is impossible. Difficult in an ordinary friendship becomes absolutely impossible in the context of friendship with a survivor. I can no more walk a mile in Bill's shoes than I can cease to love my children. It is unequivocally impossible. I can, however, listen, and I can walk side by side. I can never claim that I can imagine what he went through, but I can be present to him in his life as a survivor. And so it was that our friendship developed with each new encounter and project.

Though there might be shared features, it is simply a truism to say that every survivor story is unique. It is important, however, to honor the fact that every story of survival is sacred. Each story relates the trauma of life threatened and life lost, the abuse of human dignity, and the power of the desire to choose life over death. How do we keep, therefore, from flattening the details of each account with phrases such as "everyone suffered terribly" when we cannot begin to comprehend the enormity of the murder of six million people? Elie Wiesel famously noted that while not all victims were Jews, all Jews were victims. Again, how do we differentiate one death from another in assembly line mass produced murder? How do we honor each sacred story?

When Rabbi Marc Gellman spoke as president of the Board of Rabbis at the September 23, 2001, prayer service held at Yankee Stadium as the United States reeled from the attack of September 11, he suggested an answer. He counseled that while it is hard to understand the mass deaths of thousands or millions, everyone knows what it is like to lose a single loved one to death. With the world watching, he offered a perspective steeped in the Jewish experience of the Shoah:

> The real horror of that day lies not in its bigness, but in its smallness. In the small, searing death of one person, 6,000 times. And that one person was not a number. That person was our father, or our mother, or our son, or our daughter, or our grandpa, or grandma, or brother, or sister, or cousin, or uncle, or aunt, or friend, or lover, our neighbor, our co-worker, the woman who delivered our mail, or the man who put out the fire, or the man who arrested the bad guys in our town.[2]

Before September 11, and despite the fact that Bill was a survivor, he became for me the face of the one person who died six million times in the Shoah. He was a passionate Holocaust educator and he worked to give voice to those whose voices were cut short, he worked to honor all those who suffered, and he worked to honor the rescuers. When I had the privilege of listening to him and of walking and working with him, he taught me what the Holocaust meant for one person—and six million became comprehensible, small, and personal. The Holocaust became meaningful in a way impossible without my friendship to Bill.

Working Together

In our first meeting, I had learned the highlights of his family's story. His parents were highly regarded professionals in Warsaw. His father was an editor of a daily Warsaw newspaper *Ostatnie Wiadomosci* [Latest News] and his mother was a pharmacist. Improbably, this small nuclear family of three survived the Warsaw Ghetto, its liquidation in April 1943, work camps, concentration camps, and death camps, and, for

Bill, being hidden by family friends, Polish resisters, and Catholic nuns. The pride in Bill's eyes and voice was palpable as he told me how his parents were reunited. Leona, Bill's mother, had returned to Warsaw, managed to find their friend Maria, who had secured Bill's place at the Catholic orphanage, and together they were able to retrieve Bill. Leona started working to arrange donations of pharmaceutical supplies at the office of the Central Committee of Polish Jews. As survivors returned to Warsaw, they would register at these offices and search lists looking, mostly in vain, to find family or friends who may have survived. Bill was a great storyteller and the picture he painted of his mother working for the committee, and renewing her hope daily that her husband would return, was vivid. My breath was taken away as he recounted his father walking into the office amid so many people waiting for a loved one to return and his mother recognizing him. As they fell into each other's arms, the remnant of their neighbors and colleagues surrounded them with cheers and tears as they witnessed the miraculous reunion of wife and husband, father and child—a nuclear family not destroyed by the crematoria of Auschwitz.

I came to know Bill's parents from his stories and also from the exquisite memoir written by his father, Alexander Donat, née Mojzesz Grynberg. During that first meeting, Bill told me proudly that William Safire's "On Language" column for The New York Times had credited his father's The Holocaust Kingdom[3] with the first use of the term "Holocaust" with an uppercase "h" as applied to the destruction of European Jewry under Hitler.[4] My first act of walking with Bill was to read the memoir very carefully in order to hear Bill's story. To be in relation to Bill, I also had to understand his parents' stories of survival. It was a first step, though I did not know it at the time, toward becoming someone who would witness to the story, who would honor the memory, and keep it alive. Bill turned six million into one. I could no longer do theology with my back toward Auschwitz, in Metz's famous phrase, because I was now in relationship with someone whose parents had suffered there; I was becoming friends with someone who narrowly escaped the transport that would have claimed his life; a boy who had nearly starved to death at five years young was entering my life, a life that had never known mortal danger. Being friends with Bill was an ongoing deepening of understanding what it is to live in an anamnestic culture, to hear memory, to honor memory, to have past pain made present, to attempt healing and reconciliation. The cries of those who suffer make claims on our consciences. It was a privilege for me to become part of a Holocaust survivor's life, but it was also a contrast experience. And the critical and productive protest against the experience was to collaborate with Bill.

Bill's Story

Bill, a proud graduate of Colgate University with a BA in French language and literature, lived the change in Catholic teaching about Jews and Judaism in a very particular way. By profession he was a printer and publisher, by avocation he was a linguist and an historian of the Holocaust, and by lived experience he was an expert in Polish-Jewish and Catholic-Jewish relationships. Shortly after we met, I invited Bill to offer the annual Shoah commemoration lecture at my college and we began a series of educational collaborations for the students and the surrounding community. As I learned more as we worked together, I was alternately humbled by this gentle, good man and shamed by my own religious tradition. The nuns who hid Bill in a town outside of Warsaw insisted on baptizing Bill. Of course, it was done without permission of father or mother imprisoned in camps, or of the family friend, "Auntie" Maria, who had engineered Bill's escape to the nuns. The sisters were classical supersessionists. Though they heroically risked their lives and potentially the lives of the other children at the orphanage to save him, they did not count physical survival as their most important value. Eternal salvation required that they teach Bill to reject not only his Jewish heritage but his parents as well. By catechizing Bill, the nuns were living out the consequences of two millennia of church teaching that the Jewish people were a deicide people. The boy was only five and his soul could be claimed, it must be claimed, for Christ.

For those whose anti-Jewish theology ran deep, baptism was important but in a sense suspect. John Connelly has explained in detail how being Jewish was considered to be a genetically inherited or second original sin.[5] Was baptism enough to redeem both original sins or would it take a couple of generations "to stick," so to speak? Imagine, if you will, a small boy with curly blond hair and bright blue eyes whose parents loved him so much that they entrusted him to a Gentile friend knowing that if they somehow survived the ghetto, the chances of surviving deportation were virtually zero. Now imagine the nuns who cared for and loved the child as they periodically combed through his blond locks looking for any growth of devil's horns. The Christian perception of Jews as demonic is well illustrated in medieval artwork depicting Jews as half human and half animal, through paintings of Jews consorting with the devil, and by the accusation of blood libel. The brave nuns were committed to saving Bill, but for them it was a bigger project than life and death—it was good versus evil. In their mind, the little boy would probably turn demonic, so baptism was an absolute necessity.

To be fair, it was extremely dangerous to hide a Jewish boy, because no matter how Aryan he looked, the authorities could always check for the telltale sign of the Covenant, the *b'rit milah* (circumcision). The rejection of his past, however, had to be complete for the nuns. Bill's parents had already prepped him to live with their Gentile friends: you are Polish Catholic, your mother is in the country, your father is a Polish Army officer prisoner of war. You are not Jewish. The Donats spoke Polish not Yiddish and this aided Bill's survival as he would have to recite the Pater Nostra and the Ave Maria as if he were a cradle Catholic—any hint of a Yiddish accent would have betrayed the ruse. How painful for parents to teach their child to renounce them! How ironic that this selfless act by Jewish parents could have been interpreted by Christians within their own theological world view as a christic act of self-sacrifice for the salvation of the child, yet the Catholic sisters who hid him taught the same child to renounce the parents literally because their anti-Jewish theology used the self-sacrifice of the cross as an instrument to damn the Jews.

As far as the nuns were concerned, Bill represented a living, breathing version of classic anti-Jewish tropes. Judaism was a moribund religion. The Jews no longer had a role in communicating God's revelation. The crime of deicide voided the Jewish covenant with God and therefore the Jewish claim on the homeland of Israel. The nuns' only course of action, their obligation in their worldview, was to give Bill life with God by making him a Catholic. They were quite successful.

It was unsettling to hear Bill's story. As a theologian, I knew the sordid Christian theology of Judaism, but it was from a different time. It was not my theology. As a friend, to hear Bill describe his time in the orphanage was once again to make the millions singular. It is nearly impossible to describe my feelings when I first heard Bill say that he would regularly pray on his knees for "Jesus to forgive me for the sin of being born Jewish." What an image! A child who miraculously survived being marched to the *Umschlagplatz*, the gathering place in Warsaw to board trains for deportation, a child who survived a raid of Polish collaborating police after his presence in his Auntie Maria's apartment had been revealed by neighbors, a child whose parents did everything they could to save his life, was on his knees, having disavowed his heritage and his parents, praying for absolution from his Jewish reality as his parents fought for their own survival so that they could return to him. I searched Bill's face for signs of anger or disgust as he told me about his prayer, but found none. I, however, was angry that my tradition for so long had taught such contempt for the Jewish people. I alternately felt revulsion at the image and compassion for a little boy who was alone in a place that simultaneously cared for him and rejected him. When I queried Bill, he counseled me that he could not be angry at the nuns. Time and again he would say that they only did what they knew, what they had been taught. The countryside outside of Warsaw in the early 1940s, he often said, was not very different from pre-Modern, medieval Europe. The nuns risked their lives to save him, and he would always be grateful to them. He loved them.

Though the nuns actively taught him to reject his mother, using vile Polish epithets to refer ignominiously to Jewish women even as the other boys at the orphanage hurled equally offensive names at Bill, though the nuns were not quite certain his baptism had saved him, though, as an adult, Bill studied and understood the historical context of the Christian anti-Judaism that he lived, he loved them. Bill taught me understanding and compassion in new ways. I am a better Catholic because of him. As a putative orphan child, he bore the negative consequences that the Cross has had for Jews, but as an adult he harbored no animus toward Christianity or toward any individual Christian.

Bill retained his fervent Catholicism after his parents managed, with the help of a prewar publishing friend, to move to the United States. He would recall his mother's patience and wisdom with the wistfulness of a parent who hoped he had done as well by his own children. When he wanted to go to church, she let him; when they were out for a walk and passed a church and he wanted to go in and pray, she let him (always declining his offer to accompany him); when he spoke in anti-Jewish ways about family members, she gently redirected him, but never attacked his adopted faith. Bill would bring audiences to outright laughter when he would describe an incident that illustrated his love for the American West as well as his attachment to Catholic culture. He was all of seven or eight when a family member gave him a pair of cowboy boots for his birthday. He was so excited by the gift that he spontaneously crossed himself in thanksgiving—he was a true American now, and still a Catholic.

Theodicy

Bill was my partner in the classroom as frequently as possible. I could teach Jewish-Christian relations or provoke discussion about the relationship of Christian anti-Judaism to the Holocaust, but Bill's authority came from having lived the reality I labored to convey. There have been a few times when students actively objected to learning the historical reality that Jesus of Nazareth was Jewish and there have been times when they completely rejected all analyses of Christian responsibility for the Shoah. But then Bill would come and engage my students and they were captivated and converted. They listened and learned not just because Bill was a survivor (often the only one they had ever met), but because he was without rancor. Students always described him as angelic and saintly as they connected to his warmth and marveled how he could live without anger and bitterness after what he and his family had suffered.

I never asked Bill the "God question." I knew that if he wanted to discuss it, we would. Instead, we spoke of his gradual return to Judaism as an older child and young adult, his raising his children in the Jewish faith, and his adult participation with synagogue education programs for youth. One day on a trip to New York City to the Museum of Jewish Heritage—A Living Memorial to the Holocaust, some of my students asked him directly about his belief in God. I was leading another group of students through the museum and was not present. Again, Bill's respect and professionalism for me and for the students was absolute as he reported the story to me as soon as he could and asked me if it was alright that he told them the truth. I reassured him that he had of course acted appropriately and that he did not need my permission to speak candidly with the students; but, I wondered, might he let me know what he said. Ambivalence and doubt were the answers. He told them that he honestly was not sure what he thought, and he wondered if God could be God and let the Holocaust happen; however, he also emphasized for the students that he was nonetheless a proud and active Jew.

It was a fitting question in a fitting place. Not only was Bill a regular docent at the Museum, his mother and father were represented in it. A quotation from his mother's memoir was part of the Warsaw Ghetto portion of the exhibit along with her Auschwitz tattoo number: "They made adroit pricks in the skin with a tattoo needle on the left forearm. It was not too painful, but every prick of that needle pierced my heart. My number was 49397."[6] The end of the second floor exhibit of the War against the Jews displays a quotation from his father reflecting on his liberation on April 29, 1945: "In that hour of liberation we wept as we had not wept during all the years of martyrdom; we wept tears of sorrow, not tears of joy. Our liberation came too late; we had paid too high a price...What would we look forward to? What was there for us to return to? And where?"[7] These are, if we are not to descend to sentimentality, haunting and depressing sentiments. Often, when I am in the Museum, I think how son and father were not alike—the despair of the father that emanates often from his memoir, as evidenced by the quotation above, contrasts sharply with the joie de vivre that was Bill's customary modality. Such a comparison, however, is neither entirely true nor fair. One cannot compare the horrors an adult endured to survive a variety of camps with the sufferings of a hidden child. Additionally, after the war, Bill's parents worked very hard to provide him with the typical American life, of which he spoke so lovingly. Bill spoke freely about how hard survival was for his father. Writing the memoir helped his father, but Bill said life remained very difficult for his father till the end. Eventually, Bill allowed me to see the rough edges of his own survival.

The fear and concern, perhaps despair, in the father's words came through to me from Bill at times as our relationship deepened. The nuns had been wrong about him: he was not a demon. My students were wrong about him: he was not an angel. Bill was human and though he did not carry the burden his father carried, living under Nazi occupation from age two to eight took its toll. My first insight into the deepest meaning for Bill of our work together was from his wife Ellen. It was early in our friendship and Bill was teaching a ten-week adult education course in the history of the Holocaust with a section on antisemitism and Christian anti-Judaism. Together, we had developed this course for the public series that my position offers to the communities surrounding the college. Ellen surprised me when I called to discuss some course details with Bill; as she answered the phone, she thanked me for arranging the course. Then, in a tone so serious that I knew the previous expression of gratitude was far more than quotidian politeness, she told me that I had no idea how much teaching the course meant to Bill. Ellen took other opportunities during the course of that semester, and later during other collaborations that Bill and I engaged, to emphasize to me the absolute meaningfulness and importance for Bill of these teaching opportunities. Gradually it became clear to me that teaching classes to my students, or lecturing to bar/bat mitzvah students from Vermont—who would stop at his temple on the way to the United States Holocaust Memorial Museum specifically to learn from him—or simply talking to me over lunch, were important aspects of Bill's lifelong journey toward healing. It was part of how he confronted the despair explicit in his father's words at liberation. Bill had constructed a place and a life to which he could return. Though I never saw Bill weep, I know that his tears were not just tears of sorrow, but tears of joy mixed with sorrow. I was privileged and honored to be a small part of his arduous journey to reconcile the destruction of the Shoah with a new life—"a normal American life," as Bill would often remark.

One day of Bill's journey stands out for me particularly. It was late autumn 2003 and Bill called sounding very uncharacteristically urgent and agitated. He needed to see me as soon as possible. We set a date for lunch and I met him at an Italian restaurant he favored close to campus. Charming and genteel as ever, Bill held a chair out for me, made sure that I had something to drink, and ascertained that I was comfortable before our conversation began. Usually we spoke first about my children and his grandchildren, but on this day, as soon as he had completed the first tasks of hospitality (he was always host; he said his father would never forgive his lack of manners if he let me take him to lunch!), he launched headlong into the topic upsetting him. Had I heard of the new Mel Gibson movie chronicling the last 12 hours of Jesus's life? It was to debut on Ash Wednesday 2004. Of course, I knew of the film, but I let him explain everything. He spoke about all the articles he had read about the antisemitism inherent in the film. He told me about his conversations with other survivors and how all of them were experiencing a return of their nightmares. He spoke about how survivors feared outbreaks of violence against Jews around the world once the movie was released. He was angry and he was scared, and never before had I seen him in that way. His deep blue eyes penetrated me to the core when he asked me in all earnestness what could be done to stop the film and to protect people. I felt completely inadequate to assuage my dear friend's fears. But I sat with him and I held his fears with care. I told him about scholars' efforts to contact Gibson asking for modifications to the film. Even though they were not successful, it reassured him to know that there were Christians willing to contest Gibson and his juggernaut publicity machine for *The Passion of the Christ*. It helped Bill to know that there would be programs addressing the serious problems with the film. He began to relax a bit as lunch progressed, but we kept returning to that topic during our lunch. I could not help but remember how Bill had told me how terrorized he felt when Nazi collaborators who stormed his first hiding place took his favorite toy from him (a rocking horse) and I thought that his fear-filled eyes at lunch were the very eyes of that toddler.

The anger that I felt toward my tradition when I learned that the child Bill had prayed for forgiveness for being born a Jew was the anger that I felt at that lunch because my adult friend was living in fear and pain due to a commercial rendering of the paschal mystery. It was a silent moment of recommitment to working for a robust positive Christian theology of Judaism and to the work of Jewish-Christian reconciliation. It was a poignant lunch that taught me in a new way about the consequences of the Christian millennia for Jews. Millions became one, a lesson to be learned time and again, ever new. Bill's demeanor had changed toward the end of the lunch and so I thought, I hoped, I had been a little helpful. In the face of Gibson's *The Passion of the Christ*, what could I say to that toddler taught to reject his mother should she return and attempt to take him away from his Catholic life? What did I have to offer to the successful businessman, Holocaust educator, and grandfather? I only know that we were all part of that luncheon conversation. And the psalmist's words, "How good it is when people sit together as one," seemed to hover in the air.

Righteous Gentiles

Bill valued precision. He was famous among his family and friends for repeating "everything has to be yare," a nautical phrase imported from his hobby as a boating enthusiast. As a sailor, as a business owner specializing in printing and graphic arts, there was good reason for precision. Such appreciation for detail carried over into his work as an educator. As much as Bill wanted people to understand the depth and breadth of the Final Solution, he also wanted to give credit to people who courageously attempted to rescue Jews from certain death. Without the rescuers, Holocaust education would not be accurate, not precise, not yare. Bill was a board member of Thanks To Scandinavia, an institute of the American Jewish Committee dedicated to education about the Scandinavian rescue of its Jewish population. I marveled at Bill's passionate involvement with so many people and organizations. If he had only offered presentations about his family's experience, it would have been enough, "*dayenu!*" as the Passover Seder song goes. Yet Bill spent his life learning as much as he could about all aspects of the Holocaust. Thanks To Scandinavia supported the research for the development of an opera based on the rescue of the Danish Jews. In February 2008, Bill invited me as his guest to the premier of that opera, *The Yellow Star: Celebrating Extraordinary Acts by Ordinary People,* at which he would be offering a brief comparative analysis of the Danish and the Polish situations. Eight months later, Bill, the librettist/composer Bradley Detrick, and I produced the same opera at my institution. It seems to me that Bill in part confronted the rigors of being a survivor through his enthusiastic approach to programs, such as *The Yellow Star,* that were able to reflect on some hope for humanity, in this case the rescuers, while still presenting unvarnished truths about the traumatic experiences of the Holocaust. Bill wrote, "the overwhelming response of the entire Danish population to save its Jewish minority from the Nazi terror, must be recognized and lauded for all time."[8] Bill's ability to avoid collective guilt and blame, his moral courage to name accurately perpetrators, bystanders, and rescuers, all contributed to his equanimity of spirit that students remarked as saintly. He was a constant model of fair-mindedness, of hope, and of gratitude. Without saying a word, he challenged me to live more deeply the fundamental virtues that our two traditions shared.

Again, we found ourselves at lunch, at "our Italian restaurant," and Bill was excitedly telling me about being contacted by a Polish woman who claimed to have been one of his rescuers. I always experienced Bill as a gentle dove, but he was also wise as a serpent and he was not going to let his story and his parents' story be co-opted by a charlatan. He had done his best to verify the woman's story from this side of the Atlantic and he still was not sure that this woman was genuine, but he had decided to return to his homeland and to go to Warsaw and meet her. Through a series of questions whose answers could not be found in any of Bill's or his parents' publications, Bill ascertained that the elderly woman who had called him to Poland, Magda Rusinek, was indeed the teenager who hid him when Auntie Maria was betrayed by neighbors. I recall laughing with Bill as he told me the story of how he carefully and gently, but firmly and doggedly conducted the meeting with Magda. Typically for Bill, once the truth was clear, he assented to the request from television producers to be interviewed along with Magda. I know that he felt that it was part of his responsibility to tell the story of his rescuer. He would now promote the righteousness of Magda, a light in the darkness, a symbol of hope for humanity. His own story could also, therefore, be told with more precision, but so, too, could the wider story of the Holocaust.[9] I was not, then, surprised to learn that Bill had started the application process with Yad Vashem, Israel's Holocaust Martyrs' and Heroes' Remembrance Authority, to honor Magda as Righteous Among the Nations. For Magda, he would make everything yare—precise, fair, just, right. The last overseas trip Bill took was to Yad Vashem to be with Magda as she accepted her honor. How good it is for brothers and sisters to sit together in unity.

Bill never stopped; he was indefatigable. He labored to make the reality of the Holocaust understood (as far as it is possible to give comprehensible form to great evil) to those far removed from it in time. He remembered so that he could teach and in teaching, it seems to me, he applied balm on the deep wounds of his childhood. But I hasten to emphasize that Bill was always a person for others, his parents, his children, his grandchildren, his friends, his rescuers, and students anywhere. He was not thinking about himself when he engaged in Holocaust education; rather, he was making the past present in each new moment so that the future could be protected from further genocides. He made six million comprehensible to, probably, thousands of students over the course of his volunteering. I am ever so grateful that he invited me to participate with him in his work.

Our friendship affects how I think theologically. People's lives are at stake when bad theology is written. Truth is about looking someone in the eye and saying nothing, absolutely nothing, that cannot be said, as

Rabbi Irving "Yitz" Greenberg has famously taught, in the presence of a child standing in the fires of Auschwitz—or in the presence of a perfectly composed and gentle man who once prayed to be forgiven for the sin of being Jewish.

Final Conversations

Bill and I had been out of touch for several months when I received a letter from him explaining that he had been ill but that he wanted to get together. As always, we met for lunch. I listened to him describe a nightmarish story of misdiagnosis. The prostate cancer was finally diagnosed and under treatment and he was eager to get back to his customary schedule of speaking and of collaborative projects. Soon thereafter, however, Bill contracted a rare reaction to an aggressive treatment and his health declined precipitously. Ever the survivor, he was battling valiantly and did not want a little thing like cancer to get in the way of helping me to teach my students. We set a date for him to come to class. He apologized to me for asking if I would mind if he taught the class from a seated rather than a standing position. The treatments had made his legs very weak. I was more flabbergasted than when years earlier he had offered me references. Again, it was his life being put at the service of others—a life I cherished, a friend who did not need references and certainly did not need to stand to exude the natural authority of an eminently ethical and unfailingly kind human being. "No, Bill, not to worry; we'll all sit together in a circle; it's a small class this time. How good it will be for us to sit together."

Ellen called over the weekend to cancel. Bill was not strong enough to come this week. In the background, I could hear Bill trying to say something. Ellen put him on the phone and Bill made me promise to call the following Sunday. If he had a good week, he would come. "Could I adjust my course schedule?" was his question.

"Of course, Bill, I would adjust any schedule for you. Just focus on getting healthy, don't worry about us."

But he made me promise to call and so I did. I called each week for probably six weeks and our conversations were of varying lengths depending on how he was feeling. He was never quite up to coming. The spirit was willing, but the flesh was weak. And then came the conversation.

"Bill, how's it going this week?" I asked.

"Well, I've hit a setback and have to go to the hospital. Will you visit?"

"Absolutely, Bill."

"Ok, Ellen will give you the details."

Ellen got on the phone to explain the possible hospitals they might use. She told me that the prognosis was far from positive. We arranged a plan for updating information that included Grace, a colleague from another institution, so that Ellen would not have to make multiple phone calls.

Bill got settled into a hospital for additional evaluations. I knew that this would be a temporary admission because Ellen was trying to secure a space at a hospital specializing in hospice care for cancer patients. I went to visit. It was a Friday evening, Shabbat, and I had to leave for a conference on Jewish-Christian relations the next day. I hovered in the hallway until Ellen saw me. She told Bill that I had come to visit and she would leave us alone. She came out to the hallway and in hushed tones told me that the doctors estimated six weeks; they would transfer Bill to Calvary Hospital on Monday.

Breathing deeply, I braced myself to see a man, whom I had only ever seen as robust and impeccably dressed, laid low by disease and clothed in a hospital gown. I entered the room and Bill opened his arms in as wide a welcoming embrace as the tubes to which he was attached allowed and exclaimed, "Elena, I am going home!" To which I replied with a huge smile, "Yes, Bill, and I know the rabbi in charge!"

The irony of the situation was not lost on either of us. It was a painfully poignant moment. But it was also a graced and humorous exchange that while reflecting Bill's luminous spirit also managed to encapsulate a revolution in Jewish-Christian relations. A Jewish boy was ravaged by a war that intended to destroy all Jews, separated from his family, and saved—but reviled as Jewish—in a Catholic orphanage. A Jewish man ravaged by disease, in imminent danger of being separated from his family by death, and on his way to finding palliative care at a Catholic hospice. And not just any Catholic hospital, but one called Calvary! The interpretation of the cross that had Polish nuns baptizing the boy out of fear of the devil had yielded to a more authentic interpretation of the Cross, one of infinite compassion and love, so that the man could face his end in dignity. Could there be any more powerful representation of the change in Jewish-Catholic relations since the Shoah than that of a Jewish man calling a Catholic hospital home (with no rancor and no fear of forced conversion) and meaning it? The fact that the chief chaplain was a rabbi with whom I was friends only added to the intensity of the exchange. We did not know whether to laugh or cry and for that moment we laughed. It was all so true; he was going home.

Levity faded quickly as Bill's body betrayed and embarrassed him. He flashed anger and frustration that I had never seen in him. He adjusted his bed sheets to maintain his dignity. "No Bill, I am not offended. No Bill, I am staying as long as you want me." He calmed. "Look, I don't quite know the set up at Calvary. But let me get settled and learn the routine. They must have a sitting room. You can bring your students to me two or three at a time and I can talk to them there."

"Okay, Bill, but you just focus on you for now."

"But I can do it. I want to do it; I just don't know the setup yet."

"Okay, Bill, I will bring them."

What generosity of spirit, what fierce determination to teach against hate and intolerance that in the grip of crippling pain and in the face of death, he was still trying to help me and my students. Bill embodied selflessness. He was teaching me to the end. Bill asked me some questions about my children and the conference to which I was headed. He caught me with tears in my eyes and wagged his finger at me emphatically. "No, no, you can't do that! You have to be strong for me."

He tired and I knew it was time to leave. I told him that I would be out of town until Monday night. I wanted to tell him that I loved him, but I knew I could not speak the words without descending into weeping—which he had expressly forbidden—and so I bowed deeply in a gesture of loving respect, forced a smile, waved, and promised that I would be back on Tuesday. How good it is when brothers and sisters sit together.

But the call came early Tuesday.

Beyond the Veil

I drove toward the funeral perhaps too fast and too furiously. I kept hitting seek on the radio and would stop on any extremely noisy, busy, screeching piece of music I could find. I kept turning up the volume because I could not find any piece loud enough to drown out the cries in my heart. I searched for music to match my despair.

When the youngest of Bill's grandchildren skipped into the Temple's sanctuary with a huge smile on her face and her even larger blond curls bouncing on the nape of her neck, I gasped and thought to myself that this was a vision of Bill. I felt as if I were seeing him in another time and place. She looked exactly like he did in the one toddler picture of him that had survived the war because his parents had sent it to relatives in Palestine. I could not help but think of him playing hide-and-seek with his Auntie Maria as she literally hid him to save his life, but he thought she was playing. The child captivated all of us as we waited for the service to begin. While watching her play, the edge of the pain we felt was dulled for a few moments. I heard Bill's soothing voice say, as I had heard him say so often to my students: "In your face Hitler. We survived. And, we thrived!" And I saw Bill's eyes twinkle as he smiled his benevolent smile.

Four months after Bill died, I landed in Warsaw for the first time. I gathered my students around me and I told them about Bill as I clutched several obituaries in my hand. Spending a week studying in Auschwitz is not a trip into a distant history. I told them that the Holocaust affects people today. We study for the living and the dead. Our study will make us witnesses who must speak out against philosophies, theologies, and all manner of ideologies that cause such evil. We must remember for the mother, the brother, the husband, the sister, the aunt, the friend, who can no longer speak. Our remembering must make them real and present so that their stories are not lost in the fog of incomprehensibly large numbers or relegated to a computer that cannot remember the beauty and meaning of their sacred stories, their lives.

Bill will continue to be my one in six million—a survivor of hate, a survivor of the shadow of anti-Judaism on the cross of Christianity, and an animator of love and forgiveness between Jews and Christians. Bill remembered, as any good Jew or Christian does, to make the sacred present. He remembered so as to heal, not open, wounds. How good it is when brothers and sisters sit together in unity. He has blessed my life and my teaching with his friendship.

May his name be for a blessing.

Notes

* This chapter title alludes to Psalm 133:1, which the Jewish Publication Society translates as "How good and how pleasant it is that brothers dwell together." Other translations use an inclusive "brothers and sisters," other translations use "sit" instead of "dwell," and contemporary musical renderings of the verse may add "in peace" after "dwell together."

1. *Nostra Aetate* (Vatican, October 28, 1965), 4, accessed June 11, 2014, http://www.vatican.va/archive/hist_councils/ii_vatican_council/documents/vat-ii_decl_19651028_nostra-aetate_en.html.

2. "United in Prayer," CNN.com, September 24, 2001, accessed June 11, 2014, http://edition.cnn.com/2001/US/09/23/vic.service.quotes/.

3. Alexander Donat's *The Holocaust Kingdom* was originally published in 1965, by Holt, Rinehart and Winston. In 1978, it was republished by Holocaust Library, an imprint of Holocaust Publications, which was founded by Alexander Donat. Page references herein are to a new edition published in 1999 by the United States Holocaust Memorial Museum, which features an "Afterword" by William Donat.

4. The column was reprinted in William Safire, *Coming to Terms* (New York: Doubleday, 1991), 185.

5. See John Connelly, *From Enemy to Brother: The Revolution in Catholic Teaching on the Jews 1933–1965* (Cambridge: Harvard University Press, 2011). See especially the notion that "Jews could not become Catholic in a single generation…" (32).

6. Donat, *The Holocaust Kingdom*, 260.

7. Donat, *The Holocaust Kingdom*, 248, 250.

8. William H. Donat, "Thanks To Scandinavia: A Scholarship Fund," September 1, 2003, accessed June 17, 2014, http://thankstoscandinavia.org/index.php?s=William+H.+Donat.

9. Magda Rusinek was part of the network of the now famous Irena Sendler. Rusinek appears with Bill in the documentary, "Irena Sendler: In the Name of their Mothers" (PBS, May 1, 2011).

4

Faith and Friendship

David B. Burrell, CSC

Interreligious friendship, since it is a virtue, entails not only values, but skills as well. I began to recognize the value of friendships that cross over the barriers that religions can place between us while living in Jerusalem in the early eighties. It was in Jerusalem that I began to acquire the skills demanded by interfaith friendship as well. I am blessed to have had a number of great teachers in this regard. In this chapter, I want to tell stories about my teachers and their struggles with interreligious friendships, and how the friendship they extended to me transformed me as a philosopher and as a man of faith.

My first teacher was Marcel Dubois, OP, a fellow philosopher with an amazing gift for friendship. Inspired by Jacques Maritain, Marcel had come to Israel in 1962, in the early period of the Jewish state (inaugurated in 1948), expressly to serve the Jewish people. As a Frenchman, a backlog of residual guilt no doubt spurred his mission, making it a personal and ecclesial round of amends. I came to live with Marcel and his fledgling community in Isaiah House after an initial year in the Holy Land serving as rector of Tantur Ecumenical Institute, a Christian initiative poised between Jerusalem and Bethlehem, Israel and Palestine. Tantur's setting between the worlds contrasted with Isaiah House's location in Israeli west Jerusalem, though it was but a short walk to Jaffa gate in the old city of Jerusalem. So I found myself chafing at the way Marcel and his friends would speak of "Arabs," as though an irritation to Western-oriented Jews settling the land promised their fathers. His coterie was composed largely of old-line Zionists who simply presumed theirs to be a "civilizing mission" of Palestine, so it fit all too neatly into a French colonial mindset. Raised in Europe, they exuded Western liberal values. Marcel took the proper acculturating step of learning Hebrew (with noticeably Gallic intonation) so before long became a lively presence in the sophisticated intellectual world of Hebrew University. That was his world.

During the year at Tantur, I had taken an initial step toward Arabic, through Hebrew, in the Israeli *ulpan* (instruction) system, thrown (in 1980) with Jewish exiles from the Khomeini revolution in Iran. So their presence considerably enhanced my acquaintance with the milieu into which Marcel has deliberately inserted his Dominican philosophical skills, though it was my first year in Israel/Palestine, and he had become an Israeli citizen after some 30 years in the land. All that helps sketch the polyglot and variegated milieu into which I had been thrust at 47 years of age, needing to continue to explore Judaism after serving as chair of theology at Notre Dame, where we had inaugurated a Judaica chair with the help of colleagues more seasoned than I: John Howard Yoder, Joseph Blenkinsopp, Robert Wilken, and Stanley Hauerwas. In addition to Hebrew, I was intent on learning Arabic, to pursue a triadic study of Judaism, Christianity, and Islam. So when Marcel, currently serving as chair of Philosophy at Hebrew University, invited me to conduct a seminar on Moses Maimonides and Thomas Aquinas, I jumped at the chance. I thought that their thought might serve as a model of the triadic inquiry I had dreamed of undertaking, for Moses ben Maimon lived in the Islamicate and composed the *Guide of the Perplexed* in Judaeo-Arabic and had a major impact on the thought of Thomas Aquinas. Yet absent the personal witness of Marcel Dubois, whose instinct for friendship ever engaged both heart and head, all this could have been an academic exercise. In fact, a weekly seminar with Yesheyahu Leibowitz set the tone. Convening each shabbat evening at Isaiah House with a half-dozen students to overhear them, we watched two great minds and hearts wrestle with issues compelling for each, only to reach for ways to "agree to disagree"—Marcel's summary phrase for their relentless journey together as friends. This philosopher and physical chemist, editor of the Israeli Encyclopedia, would later react to Israeli occupation of biblical Palestine in the touted Six-Day War with the prophetic: "Give it back! I am a Zionist, promoting a Jewish state in the Holy Land. Yet if we incorporate the people whom we have just conquered into our state, it can no longer be ethnically Jewish. But if we refuse to incorporate them, it cannot be ethically Jewish!" How prescient!

Nothing "Judeo-Christian" about this endeavor, as the sharp edges of their well-honed philosophical minds dissected issues dividing them from each other while animating the personal inquiry of each. Put starkly, while Christians and Jews both pray the psalms, one community sees Jesus as the very "Word of God through whom the universe is made," "splendor of the Father's glory," while the other regards him as "some other guy," an unwelcome interloper whose legacy poses intractable conundra for human thought as well as spawning centuries of bloody conflict. Yet, in the midst of this maelstrom, contended two great spirits who cared deeply for their respective traditions and for one another. What a witness for those of us—Jews or Christians—who sought "mutual illumination" from sparks generated in their debates! The depth and passion of these two great minds was one of my first great lessons regarding the value of, and the skills demanded by, interreligious friendship.

At the center of this crucible stood a student of Marcel more nearly my age, Avital ("Tali") Wohlman, whose razor-sharp mind brought out the best from us all, while her heart animated our evening proceedings. Like Marcel Dubois and Yesheyahu Leibowitz, Tali also taught me wonderful things about interfaith friendships. Though Tali lived in her own "digs," she seemed to spend every waking hour at Isaiah House, where our minds came ineluctably together. A self-professed "atheist," I would come to discover how deeply Christian were her sensibilities. Indeed it was those sensibilities that led her to reach out to Palestinians, and categorically reject the pretenses of Zionism. When she later took up residence with Marcel after the official demise of Isaiah House, there began for Marcel a painful weaning process from what he would later describe as his "naive Zionism." It was in fact a veritable opening of mind and heart into a much wider world, embodied in the person of Mahmoud, a Palestinian engaged to care for the garden, whose unmistakable faith, refined through suffering, displayed a God whom Marcel had also come to know, albeit under different names. So they connected, not just as employer/employee, but as friends too. Marcel's unerring sense for the authentically human found a soul-partner, not long before his sturdy Norman constitution began to give way to old age. Since I was by then resident at Tantur, a half-hour walk from their home in Beit Safafa, an Arab village surrounded by Jerusalem, I was privileged to witness this transformation in this French intellectual, lionized by cultured Israelis ideologically rendered insouciant for the land's long-term inhabitants and now as a friend to a Muslim.

In his early eighties, having long enjoyed an energy supported by good health and stimulated by unceasing inquiry, Marcel slowly morphed into a Christian counterpart of the faithful Muslim, Mahmoud. As their friendship grew apace, unimpeded by cultural disparity, the results in Marcel were arresting: a simpler human being, chastened by a humiliating realization of the ways the blinkered world into which he had assiduously inserted himself, amid ready adulation and appreciation, had effectively distorted his otherwise unerring sense for humanity—something only Mahmoud's humble presence could restore. So I was witness to a friendship among an ethnically Jewish woman, herself a loving companion to a resolutely Catholic Dominican friar, and a Palestinian peasant whose simple faith trumped them both. Who was I? A participant-observer who loved each of the principals of this drama, and learned so much from their interaction that this story emerges as a spontaneous example of interfaith friendship in the Holy Land.

Our Mediterranean location proved to be intimately linked to discovering the inner affinity between Thomas Aquinas and Moses Maimonides, together with Ibn Sina [Avicenna], since better medievalists than I had let it pass relatively unnoticed. So a fresh intellectual program emerged in Isaiah House among the three of us—Tali, Marcel, and I—as we explored together this rich interfaith period of medieval inquiry. Curiously, the superior formation in Thomas Aquinas that Marcel had enjoyed at Le Saulchior in the rich ressourcement period of the 1940s had passed over these interfaith linkages. It seemed to require the Mediterranean milieu of Jerusalem to tease out the side of Aquinas that northern European scholarship had quite overlooked, despite patent references in his text.

How privileged I had been to be located at Tantur, to come to appreciate what libraries alone can never provide: an interfaith perspective richly imbued with history and the prescient friendship among the three of us, which would shape decades of scholarship for Tali and me, as we each retooled in Arabic so that we might mine the riches of Islamic philosophical inquiry. Marcel continues to be an absent presence to both of us. Always preferring to compose in French, Tali produced a penetrating study of Marcel, and his times and place.[1] She also edited with Yossef Schwarz a collection of homages to Marcel.[2] The truly outstanding feature of Marcel for many of us was his faith. One could describe him as endowed with the intellect of a philosopher, the soul of a poet, and the faith of a Breton peasant. Realizing how it is virtually impossible to assess the faith of oneself or of another, Marcel's faith seemed rather to be given to him for others, much as Jesus prayed (in Peter's presence) that his faith might be strengthened, to strengthen that of his brothers and sisters. In that respect, I suspect his faith supplied for many unable even to use the term—for those, like Tali, who find themselves personally bereft of what they suppose the reality might be.

Yet, the distinguishing feature of our tripartite friendship lay in a shared passion for philosophical inquiry. Much as a neo-Platonic philosophy had facilitated the exchanges we find among Avicenna, Maimonides, and Aquinas, despite the absence of an overarching interfaith atmosphere, we could still use the idiom of philosophy to share in each other's traditions. Yet if the person at the center of this tripartite friendship had the intellect of a philosopher, he was further endowed with the soul of a poet and the faith of a peasant. And, each of these, as we know, plays a key role in friendship. Moreover, bonding among friends seems hardly affected by differences in faith-orientation (or even a professed absence of faith). If, in fact, Aristotle is correct in stating that a friend is "in on" the very relation whereby one relates to one's own self, then the bonding is already metaphysical in tone, linking friends together at what Louis Massignon called "the virginal point" where creatures come forth from an eternal creator. That puts the empirical question "How much can very different persons share?" in a new light.

One way of trying to express this is to reflect on the bonding effected by hours of zazen (Zen seated meditation) together in a *sangha* (Buddhist community). On one level, nothing is shared; on another, life-giving breath is transmitted. One result is that difference can be shared as well, so bonding is hardly affected by manifest differences. The image of sharing life-giving breath seems appropriate to friendship, which operates at a level more organic than agreement or disagreement, as its natural expression of sharing in food exemplifies. So the bonding among friends is as mysterious as each one is to oneself. What more can be said?

The Charm and the Anguish of Jerusalem and Israel-Palestine

I also want to tell stories about how interfaith friendships with oppressed peoples has enriched my own faith. First, I will tell of my friendship with two Muslim families. Let us shift our lens to the Mount of Olives overlooking the Haram ash-Sharif (Temple Mount), and the Abu-Sway family who has lived there for generations, and then to Gaza for the Hamad family, with similarly longtime residence. In each family, the father is a graduate of Bethlehem University, an initiative of the Vatican and the Catholic community of de la Salle Brothers, catering to young men and women in the southern occupied West Bank. Mustafa Abu-Sway lives with his wife, Iman, and their family in a home overlooking the Dome of the Rock, the signature of Jerusalem, in Ras-al-Amoud. He and I would describe ourselves as students of al-Ghazali, the Muslim philosophical theologian (d. 1111), whose intellectual acumen can best be compared with St. Augustine in Christian tradition. With a BA from Bethlehem University (1984) and PhD from Boston College (1993), Mustafa was recently appointed the first holder of the Integral Chair for the Study of Imam Ghazali's Work at Al-Masjid Al-Aqsa and at Al-Quds University. I shall tell you more of Mustafa and Iman later, but I first want to pair them with Jihad [Gahad] Hamad and his wife, Manar, a family from Gaza now resident with their children in London, Ontario, Canada. To come to know a Palestinian is to come to know their families; such is the receptive ethos of their world. It is also to learn to taste a mode of suffering, as we shall see, that taught me how far authentic hope surpasses optimism.

I came to meet Jihad as one of the outstanding MA students in the Kroc Institute for International Peace Studies, chosen for their involvement in ventures to facilitate peace in their respective conflicted milieux. So, Jihad had been paired with an uncompromising female Zionist colleague—part of the enculturation process in this volatile mix of students learning to live together! He chose to continue for the doctorate at Notre Dame in Sociology, but only after returning to Gaza and marrying Manar, the daughter of the administrator of south Gaza. Less than 20 years in age, but honed in a taxing environment, Manar immediately began a BA at Indiana University South Bend in women's studies, and soon contributed mightily to Notre Dame's University Village community, with 132 residents, 150 children, and 27 nationalities, where I was privileged to serve as chaplain. Before long, their first child was born, a son whom they named Salaan [peace]. So, when Yitzhak Rabin, the bold Israeli prime minister who advocated peace, was assassinated by an ultra-Zionist settler, I took Jihad with me to Beth Israel synagogue, where the South Bend Jewish congregation heartily invited this Palestinian to mourn with them for Rabin and a fractured Israeli polity.

After receiving his doctorate, Jihad was engaged by the fledgling Arab-American University near the northern Israeli West Bank city of Jenin. While visiting him there, as his students overheard our conversation about interfaith matters, they asked him how he knew so much about Christianity. His response, "I guess I am sort of Catholic Muslim," was echoed by mine, "and I a Muslim Catholic!" (Yet, I had the venerable French Islamicist, Louis Massignon, as a guide, while Jihad was forging a path of his own.) Jihad's academic post did not last long, for when he returned to Gaza to attend his father in a delicate eye operation, the Israelis would not permit him to enter the Jewish state, so he switched his post to al-Azhar University in Gaza, much to Manar's delight to return to her family. Another Kroc Institute fellow and confrere, Patrick Gaffney, and I, were welcomed royally by Jihad's family in Gaza just after their lemon orchard had been wantonly bulldozed by Israeli troops. His father was slowly and deliberately turning the ground for new planting—the kind of determination and hope that characterizes Palestine.

But increasing Israeli terrorizing of the population of Gaza—epitomized in jets deliberately breaking the sound barrier at 2 a.m. with predictable results for sleeping children and adults—before long made living there intolerable. So, with Manar's encouragement and valiant assistance, they engineered a quick exit to Cairo in one of the few breaks in the infamous fence, taking the family to live with Jihad's physician

brother there. I managed to visit them there, to experience two families crowded into a Cairo apartment, and appreciate why Jihad worked
day and night to arrange passage to Canada. When I last visited them in
London, Ontario, he had managed to parley a part-time teaching position
into President of the Canadian Palestinian Social Association (CPSA), a
non-profit NGO for volunteering. Two young people from distinguished
families can always find enterprising ways of overcoming oppression!
When I had periodically called them in the midst of the prolonged siege
of Gaza, asking how they were, the predictable answer would be *al-hamd
il-Allah* (God be praised!) That is my enduring image of Muslim faith in
God's presence and action in our lives.

Life in Occupied Jerusalem

If Mustafa and Iman's story sounds less dramatic, living in the Ras
al-Amoud quarter of Jerusalem overlooking the Haram ash-Sharif
invited daily harassment which might have debilitated lesser folk. The
division of Jerusalem into separated quarters for Jews and Arabs, dating
back to Ottoman times, may sound like "segregation" to Americans, but
becomes a vital factor in such different cultures living together. So when
Arab families succumb to "big bucks" to sell their property to Zionist
entrepreneurs, the neighborhood is instantly ruined, as large apartment
blocks disrupt an aesthetic Palestinian landscape, only to be surrounded
by impenetrable fences and glaring security lights, to say nothing of loud-
speakers broadcasting rock music to enhance the settlers' recreation! It is
hard enough even to think about, but experiencing daily is an insufferable
reminder of oppression. And, when it is financed by an American Jewish
gambling king, abetted by Christian Zionist pastors, insult compounds
the injury. Nor is that all: attempts by the Abu-Sway family to enlarge
their family compound have regularly been denied by Israeli authorities
refusing building permits, after having extracted large sums of "earnest
money." And, so it goes. Yet, Mustafa and Iman are dedicated to interfaith
dialogue!

For that is how we met, and continue to interact, though now from
afar. When I was directing the Notre Dame student program at Tantur in
1999–2000, Mustafa and I teamed with an Israeli academic, Alon Goshen-
Gottstein (now directing the Elijah Interfaith Institute) to help our stu-
dents understand "Abrahamic faiths"—a pregnant phrase borrowed from
Louis Massignon to capture the potential for interaction among Jews,
Christians, and Muslims. He has also worked extensively with a longtime
American-Israeli friend and scholar, Yeheskel Landau, currently teaching

at the Duncan MacDonald Institute for Muslim-Christian relations at Hartford Seminary. We have come to appreciate how our respective faiths have animated each of us, and how our friendship can enhance that faith incalculably in each of us.

Reflection on Friendship in the Conflicted Milieu of the Holy Land

Nicholas Wolterstorff, now Noah Porter Professor of Philosophical Theology emeritus at Yale, taught most of his academic life at Calvin College in Grand Rapids, Michigan. His life as a philosopher and a teacher has never failed to reflect the demands of his Christian faith. His recent reflections on the way experience with oppressed people quite reshaped his own ethical reflections, offering telling testimony to the power of friendship to open new vistas of life and action for philosophers.[3] In his case, it was black South Africans, native Hondurans, and Palestinians—as well as individuals from the societies dominating them who came to stand with them. It is clear that interfaith friendships helped to usher this philosopher beyond the blinkers of a Western academic world to face the realities talked about there, but never illuminated by lived experience. What made the difference? Once he learned there was "something right about writing from the wronged," it was but a small step to realize how insulated from reality is any Western academic. My friendship with Nick, while he was working at Tantur Ecumenical Institute, allowed me to witness firsthand how the solidarity that comes with interfaith friendships can give a depth to our academic pursuits that no library can supply. Once again, I came to learn how critical the location a scholar occupies can be. And, even more critical are the friendships that the scholar develops there. And, while Nick's friendships are less focused on interfaith, the theme of friendship in the midst of conflict and prevailing injustice pervades his humane study.

That observation, along with Nick's corroborating witness, allows me to illustrate how interfaith friendship in a conflicted world can help to break open a rarified academic world. And, once we realize how integral is the dimension of faith to that awakening, it is immediately obvious how an interfaith dimension can only enhance (rather than dilute) the originating faith. In fact, any suspicion that it might dilute one's own faith-commitment turns out to be abstract and ideological. For when I marvel at the staying power of my Muslim friends in Gaza in the face of an unrelenting power meant to cow and demean them, I can only thank God for their presence and witness. And, that the one God we share is abundant in mercy is also part of our distinct heritages. So, what can we say except *al-hamd'il-Allah* (God be praised) as we try to walk together in faiths which celebrate difference? And, in my current venue in Bangladesh, serving the Congregation of Holy Cross, yet we may conclude with a simple image of the way friendship can utterly transform "interfaith dialogue."

For one of the annoying features of the very term "dialogue" is its way of falsifying the intimate relations which the activity can foster—for the image of "dialoguing" suggests two (or more) persons facing each other talking *about* their faith. Yet, interfaith friendship can only be imaged by two seekers walking side-by-side, lured into a mysterious companionship by a sustaining power beyond each of them. And, that lure becomes an imperative when they are each brought face-to-face with realities, traumas, or reversals in fortune or health, which neither can sustain alone. It is there that they will call upon their respective faiths, and as they walk together, experience those disparate faiths enhancing each other: bonding in difference! So, if we initially seek friendship as a way of insulating ourselves from the harsh realities of a faceless economic world, the very experience invites us to discover ways of transforming that world, from within ourselves, yet nourished by the faith that binds us together, different though it may be!

Notes

1. Avital Wohlman, *Quand un chrétien aime Israël: L'œuvre-vie du frère Marcel-Jacques Dubois (1920 Tourcoing-2007 Jérusalem)* (Paris: Cerf, 2012).
2. Yossef Schwartz and Avital Wohlman, eds, *Le Chrétien poète de Sion: In memoriam Père Marcel-Jacques Dubois (1920–2007)* (Paris: Cerf, 2009).
3. Nicholas P. Wolterstorff, *Journey to Justice* (Grand Rapids, MI: Brazos, 2013).

5

Friendship: Cultivating Theological Virtue

Marianne Farina, CSC, and Masarrat Khan

Friendship overcomes boundaries; boundaries set by cultures, nations, or faiths. Throughout history many stories have been written, and movies made in memory of alliances between persons who have braved the barriers set before them. That persons will have more in common with others of their own kind, be it gender, language, nationality, or faith, is a recognizable phenomenon. But human need for contact and for deeper bonds urges individuals to ignore or sidestep the differences that their worlds have created. These differences can become avenues to new thought, and reveal the vision and ideas of distinctive beliefs and ethical actions. Too often, history documents how religions have been pitted against each other for power and political gains. However, through friendship, we learn ways to respect religious traditions and we develop a desire to learn from these teachings. The mutual love and affection between friends helps each to overcome prejudices and develops tolerance and empathy. It cultivates a sense of dignity for all faith traditions through a deep appreciation of their own faith, as well as that of another's faith.

As such, interreligious friendship holds the promise for a greater degree of tolerance and understanding and a stronger bond among religious differences. James L. Fredericks reflects on the role of virtues in cultivating friendships and proposes that we should consider interreligious friendship itself as a virtue.[1] He posits that cultivation of virtue, practices of hospitality, and types of friendship addressed in philosophical and religious teachings are powerful resources for helping people live "creatively and responsibly with people whose religions view the world significantly different from our own."[2] He maintains that friendship "as the preferential love (*philia*) arising out of our need for self-fulfillment through relatedness" positions us to experience transformative relationships.[3] Like other friendships, interreligious friendship implies a "conjunction of values and skills." This is especially true when suggesting a "virtue" of interreligious friendship. Fredericks notes that virtues have histories and these histories inform the way we acquire them and exercise them. Personal stories about personal preferences as they contribute to the development of virtue, in particular, can help "truths foreign to my own tradition become real possibilities for shaping and giving direction to my life."[4]

In the Indian subcontinent comprising now India, Pakistan, and Bangladesh, Hindus and Muslims, for centuries, have fought for control and supremacy over their respective regions. Their actions also have affected other minority communities, as misinformation and superstitions were spread to keep communities apart. Yet, the subcontinent also is known for its unique blend of diverse cultures, for the myriad of different religions and ethnic groups that coexist. Muslims, Hindus, Buddhists, Sikhs, Christians, Parsis, Jews, Tribal Groups, and Animists live together sometimes in harmony, at times in conflict. Despite differences, similarities exist in language, food, and attire. The subcontinent has also witnessed a type of inter-mingling that has fostered cooperation among these groups. Although intermarriage is still discouraged, it is not uncommon. From these alliances, respect and a deeper knowledge of each other emerges.

Education has encouraged a better understanding and exchange of views and values. As a result, many traditional taboos and prejudices regarding different ethical systems have been overcome. Educational institutions provide an opportunity for diverse communities to share common goals, fostering learning for the good of persons and society.

Interreligious, cross-cultural friendships lead those engaged in these endeavors to promote projects that can seek a more congenial world. Less friction and tensions, created by thoughtless derogatory remarks or actions, pave the way for a greater awareness of each other's sensitivities. Friendship counters the animosity caused by ill-motivated individuals and reduces misconceptions and prejudices arising from different lifestyles; friends help and sympathize during times of stress and turmoil. In 1947, Hindu/Muslim friends helped each other during the riots that erupted over the India/Pakistan partition. In 1970, Bangladeshis from various traditions also formed the communities to help each other during the liberation war. These memories restore one's faith in the innate goodness of all people.

There is a saying in the Bangla language that the fingers of one's hands are not the same length, which is why hands are strong and useful. In the same way, in diversity is our strength and beauty. Meeting people from various faiths or cultures stimulates learning new ideas, different ways of worship, and the particular ways that each tradition approaches God, and to the world, in general. People travel to different countries to visit beautiful, historical, and novel sights, to savor the food, in short to experience the "exotic" cultures. Some work in foreign countries either by assignment or because they wish to experience different cultures.

We, Masarrat Khan and Marianne Farina, are friends of 30 years. For this chapter, we reflect on our history as emblematic of interreligious dialogue. Together we read Christian and Islamic texts about love of God and friendship and connected these with the teachings both traditions maintain concerning interreligious relations. Recollecting, reading, and reflecting have led us to consider friendship as a theological virtue that includes infused moral virtue—God-given capacities to love God and the grace to see God in others. The various acts of particular ways of loving represent who we are as persons and as friends. Through them, we embrace the "conversion" to the flourishing that God seeks in us and all creation. Moreover, our experience of interreligious friendship serves as a witness to the possibility of Christians and Muslims living in, and acting with, greater solidarity.

My Friendship with Marianne Farina: Masarrat's Reflection

Leaving home to work in Bangladesh takes courage. In doing so, Marianne Farina entered a completely different environment in 1983, a place fraught with political turmoil and natural disasters. We met as colleagues at Holy Cross High School in Dhaka and became friends. Marianne's sense of humor and her helpfulness first attracted me. Over the years, we have shared our families, our problems, our thoughts, and our love for one another.

After three years, our interaction became more irregular because Marianne had been transferred to another mission outside Dhaka, and I had left teaching at Holy Cross School. Through mail and mutual friends, we shared our busy lives—Marianne with her new ministry and I with my three lively children and husband recovering from heart surgery. There were opportunities, though, for us to join in on projects. Marianne needed books for the rural education program she developed; and she sought my help in getting them from the Bangladesh Rural Advancement Committee (BRAC), an NGO based in Dhaka that had developed a successful nonformal system of education. After collecting the books, I traveled to Jalchatra with my family to visit Marianne, who was working with the Mandi tribal community in Tangail. She took the girls for an unforgettable motorbike ride to see monkeys in the nearby jungle. In 1994, Marianne returned to the United States for further study. Periodically, I heard about her from the sisters at Holy Cross School. A few years later, she enrolled in doctoral studies in theological ethics at Boston College. When Nehrir, my daughter, went to Boston for graduate work, Marianne contacted her and offered help and advice. When Marianne returned to Boston in 2004 to defend her dissertation, she stayed with Nehrir. While there, and via long-distance phoning, I reconnected with Marianne after a long interval. We had kept in touch through infrequent e-mail, as I was still not very skillful with the computer.

On a visit to the United States in 2010, Marianne and I met after many years. Together, we went to visit her sister and spent a week with her family. The days were filled with discussions about family and mutual friends, but invariably we turned to other issues like religion, politics, current affairs, and books. During our stay, I prayed regularly and found Marianne encouraging and respectful toward my practice. When I attended Sunday mass with her, she explained many of its rituals to me. Our lives are so different; and yet, when we are together, we realize we have so much to share and appreciate.

This is the age of cell phones and the Internet, and it is easier to stay abreast of each other's lives. We have long conversations whenever possible. We talk about many things, but our favorite topic is religion. Marianne has studied Islam, and I have had much interaction with Christian communities. As a Muslim, not only do I follow my faith with deep devotion, but I also seek to delve deeper and learn more about Islam. I am also interested in interreligious dialogue. Discussions help. We offer to one another books, movies, and websites about religion, culture, and dialogue. Thus, through Marianne, I learn of new authors, seminars, and dialogue meetings. Dialogue is critical, and we have some programs in local communities, as well as the formal study of dialogue in the Philosophy Department at Dhaka University. However, dialogue needs even greater promotion. We have many different communities living side by side for centuries, and we participate in each other's festivals, holy days, and marriage ceremonies. And though we note many similarities between our customs, there are still tensions when groups only highlight differences. We need to find ways to foster positive, personal, and social relations among religions, searching for that bond that connects us to God and one another.

In *The Four Loves*, C. S. Lewis describes friendship as a rare form of love that has great value to communities.[5] While same-gender friendships may raise suspicions in the western world, Bengali accepts and celebrates friendships among women. In fact, the Bangla word *shokhi* means a deep, loving relationship between two women. A *shokhi* is more than a sister, mother, or daughter; she is one in whom the other confides and draws comfort from, in short, a soul mate. Some treasured stories in Bengali literature, for example, *Badhon Hara* by Kazi Nazrul Islam, describe this kind of friendship.

Lewis further notes that friendship is one form of love for God.[6] It is a blessing, a grace that many of us fail to understand. He writes that friendship is a combination of three loves—Need-love, Gift-love, and Appreciative-love—and, ultimately, Charity: God's friendship with us and ours with God.[7] Lewis describes "Need-love" as that which cries out to God in our poverty, or to another, recognizing that we are lost without him or her. "Gift-love" longs to serve God, or longs to give happiness to another. "Appreciative-love" gives glory to God and "holds its breath and is silent, rejoices that such a wonder should exist."[8] In actual life, "the elements of love mix and succeed one another, moment by moment," and Lewis illustrates this by exploring the four loves: affection, friendship, romance (*eros*), and unconditional love of God (*caritas*). He describes the natural ways of the first three loves and ways these might prepare us for the grace of unconditional love, that is, Charity. God's love for us establishes "a supernatural Need-love for God and a supernatural Need-love for one another."[9] God's love does not substitute for the natural loves, but they are "summoned to become modes of Charity while also remaining the natural loves they were."[10] C. S. Lewis shows how friendships can tutor us in all elements and forms of love, as long as we remain open to the movements of God's grace in these friendships.[11] If my friendship with Marianne is chosen by God, then it is our destiny to be friends, to appreciate and to give comfort and love to one another. In this way, our friendship contributes to the quality of life in our faith communities and cultures.

These ideas remind me of the Sufi teachings of Maulana Rumi, Al Mansur, and Rabia Basri. The Sufis also advocated love as a means to reach their beloved "God." To them, the search for one's beloved transcends religions, class, and nations. Anyone can practice love, humility, and charity toward their companions to come closer to the ultimate goal—God who is All Love. To achieve bliss in this life, one has to be tolerant, forgiving, and kind; one must pray and ask for God's mercy. Only the deserving achieve bliss/ecstasy/oneness with God. My friendship with Marianne is an opening to experience blessings from God and helps me to realize how these blessings can be shared with others.

My Friendship with Masarrat: Marianne's Reflection

Reflecting on my friendship with Masarrat reminded me of the original challenges I faced when coming to teach at Holy Cross High School in Dhaka, Bangladesh. For over a hundred years, Holy Cross men and women have engaged in all types of ministry and service with the people of Bangladesh. Our primary focus has been to contribute to, and strengthen, educational and vocational training programs in the country.

Holy Cross' presence in Bangladesh seeks to proclaim the Gospel through our ministry of education. The philosophy of Holy Cross education calls for educating the whole person. Blessed Basil Moreau, founder of the Congregation of Holy Cross, maintained that fostering the intellectual over the spiritual was a flawed pedagogy. Moreau believed that the knowledge was at the service of moral formation, and that this formation moves persons beyond their own personal fulfillment as they seek the transformation of church and society.

In the rich diverse religious and cultural heritage of Bangladesh, this formation takes on a new dynamism. It is one of accompaniment, mutual witness to, and conversion toward the truth and goodness found in all these traditions. Friendship with Masarrat Khan was my initial entry into this formation.

I came to Bangladesh in 1983 and met Masarrat as English teachers at Holy Cross High School. She taught the upper division classes, while I taught the middle grades. I consulted with Masarrat about the curriculum and teaching techniques. Soon, the faculty room became more than a place for me to share tea with her and discuss teaching. We began discussing other topics related to the religions and cultures of Bangladesh.

Though most of our conversations were in English, I did experiment with speaking Bangla. Masarrat gently corrected me and also taught me the origin and contexts of words and phrases, thus helping me to appreciate Bangladesh's rich cultural heritage. She generously invited me into all aspects of life in Bangladesh, which gave me courage to continue my ministry and learning. Over the years, our willingness to explore new vistas for learning together and a readiness to accept the challenges posed by our new knowledge of one another has nurtured our friendship. Though months, even years, can go by without much contact, we remain "in dialogue" with one another and our "conversion" deepens.

One of my first experiences with encountering the Muslim community took place in her home. Early in our friendship, Masarrat invited me to her house for Eid al-Adha (the feast of sacrifice). Colleagues and benefactors often invited Holy Cross Sisters to Eid celebrations; however, our relationship let me ask direct questions about the Muslim festival and witness how families celebrate Eid. She explained to me how Eid al-Adha commemorates Abraham's obedience to God in his willingness to sacrifice his only son and the celebration recalls in prayer and ritual the story of Hagar's radical trust to God. Muslims share in the spirit of this event by rededicating themselves to God through ritual observances of the Haj (pilgrimage) in Makkah (Mecca).

Throughout the day, as an expression of thanksgiving to God, Muslims invite the poor to share in the meal. I saw in Masarrat's home how the meal was prepared and served with equal regard for the poor, family, and friends. Being new to the experience of Islam, this was my initial insight into the way Islamic beliefs connect directly with ethical communal action, especially in service to the poor.

Masarrat also shared with me that a Muslim's outreach to the poor and oppressed is not restricted to certain festivals or to Muslims alone. Islam, she noted, was about learning to see the needs in the community and respond to them. This encounter, and the many others throughout the years of our relationship, taught me much about the daily life of Muslims and the importance of interreligious friendship.

Theologian C. S. Song speaks about such quality of relating when he marks out steps toward a "dialogical conversion" of faiths.[12] He describes seven stages using the metaphor of Alice's journey through the looking glass in the story of *Alice in Wonderland*. The first four stages of an encounter help us recognize that the other faith tradition is indeed different. In these "rooms," we check the "creeping imperialism" that can frame these meetings. Song reminds us that at these initial meetings, dialogue has not begun, but the intentions for the dialogue are purified because we refrain from stereotypical assessments of the other, trying not to evaluate them from our own lenses of beliefs. Recognizing differences creates the honest environment necessary for deep learning. Each tradition tells its story without the fear of judgment by the partner. The final stages require a commitment to learn from the other traditions. We ask more questions and continually correct our conception of their "world." As Song states, there is "nuance, responsiveness, explicit and implicit meanings inspired by the rhythms of life and touched by visible and invisible powers and people's identity as well as meanings of cultures/religions."[13]

In stages five and six, we learn to cultivate virtues for relating to the religious other without reducing the differences between us. This phase is essential to healthy friendships among religions because we "do not lose track of the enduring otherness of the friend."[14] As Song notes, these stages are honest efforts in building relationships. "We have seen another and they have seen us."[15] Trust develops and we seek the knowledge and skills that might help us converse more openly. The seventh and final stage is that of "dialogical conversion." It is dialogue because we have learned how to listen and speak with each other honestly. It is conversion because, under the rubric of "mutual learning," we recognize the need for internal conversion; that is, living our faith authentically, not leaving our faith tradition.

My friendship with Masarrat has tutored me in this mutual learning. Our relationship reveals God's love for us, and this love continually calls us to deeper communion with God. It becomes a way of perfection. HRH Prince Ghazi, in his book *Love in the Qur'an*, speaks of love as an abundance, in which the soul is perfected and renewed. "Virtue of soul, to faith and tranquility" is the way of Beauty.[16] His study offers an etymology of the word "love" in Arabic, detailing over 37 different types of love mentioned in the Qur'an. The lexical analysis serves as a typology exploring the various qualities and stages of love. Divine Love, God's Love, is a free gift coming to the creature and is Beauty itself. Our human love is an inclination to divine Beauty experienced in human relations and worship of God. Ultimately, the "dialogical conversion" is a turning toward this Beauty.

Prince Ghazi also describes various stages of love showing how God guides souls through love "to their true inner selves [where God dwells] and God graced them with something deeper than tranquility, namely the *Sakinah* [Qur'an 48:18], the Peace of the Heart."[17] Friendship, in this light, increases our awareness of the inner beauty of God in others, and this is the source of our growth in knowledge and virtue.[18] Masarrat and I are companions on this journey, and the graces we receive deepen our own faith and provide insights for how we might share this gift with others.

Reflecting on Muslim-Christian Dialogue and Friendship

As discussions for this essay emerged, we discovered that—though we did not become friends in order to dialogue about our faiths—understanding interreligious friendship as a virtue connects our personal histories with the efforts of both our traditions concerning interreligious dialogue. Recent teachings in Islam and Christianity point to the need to cultivate dialogue among world religions. They recommend ways that communities can grow to a deeper understanding of one another and outline means for sustaining such relations. These recommendations offer a helpful foundation for the cultivation of friendship as an "infused theological virtue," something which we both experienced in our friendship.

The documents of Vatican II in general, and *Nostra Aetate* in particular, opened up the possibility for this type of engagement. In this encounter with other religions, differences are acknowledged, but so is an "emphasis on seeking out and highlighting the positive, shared understandings."[19] In a brief five sections, *Nostra Aetate* raises critical ideas concerning relations among religious traditions. Central is the recognition that one common area of concern, regardless of national, cultural, or religious origin, is the human quest for meaning. We all ask questions about life, good and evil, suffering, sorrow, and happiness. Moreover, the document states, "From ancient times down to the present, there is found among various peoples a certain perception of that hidden power which hovers over the course of things and over the events of human history."[20] Noting how this quest and awareness support a profound religious sense among people, the document further teaches, "The Catholic Church rejects nothing that is true and holy in these religions."[21]

The third and fourth parts of the statement reflect on relations with Islam and Judaism. These sections illustrate the special relationships that exist between the Catholic Church and these two other branches of the Abrahamic tradition. Regarding Islam, the document cites significant aspects of Muslim faith that related to Christianity. Muslims "adore the one God," and take "pains to submit wholeheartedly to even His inscrutable decrees, just as Abraham...submitted to God."[22] They also honor Jesus "as a prophet" and "Mary, His virgin Mother; at times they even call on her with devotion."[23] Acknowledging that there have been "not a few of quarrels and hostilities" between Muslims and Christians, the Catholic bishops exhort us "to forget the past and to work sincerely for mutual understanding and to preserve as well as to promote together for the benefit of all mankind social justice and moral welfare, as well as peace and freedom."[24] The final section expresses a commitment to fight against discrimination among peoples because of their "race, color, condition of life, or religion."[25] The synod of bishops proclaims boldly, "We cannot truly call on God, the Father of all, if we refuse to treat in a brotherly way any man, created as he is in the image of God...'He who does not love does not know God (1 John 4:8).'"[26]

Following Vatican II, the Roman Catholic Church formed special commissions, held interreligious gatherings, and created documents and guidelines to promote good relations among religions. These efforts indeed have fostered four key areas of dialogue: dialogue of life, dialogue of common (social justice) works, dialogue of spiritual experiences, and doctrinal dialogue. All forms are critical to sustaining the dialogue with religious communities, and in particular ways, each leads to a deeper understanding of the teachings and lived experience of the religious other. In Bangladesh, we see many examples of this experience. The work of Caritas, which employs Muslims, Hindus, and Christians in its development work, has been a model of the way these forms integrate to promote cross-cultural and interreligious understanding. As projects unfold in the various cities and villages, especially those concerned with promoting social justice, communities that might not have had the opportunity to know one another discover ways to collaborate. These positive experiences inspire others to seek opportunities for interreligious encounters and learning. In addition, Christian theological seminaries and formation houses study Islam as a formal part of their education. The Catholic Church in Bangladesh believes that leaders of communities need good information about Islam and Muslim faith practices, so that they can contribute to build positive relations among Christians and Muslims in their ministries.

For the Muslim community, institutes for Islamic study and agencies promoting human development have also provided resources for positive engagement with other religious traditions. Rooted in the tradition of the Qur'anic mandate for mutually transformational dialogue,[27] these initiatives serve as directives for Muslims. Though history shows that premodern exegesis held varying, and at times conflicting, views regarding the interpretation of these mandates, scholars such as al-Zamakhshari (d. 1144) and Fakhr al Din al-Razi (d. 1210) clearly encouraged dialogue. As Asma Afsaruddin notes, the examination of key verses about relations of Muslims with non-Muslims offers an "interpretative stimulus today for the emergence of a genuine pluralism in Muslim ethical and moral thinking vis-à-vis other religions and peoples."[28] Programs, documents, and guidelines developed in recent times support her insight.

In Bangladesh, we both experienced the work of BRAC, whose programs include microfinance, education, healthcare, and access to legal services for the poor and disenfranchised. The organization began in Bangladesh, but is now present in 11 countries. The programs are successful because of BRAC's commitment to involve all members of a community regardless of religion, culture, or status in these works in laying the foundation for developing personal agency and group direction.

Islamic academic centers and programs often provide guidelines for interreligious dialogue. Muhammad Shafiq and Mohammed Abu-Nimer, in collaboration with the International Institute of Islamic Thought (IIIT), published their guidelines for interfaith dialogue.[29] They emphasized that dialogue means "building bridges" among various groups of Muslims and between Muslims and non-Muslims. The goal is to promote respect, tolerance, and peace according to God's Will. Thoughtful, open, patient, and honest dialogue, as outlined in the Qur'an—such as the "etiquette for dialogue"—is the way to attain this goal. The guidelines draw from Prophet Muhammad's life examples of how Muslims can remain steadfast in these efforts, especially when challenged by negative forces.

In 2007, a group of Muslim scholars and leaders published an open letter to Christian leaders, titled "A Common Word between Us and You." Averring that "the future of the world depends on peace between Muslims and Christians," the letter represents one of the most energetic initiatives taken up by the Muslim community to promote dialogue. The drafters maintain that, "the basis for this peace and understanding already exists. It is part of the very foundational principles of both faiths: love of the one God, and love of neighbor."[30]

The Muslim community has organized and financed a constellation of conferences and documents to address the various aspects of this letter, offering creative and helpful interpretations of *kalimat sawa'* (a word of justice) as "love of God and neighbor." The embrace of this discourse by Christians and Muslims, though mostly in academic circles, serves as a model for local communities as well. The document recognizes that "finding common ground between Muslims and Christians is not simply a matter for polite ecumenical dialogue between selected religious leaders" but agenda for all communal action.[31] The basis for relating to the religious other is belief in God, God's love, and God's desire for divine goodness as witnessed by concern and care for others.

For this essay, Masarrat and I reviewed these developments in interfaith dialogue, and we agreed that dialogue between Muslims and Christians is essentially theological. Our "dialogical conversion" is boundless as we remain open to the God's spirit. Dialogues and common endeavors are seeds for the virtue of interfaith friendship. Nurtured and cared for, these relationships help our communities excel in goodness consistently, with "insight, perceptiveness, and intelligence."[32] Certainly, the experiences we shared as teachers in Bangladesh were seeds for this growth.

Furthermore, Fredericks's analysis of interreligious friendship demonstrates that it is not only a virtue, but a theological virtue.[33] The skills we develop—for example, interpreting our tradition in new ways and using our imagination skillfully—become permanent.[34] Through this excellence, we become people skilled "in goodness because we have sought and practiced the good often enough so that the good [of befriending] is a genuine expression of who we are."[35] Created in God's image, God continually guides us toward the goodness that fulfills us; love for God, who is all Goodness, flourishes. In this way, friendship with each other and love for all others thrives. Similarities and differences bathed in this dwelling place of trust reveal the Divine to one another, and encourage us to see God in many others. While weeks, months, or years separate us, our friendship continues to form us as persons who draw near to God and others. Our lives witness to God's call to perfect happiness or real blessedness (*beatitudo* or *as-Sa'ada al-Haqiqiya*).

As we speak of interreligious friendship as a theological virtue, we also realize that as such this virtue brings forth all the infused moral virtues. For the goal we seek transcends us, and we need God's special assistance. Infused moral virtue elevates or transforms human actions so that they reflect the blessedness, peace, or perfect happiness in the fellowship of God. Islam speaks of "doing the beautiful" (*ihsan*), which means a deep consciousness of God (*taqwa*) permeates all of our actions. Christianity speaks of charity, God's friendship with humans, as the form of all virtue. Charity perfects our nature and God's wisdom directs all that we do. As such, infused virtues give new meaning to the work of prudence, justice, courage, and temperance and their fruits. As we remain friends, these capacities progressively evolve to take on dimensions of "dialogical conversion" not simply for our own good, but also for others'. Interreligious friendship, as an infused virtue, challenges us to practice prudence as intellectual humility; courage as a heroic fidelity to remain engaged not only with our friend, but also her religious world; justice as an exercise of spiritual magnanimity toward all faiths; and temperance as a studiousness that shapes our passions into God's desire for the unity of all creation. Thus, infused moral virtues are actions of responsive and responsible love for God, particular friends, and their communities, and all others. As noted above, natural loves are taken up into Charity, God's love for us.[36] God can grant us the grace of supernatural "appreciative love," which embraces the mystery of the Divine within another person. Consistently and joyfully, we recognize the good, the blessed, the Beauty in this person. In this vision, dialogue continues and deeper conversion awaits us.

Dialogue and the Theological Virtue of Interfaith Friendship: Final Thoughts

We, Masarrat and Marianne, have been blessed by our friendship. We continually learn from one another and remain open to the ways God guides us, giving witness to the importance of interreligious friendships in our communities. Believing our friendship is a gift, we wish to share some closing thoughts about cultivating virtue and solidarity among religions.

Muslims and Christians teach that the goal of interreligious dialogue is to discover common ground between religions and cultures. They also recognize that dialogue is a form of learning about God and one another.

More than simply a means for cooperative social action, these dialogues are an opportunity to share experiences and beliefs about God and our religious traditions. Cultivating interreligious friendship as virtue helps persons attain this goal and two skills are key in these efforts.

Moral theologians teach that the most fundamental law of nature is love, and remind us that loving well is not easy. Becoming skilled and faithful/faith-filled lovers is crucial.[37] Attentiveness to an inner conversion precedes "dialogical conversion." C. S. Lewis's typology indicates ways to love others of our own faith, not only with need-love, but also gift-love. As we have experienced in our loves, reciprocity can blossom to an appreciative-love; that is, learning to appreciate the existence of another and to see God in them. Such progress requires listening well, being attentive to the values of another, and therein present to the Beauty and complexity of their lives. HRH Prince Ghazi reminds us that we need to be tutored in the best circles of love. The circle of love in which believers live increases their faith as God "beautifies the soul, giving it greater capacity to love…"[38] An enlarged capacity to love enables us to accept the complexity within our own tradition and to dialogue with divergent views. In a pluralistic society, this is greater and more complex, making it necessary to prepare believers to face this reality. Dialogues contribute to a maturation of the faith and the skills learned are transferable to all types of dialogue.

We need to extend this contemplation by opening our circle of love. In *Ecclesiam Suam*, Paul VI speaks of concentric circles of dialogue, and the ways dialogue within and across these circles support one's faith-life. These include the Catholic Church, the Christian circle, the circle of religious traditions, and the circle of all humanity.[39] Attentiveness to any rung of this circle calls forth our presence to all others. Therefore, we need to acquire the virtue of intellectual and spiritual hospitality by praying for other faith communities, studying their traditions's, and encouraging face-to-face exchanges between members of different faiths. These venues will not water down our beliefs or shy away from "God-talk." These initial steps open the door for more intimate and theological exchanges. Such conversations foster engagement with the "complex particulars" of another's faith[40] and honor the best in these respective traditions.[41]

In these discoveries about other faith traditions, we create the setting for dialogue and practice, listening and speaking with each other honestly, testing our assumptions and correcting conclusions. Dialogues become seedbeds for interreligious friendship, because mutual learning has been cultivated and trust grows. Though diversity within and among faith traditions exists, we come to appreciate the goodness of each path as a celebration of existence itself, as that which exists in God. We encounter beauty and its splendor marks every aspect of life, community, and civil society. We become lifelong learners and believers who seek the face of God in the face of the other. Tagore celebrates the potential for such interfacing in our interfaith relations in his poem "Thou Hast Made Me Known." Here, God makes us known to each other—turning the "distant" into an intimate—and in this process, we come to know God.[42] In our 30-year journey as friends, we have come to know each other, and come to know God through each other. Such is the grace of friendship.

Notes

1. James L. Fredericks, "Interreligious Friendship: A New Theological Virtue," *Journal of Ecumenical Studies* 35.2 (Spring 1998): 159–160.
2. Ibid.
3. Ibid., 164.
4. Ibid., 169.
5. C. S. Lewis, *The Four Loves* (New York: Harcourt, Brace, 1988), 68.
6. Ibid., 78.
7. Ibid., 16–17, 130.
8. Ibid., 17.
9. Ibid., 129.
10. Ibid., 133.
11. Ibid., 90.
12. C. S. Song, *Tell Us Our Names: Story Theology from an Asian Perspective* (Maryknoll: Orbis Books, 1984), 121.
13. Ibid., 32.
14. Fredericks, "Interreligious Friendship," 172.
15. Song, *Tell Us Our Names*, 136.
16. HRH Ghazi bin Muhammad, *Love in the Qur'an* (Chicago: Kazi, 2011), 359.
17. Ibid., 227.
18. Ibid., 311.
19. Edward Idris Cardinal Cassidy, *Ecumenism and Interreligious Dialogue* (Mahwah: Paulist Press, 2005), 129.
20. *Nostra Aetate* (Vatican: October 28, 1965), 2, accessed June 17, 2014, http://www.vatican.va/archive/hist_councils/ii_vatican_council/documents/vat-ii_decl_19651028_nostra-aetate_en.html.
21. Ibid.
22. Ibid., 3.
23. Ibid.
24. Ibid.
25. Ibid., 5.
26. Ibid.
27. Asma Afsaruddin, "Discerning a Quranic Mandate for Mutually Transformative Dialogue," in *Criteria of Discernment in Interreligious Dialogue*, ed. Catherine Cornille (Eugene: Cascade Books, 2011), 101.

28. Ibid., 118.
29. Muhammad Shafiq and Mohammed Abu-Nimer, *Interfaith Dialogue: A Guide for Muslims* (Herdon: International Institute of Islamic Thought, 2007).
30. "A Common Word between Us and You," October 13, 2007, 2, accessed June 17, 2014, http://www.acommonword.com/the-acw-document/.
31. Ibid., 15.
32. Patricia Lamoureux and Paul J. Wadell, *The Christian Moral Life: Faithful Discipleship for a Global Society* (Maryknoll: Orbis Books, 2010), 117.
33. Fredericks, "Interreligious Friendship," 169.
34. Ibid., 170.
35. Lamoureux and Wadell, *The Christian Moral Life*, 116.
36. Lewis, *The Four Loves*, 133.
37. Lamoureux and Wadell, *The Christian Moral Life*, 179.
38. Ghazi, *Love in the Qur'an*, 297.
39. Paul VI, *Ecclesiam Suam* (Vatican: August 6, 1964), accessed June 17, 2014, http://www.vatican.va/holy_father/paul_vi/encyclicals/documents/hf_p-vi_enc_06081964_ecclesiam_en.html.
40. Chrys McVey, OP, "The Land of Unlikeness: The Risk and Promise of Muslim-Christian Dialogue," *New Blackfriars* 89.1022 (July 2008): 369–384.
41. Ian Markham, *Engaging with Bediuzzaman Said Nursi: A Model of Interfaith Dialogue* (Burlington: Ashgate Press, 2009), 175.
42. S. K. Paul, *The Complete Poems of Rabindranath Tagore's Gitanjali: Texts and Critical Edition* (New Delhi: Sarup, 2006), 263.

6

Ties That Bind: Interfaith Friend, Interfaith Kin

Rita George-Tvrtković

"*Ako Bog da*." These three words permeate the speech of my mother-in-law of 13 years, Izeta. It is the Bosnian equivalent of the Arabic phrase popular with Muslims the world over, *Insha'Allah* (If God so wills). Somehow these words best capture the essence of the ever-evolving relationship between me, an American Catholic, and Izeta, a Bosnian Muslim. I see our spiritual friendship as God-willed, since we did not choose to be friends. Rather, we became family first, and friends later. We are thus both interfaith friends *and* interfaith kin. A unique situation indeed, and certainly not planned on our part. Providential.

I am a theologian who studies medieval Christian-Muslim relations. I also have over 15 years of practical interfaith experience in the religiously diverse city of Chicago, and many Muslim colleagues and friends. But interfaith is my profession. On the personal side, I am a cradle Catholic, and I always envisioned marrying someone as devoted to my faith as I am, someone who would go to Mass with me, study the Bible with me, and help me teach our children how to pray the Our Father. Instead, I married a wonderful Bosnian man who was baptized Catholic, but considers himself "non-religious but hopeful about the existence of God." My husband is the product of an interfaith marriage between a Catholic father and a Muslim mother, a common phenomenon in urban Bosnia. But this essay will not be describing the ins and outs of our "interfaith" marriage (for in our case, "interfaith" means differing levels of religiosity, not different religions). Rather, I will be reflecting on the relationship between me and my husband's Muslim mother. I have made many Muslim friends over the course of my career, but there is something exceptional about an interfaith relationship with someone who is not only a friend, but family.

In this essay, I will explore two interrelated topics: (1) the unique nature of my Bosnian mother-in-law's Islamic faith and practice, and its effects on my own Catholic faith; and (2) how the dual nature of our interfaith friendship-kinship even more strongly underscores the notion that authentic understanding between religions—at both the grassroots and institutional levels—is not only enhanced by, but in fact requires the presence of enduring, personal relationships. The concept of "spiritual kinship" between religions mentioned by the Vatican II document *Nostra Aetate*[1] and later church teaching takes on new meaning when your interfaith friend is really and truly your kin.

Bosnian Mother-in-Law

My mother-in-law is a Muslim, but her "Muslimness" is conveyed in ways that are not normative for Muslims elsewhere in the world, but which are entirely common for Bosnia. For example, she does not wear *hijab* (Muslim female headcovering) or pray five times a day. An outsider might conclude that she is a secular Muslim in the same way one might speak of a secular Jew. But this is not the case. Rather, her brand of religiosity is consonant with how Islam is practiced in Bosnia.[2] She comes from a line of female religious leaders: her mother was a *bula*, which means that her grandmother most likely was one, too.[3] A *bula* is a traditional female Muslim religious leader in Bosnia, whose tasks might include leading women's prayer sessions, reciting the Qur'an, presiding at funerals, and faith healing.[4] My mother-in-law's *bula* mother did participate in the annual Ramadan fast, wear *hijab*, and memorize the Qur'an, but her daughter (my mother-in-law) does not practice Islam in this way, partly because she was raised during the Communist era in Yugoslavia, where religion was not prohibited, but not exactly encouraged either. Another reason my mother-in-law is less traditionally Islamic than her mother is because when she was 12 she left her home in a smaller town to attend a boarding school in a large city, and there are differences between how Islam is practiced in rural and urban Bosnia.[5] In general, urban Muslims in Communist-era Yugoslavia tended to be less strict in their religious praxis than their small towns and rural counterparts.[6]

My mother-in-law is not a *bula*, despite her lineage. And although she might not appear to be Muslim in the typical ways, she nevertheless identifies herself proudly as such. Furthermore, she has retained much of her mother's spiritual sense. She constantly affirms her strong belief in the one God, and is a deeply religious person to her core. The characteristically Muslim phrases that frequently come out of her mouth (*mashallah* or *al-hamdulilah*, for example)[7] *do* in fact mean something to her; they are not simply Arabic leftovers subtly distinguishing her Bosnian language from the otherwise nearly identical Croatian or Serbian spoken by her Christian neighbors. Her "Muslimness" is conveyed every time she reminds us about the oneness (*tawhid*) of God and the unity of all believers in that one God (which she reminds us of often), and in her attentiveness to cleanliness, which in Bosnia "is often seen as a particularly Muslim virtue."[8] She eschews alcohol, she dresses modestly, she celebrates *bajram* (Bosnian for *Eid al-Fitr*, the holiday which marks the end of the month of Ramadan), though she rarely fasts. She prays, but in her own way: never in Arabic, and never using the familiar movements of the formal *salat* prayer.[9] She is Muslim the "Bosnian way."

But her religious praxis does not end there. Because she is a Muslim woman who married a Catholic man,[10] she incorporates some Catholic practices into her personal religiosity, too. For example, not only does she make sure to have an annual Mass said in honor of her now deceased Catholic husband, but she also attends that Mass herself. And every Sunday when my children and I go to church, she asks us to light a candle for her husband and for other beloved dead. At home, she would be upset if we did not call her to participate in our nightly candle-lighting and singing of "O Come, O Come Emmanuel" during Advent. She sings with us. She also joins us in saying grace before meals. And she very much enjoys watching television movies about Jesus at Easter or Christmas. "Of course I want to learn about Jesus during your religious holidays," she declares proudly, "just as I watch Muslim religious programs that are broadcast in Bosnia during *bajram*." My Muslim mother-in-law keeps the "Christ" in Christmas better than many Christians do! Also, on ordinary Sundays, she sometimes attends Mass with me and my children; quite frankly, she comes more often than my husband. But the fact that a Bosnian Muslim would regularly participate in Catholic rituals should not be seen as extraordinary, because "for Bosnians, being Bosnian means growing up in a multicultural and multireligious environment, an environment where cultural pluralism is intrinsic to social order...[and] an essential part of their identity."[11]

Other aspects of Izeta's religiosity affect my own. Currently, she lives half the year in Bosnia, and half the year in Chicago with us. Since she does much of the cooking when she stays with us, she is always reminding me about fasting and Friday abstinence during Lent. Indeed, a few times she has saved me from accidentally eating meat when I otherwise would have forgotten. Once, when she asked me about the specifics of my Good Friday fast, she humbled me by telling me that her Bosnian Catholic husband ate only dry bread and water when he used to fast. This impressed me, for I was used to fasting the American Catholic way: one full meal plus two smaller meals not to equal the first. So, in effect, my Muslim mother-in-law made me more aware of the variety of *Catholic* fasting practices, and in so doing, inspired me to greater discipline. Furthermore, she regularly and gladly prepares two meals on Lenten Fridays, one with meat for her and my husband, and another without meat for me and my children. I do not ask her to do this; she simply offers, and I gratefully accept. She does not think that preparing two meals on Fridays during Lent is anything out of the ordinary. This is because her deep religious sense is not only spiritual, but practical. She is not only interested intellectually in all things having to do with faith, but also attentive to my family's religious needs on a very ordinary, everyday level. When she is with us, she helps to create a household environment that I would call "hospitable" to faith. Her reminders about fasting, and her questions about why I pray a certain way or what we do on Palm Sunday, and why, encourage me to be more diligent in my practice. I am a better Catholic because of her, because she inspires me to be more disciplined in, and attentive to, the particulars of fasting and prayer.

Her strong faith in God and her unique brand of Islamic religiosity have not only deepened my own Catholic faith and practice, but that of our entire family also. The fact that she often comes to Mass with us is significant not only to me, but also to my children, especially since my husband rarely comes with us to Mass, or practices any aspect of the faith, for that matter.[12] It is all the more a wonder, then, that when Izeta joins in our singing ritual during Advent, my husband has not infrequently wandered over to sit silently with us, contemplating his Muslim mother and Catholic wife and children praying this ancient Christian hymn together. Her Muslim presence at, and blessing on, our quotidian religious activities helps my children to experience their Catholic faith as something familial. Yet, at the same time, they know that *Baka* (Grandma) is a Muslim, not a Catholic. They are not confused. She comes to Mass with us, but does not receive communion. She lights a candle, but does not genuflect. She offers the greeting of peace, but does not recite the Our Father. There is no "double belonging" here.[13] She knows where the boundaries are, and so do they.

One might wonder, though: in what sense is my mother-in-law my friend? Certainly, she is interfaith kin. But that does not automatically make her a friend. Friendship is a choice, and friendship must be intentionally cultivated. And indeed, our friendship has developed gradually over the past 13 years of my marriage, as I have come to understand and respect the person she is. Aside from sharing a love for my husband/her son, and for my children/her grandchildren, we also share a particular kind of spiritual sensibility. We both delight—truly delight—in all things religious, but most especially in the more mundane aspects of religious praxis: tending a grave, *Insha'Allah*, "O Come, O Come Emmanuel," praying the *tasbih*,[14] and bread-and-water Fridays. We delight in these practices, and we share them in our everyday lives (this sharing is made possible by the fact that she lives with us for six months out of the year—a living situation that is not as common among American in-laws as it is for in-laws in other countries). Even more, we spend time together discussing various religious customs. This might not seem extraordinary. But in actuality, the fact that we frequently have such conversations is a true testament to our friendship, since talking is not easy: Izeta is an introvert, and my Bosnian is adequate, but not fluent (she speaks no English).

She and I both dwell on the borders where religions meet: I as a scholar who studies medieval Christian-Muslim relations, and she as a Bosnian whose homeland has both flourished and floundered at the nexus between East and West, Christianity and Islam, religion and atheism. I think it is this ever-present curiosity about each other's faith—hers about my American Catholicism, and mine about her unique brand of Islam (which turns out to be not so unique in Bosnia)—that makes us friends. It is our shared religious curiosity that draws us together—beyond our identities as mother-in-law and daughter-in-law, across barriers of personality and language—into friendship as women of faith.

Spiritual Kinship

As described above, my relationship with my Muslim mother-in-law is unique, since she is not only an interfaith friend, but she is also kin. This fact has led me to reflect on the following question: how might the idea of spiritual kinship, which is often cited as an essential foundation for interreligious dialogue, be enriched in cases when an interfaith friend is also a member of your family?

Before this question can be explored, a brief review of Catholic teaching on the notion of spiritual kinship as it relates to interreligious dialogue is in order. The Second Vatican Council document *Nostra Aetate* begins and ends by affirming that all human beings, no matter what religion, are related to one another by virtue of our common origin in God, the creator of the universe: "We cannot truly call on God, the *Father of all*, if we refuse to treat *in a brotherly way* any man, created as he is in the image of God. Man's relation to God the Father and *his relation to men his brothers* are so linked together that Scripture says: 'He who does not love does not know God' (1 John 4:8)."[15] Section 4 on Judaism in of *Nostra Aetate* repeatedly and unequivocally affirms the spiritual kinship between Christians and Jews. For example, "the *spiritual patrimony* common to Christians and Jews is thus so great." And over 20 years after *Nostra Aetate*, the kinship between Jews and Catholics was further underscored by Pope John Paul II during his historic visit to the synagogue of Rome in 1986: "The Jewish religion is not something 'extrinsic' to us, but in a certain way is 'intrinsic' to our own religion. With Judaism we therefore have a relationship we do not have with any other religion. *You are our dearly beloved brothers* and in a certain way it could be said, our elder brothers."[16] The very same wording underscoring Catholic-Jewish kinship was repeated in the 1998 Vatican document *We Remember: A Reflection on the Shoah.*[17]

Although the Church's connection to Judaism via a common ancestor, Abraham, is strongly affirmed in *Nostra Aetate*, *We Remember*, and many other documents,[18] its connection to Islam via Abraham is mentioned in *Nostra Aetate* only in passing, and somewhat equivocally, in section 3: "The Church regards with esteem also the Muslims... they take pains to submit wholeheartedly to even [God's] inscrutable decrees, *just as Abraham, with whom the faith of Islam takes pleasure in linking itself,* submitted to God."[19] The line "with whom the faith of Islam takes pleasure in linking itself" suggests a certain level of uncertainty regarding Islam's Abrahamic connection; while the Church wished to refer, at least in passing, to the Muslim claim of Abrahamic lineage, it seemed somewhat unwilling to affirm the connection definitively at that time (1965).[20] But the Catholic theology of Islam has progressed since then, and as early as 1979, Pope John Paul II told Turkish Christians that "they [Muslims] have like you the faith of Abraham," and later in the speech he specifically identifies "the spiritual descendants of Abraham" as "Christians, Muslims, and Jews."[21] During a 1985 speech to participants in a Muslim-Christian colloquium, the pope stated unequivocally: "As I have often said in other meetings with Muslims, your God and ours is one and the same, and *we are brothers and sisters in the faith of Abraham.*"[22] The fact that the pope called Muslims "brothers" is particularly significant, observes Michael Fitzgerald, since in the early church the term "brother" was usually only reserved for fellow Christians.[23]

According to these and other Catholic documents, the notion of spiritual kinship is fundamental to interreligious dialogue. But does the spiritual kinship to which these documents refer remain only at the theoretical level? Is the idea of spiritual kinship introduced here simply a compelling reason to begin interfaith dialogue, something to be abandoned soon after? It is precisely at this point that interreligious friendship, the subject of this volume, becomes relevant, since it could be argued that real interfaith friendship picks up where hypothetical interfaith kinship leaves off. For friendships can sometimes grow out of what are initially, rather formal interfaith dialogues. The order of such interfaith relationships therefore seems to be: first spiritual kin, then interfaith dialogue partner, then interfaith friend. But what about familial relationships? How might husbands and wives of different religions, in-laws of different religions, siblings and cousins of different religions bring to life the elusive and seemingly purely theoretical notion of spiritual kinship alluded to in these documents? How might interfaith kin confound the "normal" progression of interfaith relationships as outlined above?

The Ecumenical Directory of 1993 suggests that *Lumen Gentium*'s notion of the domestic church[24] might be a practical and powerful way to further ecumenism: "these marriages contain numerous elements that could well be made good use of and develop both for their intrinsic value and for the contribution they can make to the ecumenical movement."[25] Might interfaith marriages (and families) be held up as a positive way to improve interfaith relations, too? Of course, it must always be remembered that the Catholic Church does not recommend interfaith marriage. Catholic-Catholic marriage is, for obvious reasons, presented as the ideal.[26] However, the instance of both ecumenical and interreligious marriage is growing in many parts of the world. And in some countries (Bosnia, Nigeria, Lebanon),[27] interfaith marriage has been exceedingly common both in the past and present. Yet, despite its increasing occurrence in many parts of the world today, interfaith families are often still not seen as a positive resource for interreligious dialogue. This is despite the fact that church teaching presents *kinship*, not friendship, as one of the most compelling reasons to begin interfaith dialogue in the first place. The Catholic kinship argument is as follows: you should engage in dialogue with people of other religions, because you are not as different as you think; in fact, you are related, at least spiritually, because you both were created by God the Father, and that is why you should talk to one other. After you begin to talk, you might begin to understand each other at least on an intellectual level. You might begin to respect one another. And, you might eventually even become friends.

Friendship is a choice, and there is no guarantee that a dialogue partner will become a friend. You choose to be friends with someone you genuinely like, and with whom you share certain qualities and interests. But family is different. You might choose your spouse, but you do not choose your in-laws, siblings, parents, or cousins. The word "family" expresses a unique kind of relationship, a unique kind of love. It may or may not contain elements of unconditional *agape* and the more elective *philia*; but in any case, it is not a disinterested kind of love.[28] How might the notion of interfaith kinship be helpful then, not only for its ability to *spark* dialogue between people otherwise unlikely to speak across religious borders, but also to *sustain* dialogue over the long haul, even and especially when the conversation gets difficult? Friendships fade, but family is forever. Blood and in-law connections remain, despite divorce and estrangement. They are the "ties that bind." Might this be a useful metaphor for the best kind of interfaith relationship: one that endures over time, through it all?

In short, it seems that kinship might be a more appropriate way to talk about interreligious relationships than friendship. While refocusing on relationships is good for interfaith dialogue, friendship might not actually be the best place to start. We should begin with kinship—with our most fundamental connection as children of God—and then work on friendship from there.

My mother-in-law's unique Muslim faith has deepened my own. But even more, our shared friendship, rooted as it is in an abiding curiosity about all things religious, has enhanced the faith of my entire family—husband, children, wife—in small, but significant ways. I can only wonder if (and hope that) my Catholic faith has increased and deepened my mother-in-law's Muslim faith, unique as it is. In any case, our spiritual kinship-cum-friendship has affirmed my belief that authentic understanding between religions requires long-lasting personal relationships between believers. Mere proximity to the other is not enough for such understanding to occur, as the recent war in Bosnia sadly affirms. Mere *knowledge* of the other is not enough, either. Only by sharing our lives and faith in an intentional way, only by calling the other "friend" or "sister" or "mother," can true understanding and solidarity between people of faith, and ultimately between religions, begin and hopefully endure over time. *Ako Bog da.*

Notes

1. For example: "The spiritual patrimony common to Christians and Jews is thus so great" and "We cannot truly call on God, the Father of all, if we refuse to treat in a brotherly way any man, created as he is in the image of God. Man's relation to God the Father and his relation to men his brothers are so linked together that Scripture says: 'He who does not love does not know God' (1 John 4:8)." *Nostra Aetate* (Vatican: October 28, 1965), 4 and 5, accessed June 17, 2014, http://www.vatican.va/archive/hist_councils/ii_vatican_council/documents/vat-ii_decl_19651028_nostra-aetate_en.html.
2. For an excellent introduction to the unique nature of Bosnian Islam, see Tone Bringa, *Being Muslim the Bosnian Way* (Princeton, NJ: Princeton University Press, 1995).
3. "Families would have a long tradition of religious instructors and learned men and women." Ibid., 197.

4. For a good description of the *bula*, see Bringa, *Being Muslim the Bosnian Way*, especially 206–220. Bringa also discusses the tensions between the more mainstream Islam as practiced in the cities, and the more heterodox Islam as practiced in rural areas, the latter of which often includes traditional tasks of the *bula*, such as interpreting dreams, faith-healing, and divining the future. Ibid., 224–231.

5. Ibid., 204.

6. Ibid., 8–9, 60.

7. These are two common Arabic phrases used by Muslims the world over. *Mashallah* expresses approval or congratulations; it literally means "God has willed it to be so." It could be seen as a corollary to *Insha'Allah*: just as *Insha'Allah* expresses hope that something will happen in the future (but only according to God's will), likewise does *mashallah* acknowledge (and express gratitude for) something that has happened in the past according to God's will. *Al-hamdulilah* means "praise/thanks be to God."

8. Ibid., 68.

9. *Salat* is the Arabic word for the formal, five-times-a-day prayers and ritual movements performed by Muslims, and is distinct from *du'a*, more informal supplication. *Salat* is one of the five pillars of Islam, the practice of which identifies a person as a Muslim.

10. John V. A. Fine notes that "since World War II, 30 to 40 percent of urban marriages in Bosnia have been mixed" in his "Medieval and Ottoman Roots of Modern Bosnia," in *The Muslims of Bosnia-Herzegovina*, ed. Mark Pinson (Cambridge: Harvard University Press, 1998), 2. While the Qur'an allows Muslim men to marry "women of the book" (Christians or Jews), Muslim women have traditionally been required to marry Muslim men only.

11. Bringa, *Being Muslim the Bosnian Way*, 83.

12. "It is primarily what people do that defines their membership" in a particular religious community in Bosnia. Ibid., 81.

13. For more on the notion of double or multiple religious belonging, see Catherine Cornille, ed., *Many Mansions? Multiple Religious Belonging and Christian Identity* (New York: Orbis, 2002).

14. The *tasbih* are Muslim prayer beads. There often have 33 or 99 beads, which are used to repeat praises to God, or say the 99 names of God. Remembrance of God's name (*dhikr*) is a practice encouraged by the Qur'an.

15. *Nostra Aetate*, 5. Emphasis mine.

16. John Paul II, "Speech at the Synagogue of Rome," April 13, 1986, 4: *AAS* 78 (1986), 1120. Emphasis mine.

17. Vatican Commission for Religious Relations with the Jews, "We Remember: A Reflection on the Shoah" (Vatican: March 16, 1998), 27, accessed June 17, 2014, http://www.ccjr.us/dialogika-resources/documents-and-statements/roman -catholic/vatican-curia/278-we-remember.

18. "A new future in which there will be no more anti-Judaism among Christians or anti-Christian sentiments among Jews…befits those who adore the one Creator and Lord and have a common father in faith, Abraham." Ibid., 29.

19. *Nostra Aetate*, 3. Emphasis mine.

20. The idea of the "Abrahamic faiths," that Christians, Jews, and Muslims are linked through the spiritual patrimony of Abraham, is relatively new, and can be traced to the writings of French Orientalist Louis Massignon (d. 1962), whose thought influenced the framers of *Nostra Aetate*, 3. Medieval Christians rarely spoke of such a connection between Muslims and Christians; they traced Islam's roots to Ishmael, not Abraham.

21. John Paul II, as quoted in Pontifical Council for Interreligious Dialogue, *Recognize the Spiritual Bonds which Unite Us: Sixteen Years of Christian-Muslim Dialogue* (Vatican: 1994), 23.

22. John Paul II, "Address to the Participants in the Colloquium on 'Holiness in Christianity and Islam'" (Vatican: May 9, 1985), 1, accessed June 23, 2014, http://www.vatican.va/holy_father/john_paul_ii/speeches/1985/may/documents/hf_jp-ii_spe_19850509_partecipanti-simposio_en.html. Emphasis mine.

23. Michael Fitzgerald, "Dialogue and Proclamation: A Reading in the Perspective of Christian-Muslim Relations," in *In Many and Diverse Ways: In Honor of Jacques Dupuis*, ed. Daniel Kendall and Gerald O'Collins (New York: Orbis, 2003), 185.

24. *Lumen Gentium* (Vatican: November 21, 1964), 11, accessed June 23, 2014, http://www.vatican.va/archive/hist_councils/ii_vatican_council/documents/vat-ii_const_19641121_lumen-gentium_en.html.

25. Pontifical Council for Christian Unity, *Directory for the Application of Principles and Norms on Ecumenism* (Vatican: March 25, 1993), 145, accessed June 23, 2014, http://www.vatican.va/roman_curia/pontifical_councils/chrstuni/documents/rc_pc_chrstuni_doc_25031993_principles-and-norms-on-ecumenism_en.html.

26. *Catechism of the Catholic Church*, 1633–37, accessed June 23, 2014, http://www.vatican.va/archive/ENG0015/_INDEX.HTM.

27. Nadim Shehadi and Dana Haffar-Mills, *Lebanon: A History of Conflict and Consensus* (London: Tauris, 1988). For more on interfaith marriage in Lebanon and Palestine, see Abe Ata, *Intermarriage between Christians and Muslims* (Ringwood: David Lovell, 2000).

28. James L. Fredericks stresses the importance of *philia*, fraternal love, in interfaith dialogue in his article, "Interreligious Friendship: A New Theological Virtue," *Journal of Ecumenical Studies* 35.2 (Spring 1998): 159–174.

7

Rasoul, My Friend and Brother

Bradley J. Malkovsky

In the summer of 2008, I received an unexpected phone call from my
wife, Mariam, asking me to leave my office at the university as soon as
possible and come meet her at her store in downtown South Bend. I was
surprised at this, since she did not normally work on Thursdays, but on
this particular day, and for reasons that are no longer remembered, she
had decided to pay a brief visit to one of her employees. On the phone,
she had simply asked me, "Can you come soon? I'll explain when you get
here."

When I arrived, I found her sitting at the back of the store with three
people I had never seen before. A tall distinguished looking man with
salt-and-pepper hair and a short-clipped beard in a grey sport coat was
sitting beside a woman wearing a tunic and a headscarf. In another chair,
also wearing a headscarf, was a young girl. The man was looking at me
smiling. "I'd like to introduce you to the Rasoulipours," said Mariam.
"They're from Iran." The man rose to his feet, still smiling, and extended
his hand to me. "Rasoul Rasoulipour,"[1] he said. After we exchanged names,
Mariam added, "He studied in India, in Pune." "Really?" I said. "Where
in Pune did you study?" "At the University of Poona,"[2] he answered, still
smiling. "In the department of philosophy." I noticed immediately the
refined gentleness of his speech. "I studied at the University of Poona,
too," I said, a bit amazed. "In the Sanskrit department." "Yes, I know," he
replied. "Your wife told me." Pune is the city where my wife grew up and
where I had lived as a student for five years. The friendly Iranian man and
I therefore had much in common.

I soon learned that Rasoul had earned a doctorate in the philosophy
of religion, and that he had studied the teachings of other religions in

addition to his own Shiite Muslim faith. Comparing faith traditions was, therefore, another thing we had in common, since I taught the relationship of Christianity to other religions at Notre Dame. At that first meeting, I also learned that the name of Rasoul's wife was Maryam, the same as my wife's name, only with a slight variation in spelling. Their daughter, Fatemeh, who was sitting so quietly, was ten years old, the same age as our daughter, Karina. "Well," I thought to myself, "if this is not divine providence bringing us together, I don't know what is."[3] Maryam, Rasoul's wife, had come to the store that day only because someone at the mall had recommended my wife's boutique as a place where she might find clothing more suitable to her taste. Rasoul joined her there a bit later that afternoon. The fact is that, if the two women had not met at that very hour, our families might never have met and become friends. And Rasoul might never have become my colleague in the department of Theology.

When I think back on this unlikely first encounter, I am reminded of the teaching on divine providence given in Vatican II's "Declaration on the Relationship of the Church to Non-Christian Religions," known by its Latin opening words *Nostra Aetate* ("In our time"). It is well known that this document—more than any other—ushered in a new era of positive Catholic relations with other religions. But even more than its very affirming presentations of Hinduism, Buddhism, and Islam in articles 2 and 3,[4] and with Judaism in article 4, what strikes me now when I think of my friendship with Rasoul is a passage that appears already in article 1: God's "providence, His manifestations of goodness, His saving design extend to all men."[5] That means whether we are believers, agnostics or atheists, whether we are Christians or Muslims, or belong to no religion at all, God is at work in our lives, the God who, according to Jesus, knows the number of hairs on our head (Luke 12:7, Matthew 10:30). God is active in the lives of everyone. Today more than ever we recognize that God is bringing together people of different backgrounds and faiths, in order to foster a greater unity, love, and justice on earth. Ultimately, according to the teaching of Christians and Muslims, this unity will reach its completion in the full and final communion with a loving Creator in the resurrection. I believe it was divine providence that brought our two families together that day from such great distances and across religious boundaries, and it is this shared conviction that has provided the foundation upon which our friendship has been built.

There are other examples from Rasoul's life that, in the light of faith, might be seen as instances of divine play at work. I remember during that same summer, while we were at lunch, how Rasoul asked me what had caused Notre Dame to become such a famous Catholic university. I told him that, more than anything else, it was due to the work of Father

Theodore Hesburgh, for many years the president of the university (1952–1987) and a nationally known figure. Rasoul asked me how long ago Father Hesburgh had lived. I told him he was actually still alive, though now very old, over ninety.[6] "How can I meet him?" Rasoul asked. "Not much chance of that," I said. "It's harder to meet Father Hesburgh than it is to meet the pope. He has constant visitors all day long. You would need to set up an appointment long in advance." I knew that Rasoul would be leaving the United States soon and heading back to Iran. He would have to meet Father Hesburgh another time.

Rasoul smiled, but said nothing.

The next day I ran into my friend on campus. His first words were, "I had a very nice conversation yesterday with Father Hesburgh." "You did?" I said. "How did you manage that?" Rasoul laughed. "I just went to his office to make an appointment, and the lady working there told me I was in luck, that someone had just cancelled their appointment, and if I wanted to, I could visit with Father Hesburgh immediately for about forty minutes."

In that warm exchange, Rasoul discovered that Father Hesburgh had once travelled to Iran and had visited a number of cities renowned for their spirituality and learning. Father Hesburgh spoke that day of his love for Iran and its people. He was at the same time concerned about the callous misuse of political power among those in high office. But he did not mean only abuses in Iran. His final words to Rasoul were, "You and I both deserve better presidents."

The Iran-Iraq War

I had never before met a scholar of philosophy and religion who had risked his life clearing land mines or suffered the effects of a mustard gas attack. Rasoul, whose face so often radiates such a kindly peaceful smile, has seen his share of suffering. The worst suffering occurred during the Iran-Iraq War (1980–1988), one of the longest and bloodiest of the twentieth century, a seemingly endless conflict in which the Iranians suffered four hundred thousand deaths,[7] and the Iraqis a quarter million. Though Rasoul never used any weapons himself, he did volunteer for the Iranian militia numerous times, and one of his tasks was to defuse mines planted by the Iraqis. Each man was given a hand tool to unearth the explosives, an especially difficult job at night, because many of the mines and detonating wires were so small. The work was nerve-wracking; any moment could be a man's last. Rasoul saw friends and comrades injured and killed. A close friend in Iran now lives with two prosthetic hands. Others lost legs and eyes. Rasoul himself was spared such injury, but another kind of misery still awaited him.

In April 1988, while serving as a mine-clearer in the military, Rasoul had just arrived at the Iraqi port city of al-Faw, which the Iranians had captured two years earlier. By the time Rasoul entered the city, Saddam Hussein had stepped up his operations to recapture the city. On the evening before the beginning of Ramadan, on April 17, 1988, just one day after Rasoul's arrival in al-Faw, the Iraqi military launched a surprise attack on the badly outnumbered Iranian volunteer militia. This Second Battle of al-Faw[8] resulted in a victory for Iraq in only 35 hours. The Iranians were forced to give up al-Faw and retreat to their homeland. What was decisive for Iraq's victory was its use of chemical weapons.[9]

As Rasoul tells the story, he was in the basement of a hospital in al-Faw leading 16 soldiers in the final prayer of the day when the bombs hit. No one expected an attack on the eve of Ramadan. Iraqi warplanes and missiles were dropping mustard and nerve gas on the city. The Iranians' gas masks were only two rooms away, but by the time Rasoul put on his mask it was too late; it had been contaminated.

Direct exposure to mustard gas has an immediate impact with long-lasting effects. The men began coughing and gasping for breath. Rasoul watched helplessly as two of his comrades began foaming at the mouth and then choked to death while waiting for an ambulance.

The Iranians quickly withdrew from the city, and the injured were taken to a nearby desert hospital. The men undressed and showered with anti-chemical soap, and their contaminated clothing was destroyed. Their skin began to burn and blister. Eventually Rasoul would be given the news that one of his lungs was so damaged as to be unusable, and that he would suffer for the rest of his life from chronic bronchitis.

Within a short time, all those who had survived the gas attack in the hospital basement went blind. They were transported by train over a two-day period to a hospital in Tehran specializing in eye trauma. All the men were put in the same hospital ward, confined to their beds most of the day and night. This was a time of great misery. The eye pain was constant. "Some nights we could not sleep, the pain was so bad," Rasoul told me. And there was the psychological torment of having to accept that the life you once knew has been suddenly shattered and that you do not know when your suffering and helplessness will come to an end. Life in the hospital was endless, tedium, and dark. The blind men would converse with each other from their beds while waiting for their next meal to arrive or the next dose of medicine.

I could not help but press for further details. "What about your faith?" I asked. "We prayed," he said. "Sometimes we prayed together. The others would ask me to lead the prayers or recite the Qur'an. As we prayed in bed we imagined ourselves doing the bowing and prostrating that are part of the prayer."

Each night, the blind patients in the ward were treated with eye drops administered by women volunteers from the city. The physician's hopeful prognosis was that the men's sight would be restored in three to four months. Yet, day after day, as the drops were put into their eyes, there was no sign of improvement. All day and all night, Rasoul lay in total darkness. But, one night, a new woman arrived. Rasoul did not recognize her voice. He asked her if she had come to administer the eye drops like the other women before her. The woman replied, "The medicine will not help. Only God can heal you." And then she was gone. The phrase was taken from the Qur'an, chapter 26, verse 80: "He [God] who cures me when I am ill."[10] This verse had been written in Arabic script, framed, and placed on the wall above Rasoul's bed, a handwritten gift from a friend who had come to visit him in the hospital.

The next morning, Rasoul reported to his physician that his sight had started to return. He could see shapes, but the light hurt his eyes, so he was given dark glasses. The physician regarded the sudden improvement as miraculous. Eventually, Rasoul's full sight was restored. It was only gradually that he told this story to me and to others. As to the woman who had recited the Qur'an verse, he asked several people about her, but he never learned her identity. It was almost as if an angel had come. And he is convinced that his healing was from God.

During the following four months, Rasoul and the others were transferred to a different hospital in Tehran for skin treatment. Everyday, soaps and salves were applied to the burns and blisters that covered the bodies of the men. The application caused such pain that the men would cry out in agony. Their shouting and moaning sometimes continued through the night. "We would sometimes go four nights in a row without sleep," he said. "It was terrible." He returned to the front after being released from the hospital, but from then on only as a chaplain.

Rasoul bears no ill will or bitterness toward the Iraqi military. He refers to them as "my Iraqi brothers." He knows that they were just following orders. He always emphasizes the need for forgiveness between enemies. "At the bare minimum," he says, "enemies need to keep talking to each other, to be reminded of their common humanity that comes from God." The Sunnis he calls "my Sunni brothers and sisters,"[11] despite the long history of animosity between Sunnis and Shiites. "It is the extremists in both groups that say the others are not Muslims," he told me once. "But all are Muslim. All follow the Qur'an and the Prophet Muhammad."

"Why Do You Want To Write About Me?"

It was only after much persistence on my part that Rasoul agreed to open up about the details of his life. "Why do you want to write about me?" he would ask. "I am not anyone important, and I am not a holy man." I assured him that we in the West know too little about Islam, about Shiism, and about the venerable history of the Persians. And so he consented to answer my questions, though I am well aware that in this essay I am merely alluding at best to a civilization stretching back to antiquity that has produced some of the world's greatest theologians, scholars, poets, and holy people.

Prior to the Iranian Revolution in 1979, Rasoul had excelled in math and engineering. But then the universities were shut down for two years. Only the theological colleges remained open. He entered Shahid Motahari University in Tehran, where he stayed nine years, earning a BA in Islamic Studies and an MA in Islamic Philosophy. This was during the time that he sometimes served in the militia. His BA subjects included Arabic and Arabic literature, Qur'anic exegesis, and the basic teachings of Shiite theology, such as God's activities and attributes, divine justice, prophecy of the Prophet Muhammad, the 12 Imams, and eschatology. For the MA degree, he studied Islamic philosophy, traditional and modern Western philosophy, the philosophy of science, and Islamic mysticism.[12]

The study of Islamic theology and philosophy came naturally to Rasoul, since he had spent so much time from a young age practicing Qur'anic recitation.[13] To recite the Qur'an properly involves learning sophisticated rules governing not only the pronunciation and length of sounds, but also the intonation, the cadence, the stops, and the pauses between them. While living in India, I had regularly heard the beautiful call to prayer (*adhan*) issuing from mosques all over Pune, sometimes while attending Mass; but it was not until recent years, especially through Rasoul, that I have begun to appreciate the aesthetic and spiritual significance of the Qur'an as a whole, and the precision and rules by which proper recitation should be performed.

The importance given to proper recitation has to do with the Muslim belief that the Qur'an presents to us the very speech of God. This love of the Qur'an's sound and language, not just its message, is typical of Muslims the world over.[14] The very sound of the Qur'an, even for one who does not understand its meaning,[15] has the capacity to reveal the majesty and transcendence of God—so much so that non-Muslim listeners at public recitations have converted on the spot to Islam.[16]

As a boy, Rasoul would freely attend recitation class several times a week for three-hour sessions after the regular school day had ended. There he learned that the best reciters (*qaris*) in the world were Egyptian.[17] And so one of those three hours involved listening carefully to recordings of Egyptian *qaris*. Rasoul eventually became one of the most well-known reciters in Iran. After winning the national competition for university students at the age of 19, he appeared regularly on Iranian television. Over the years, he has been sent by the Iranian government to more than 30 countries to officiate as a judge at competitions for Qur'an recitation. He is no longer able to recite as well as in his younger years, because after the chemical attack he has only one functioning lung; but he still teaches young people to recite, as time allows.[18] At the local mosque in South Bend this year (2013), he has taken time out from his academic work to teach 34 children from the ages of three to 15 to recite one hour each evening during Ramadan.[19]

Rasoul's Work In Interreligious Dialogue

Rasoul is in many ways a bridge between different worlds, between Shiite and Sunni Islam, between Islam and other religions, between philosophy and theology,[20] between thinkers and mystic-poets, between Iran and the United States. He pointed out to my students one day in class how ignorance of the other is one of the major obstacles to understanding and peace. Both Muslims and Christians suffer from ignorance. "Too many Christians think Islam is a religion of terror and violence. Too many Muslims think Christianity is a tool of the West representing imperialism and power, that Christianity is a religion of tyranny."

In 2006–2009, while retaining his position as professor in the department of Religion and Philosophy at Kharazmi University, Rasoul served as director of the Center for Interreligious Dialogue in Tehran, an institution under the auspices of the government's Organization for Islamic Culture and Relations. His experience of different religions in India and his knowledge of English made him an obvious candidate for the position. As director, he quickly began reaching out to representatives of other religions living abroad, inviting them to visit Iran for friendly exchanges and bilateral dialogues. Perhaps his most controversial move was to invite a 27-member delegation of American Jews to visit Iran in 2007. Delegations from the World Council of Churches also arrived, as did Christian groups from the United States from different churches[21] and representatives from many European countries and Russia.

Rasoul has participated in two meetings with representatives of the Vatican's Pontifical Council for Interreligious Dialogue, one of them in Rome in 2008, which took place after Pope Benedict's controversial Regensburg address.[22] The topic of the conference was "Faith and Reason in Christianity and Islam."[23] Though he was not an active participant at the colloquium, Pope Benedict XVI personally welcomed the Iranian delegation. What particularly impressed Rasoul was that Pope Benedict did not wait for the Muslim representatives to come to him. Instead he approached them himself one by one to shake hands. Rasoul added, happily, that when Pope Benedict received a copy of the Qur'an he took it to his lips and kissed it. He called it "a precious book."

As Rasoul told me, when Vatican representatives meet with Muslim theologians, they tend not to debate issues like the divinity of Jesus or the Trinity. Past experience has shown that debates and doctrinal warfare tend to lead nowhere. Instead, Catholic and Muslim theologians more frequently meet nowadays to inform and clarify knowledge of their traditions and spiritualities, and to discuss common values and teachings.[24] I myself have never felt the need to debate Rasoul on anything, even though we are aware of significant differences between our two faiths—the most obvious one being that Rasoul follows the Prophet Muhammad, whereas I follow the Jesus of the New Testament. Very frequently, he has taught me to appreciate the key differences between Shiite and Sunni Islam and to see important similarities between the Shiite community and the Roman Catholic Church, especially in regard to its hierarchical structure[25] and its rich history of mysticism and mystical theology. We have recommended to each other scholars and thinkers who are important. Recently, I referred him to the works of Karl Rahner and Catherine LaCugna on the Trinity, and Rasoul presented me with a book on Shiism by the famous Allamah Sayyid Muhammad Husayn Tabatabai (1903–1981).[26]

The issue of conversion from one religion to another has also never come up. Though other Muslims have taken my wife Mariam aside in the past and questioned her about why she left Sunni Islam and became a Catholic,[27] neither Rasoul nor Maryam have ever done this. It is clear that we four feel a strong inner connection, a spiritual bond that unites us, despite belonging to different religions. Doctrinal differences have not prevented us from seeing the work of God and the love of God in the religion of the other. We all believe in one good and gracious God. It is at the heart of our identity and the foundation of our relationship. According to Rasoul, the knowledge of God's love is the "secret inner life" of religion. He quotes the famous poet Rumi (1207–1273) on this point:

> The sect of lovers is distinct from all others,
> Lovers have a religion and a faith of their own.[28]

It is Rasoul's conviction that the main task of all religions, despite their many differences, is to promote love, compassion, and forgiveness. Love is the antidote to the illness of human alienation and anxiety, of conflict and war. And love is not only the answer to society's ills but is also the surest path to God. Our love for God is a response to God having loved us first. "People could not love God if He did not already love them. God created people out of love for them," he says, and as proof cites the Qur'an 5:54: "[the] people He loves and who love Him."[29] As a Muslim, he teaches that the human love of God will increase to the extent people follow the example and teaching of the Prophet Muhammad, purify and cultivate their souls, remember God ceaselessly, and strive to become perfect human beings. But this path of mystical ascent is not divorced from the daily observances of orthodox Shiite practice, nor does it seek to disengage itself from the world and its many needs; rather, such mystical awareness is the fruit of daily orthodox practice. Orthodox Shiite observance and spiritual growth are understood to be one. Sufism, which is found in many forms in present-day Iran, is to be distrusted whenever it follows a path that would dispense with the Qur'an as the sure foundation of Islamic praxis and spirituality. That is why expressions of Sufism that would follow an independent path of ascetic perfection and interior prayer disconnected from mainstream Muslim community life are treated with suspicion. "Sufism," then, as it is understood in Iran, is to be found not only in Islam, but also around the world in many other religions. This broad understanding of Sufism is rarely known in the Western world, a view that distinguishes between orthodox and heterodox forms of Sufism.

Rasoul has spoken of "the vast literature on Divine Love in nearly every Islamic language from Arabic and Persian to Turkish and Swahili, as well as in most of the local languages of India and Southeast Asia," all of which attest to "the significance of the dimension of love in the inner life of Islam." But among the poets it is the Persians who have brought forth the highest expression of this inner life of Islam through their devotional verse. It is astonishing to note the sheer number of Persian poets and poet-scholars who have emerged century after century with their message of love, especially in the Middle Ages: from Rudaki (858–941), Tabrizi (1009–1072), and Omar Khayyam (1048–1131), to Nizami (1141–1209), Rumi (1207–1273), Saadi (1210–1291), Sanai (11th-12th c.), Attar (1145–1221), Hafez (1325/26–1389/90), Jami (1414–1492), and many more. Of these, Hafez is the most popular. His poetry and wisdom sayings are committed to memory by countless Iranians.

God's love, Rasoul says, in keeping with this broad stream of Persian mystical theology, enables us to meet the stranger and guest as the sacred other. "It is in extending hospitality that we mysteriously meet God." Mariam and I have experienced this loving hospitality many times over the years through our visits to the Rasoulipour family. One day in particular, from this past summer, comes to mind. It was the middle of Ramadan, and Mariam and I dropped in at the Rasoulipour apartment one hot late afternoon in July for a short visit. As is the custom with observant Muslims, Rasoul and Maryam had been fasting from dawn to dusk for many days, taking neither food nor liquid. In northern Indiana this year, the fast lasted more than 17 hours. We expected to stay only a short while. We knew about the hospitality of our friends from previous visits. We agreed beforehand that when they offered us something to drink we would accept it graciously and take nothing more, since it would be awkward to eat while our friends did not. But our protests were in vain. A large assortment of snacks and drinks was placed before us, after which we were given a full meal of sumptuous Iranian dishes, followed by tea and bowls of ice cream mixed with cookies, fruits, and chocolate candies (they know about my sweet tooth). Rasoul and Maryam looked on, smiling as we ate. What they had, in fact, done was give us a large portion of the meal they had prepared for themselves to be eaten at the end of the day, after the fast had ended. It goes without saying that we were deeply moved and humbled by their generosity—and by their love.

Among his contemporaries, the man who has most inspired Rasoul as a model of faith is the late Haji Ismael Dulabi (1903–2002). Dulabi's education in Muslim theology was informal at best, but he was a mystic of great simplicity, deep wisdom, pure humility, and love, and so holy that some of the greatest Shiite scholars and political figures would go to him to receive his blessing. All his sermons and private talks began and ended with the love of God. People from across Iran would come to him for guidance in the spiritual life. He would teach them to follow the Qur'an, to strive after a pure heart, to be constant in prayer, to be forgiving when wronged, to be generous to the poor, and to be merciful just as God shows mercy to us. But he was also an agent of God's mercy in another way: as a healer. Many people would travel to the Haji's home to be healed of their infirmities. In some instances he would inspire his visitors to believe that they, too, could heal others through faith in God. When I hear such stories about Dulabi, his healing presence, his humility, his desire to put himself at the service of others, his strong faith in God's goodness and love, I think automatically of these qualities in my friend, Rasoul. Dulabi would have been proud to count him as one of his followers.

Conclusion

Since our friendship began in 2008, Rasoul has taught three times at Notre Dame and has been a popular, even beloved, teacher and a wonderful colleague, always ready to participate in panel discussions, symposia, and other gatherings, both theological and spiritual. He has been associated not only with our Department of Theology, but also with the Institute for Church Life.[30] He has taught courses on Shiism and Catholicism and on science and religion. What I found of particular interest about Rasoul's interaction with his students, and a clear indication of his humility, was that he did not reveal to them his accomplishments in Iran, his travails at war, his miraculous healing, nor his meeting with Pope Benedict. Those students, some of whom were my own students, were surprised when they learned about all this from me.

As I conclude this essay, Rasoul has just left the United States, only two days ago, and returned to Iran with Maryam and Fatemeh. A few weeks earlier, Mariam and I received an unexpected gift from them when they visited our home: a beautiful handwoven carpet from Iran that they had used each day here in America while performing their prayers. A few days later, on the day of departure, Rasoul surprised me yet again with the gift of a *misbaha*, that is, a string of 33 prayer beads, by which one recites the 99 beautiful names of God. Both gifts are a reminder that prayer is our obligation and our delight, and it is what unites our families across great distances.

So what have I learned from this friendship? I have learned to appreciate more of what it means to be a Muslim, to value not only Islam in general, but also to value *this* particular kind of Islam, that is, Shiite Islam.[31] We Americans are often exposed by our media to Iran and Shiism, but the news almost always seems to focus on political discord and violence. We seldom have an opportunity to learn about the deep spirituality of so many practicing Shiites like my friend Rasoul, with their trust in God's love and mercy. We have so little chance to discover what we have in common, not just on the purely human level, as we might discover with people we might come to know anywhere, but also on the level of faith and spirituality. And I have also come to learn about and appreciate the vast treasury of Shiite theology and Persian mystical writings.

Rasoul is, moreover, an impressive witness of what it is like when trust in God molds one's whole life. It seems to me that God is palpably blessing him and his work. He is a representative of what is best in Islam, a Muslim who is an ambassador of love, peace, and prayer. And it is a tribute to our spiritual connection that our friendship sometimes makes me forget our religious differences. During moments of deep personal exchange, I become aware that I am in the presence of God who surrounds us and blesses us. Our friendship is therefore a gift of God, a reminder of God's presence to all, and a reminder that God is greater than our religions, even when our faith traditions rightly seek to honor God and call us to submit to the divine will, which is Love.

Many of us here at Notre Dame, at the local mosque, and in other parts of Indiana and the Midwest—both Muslim and Christian—look forward to the day when Rasoul and his family would return. There are other Christians in the United States who have known Rasoul longer than I, and who could just as well have written about their interreligious friendship with him. After all, Rasoul makes friends easily wherever he goes. I am honored to have been given the privilege to write about him. My hope is that this little essay will contribute in some small way to bringing about a greater understanding and unity between Christians and Muslims, and to encourage us all to allow our passing acquaintance with people of other religions to bloom into a deep friendship. I cannot stop thinking of my friend, lying on his hospital bed, his eyes aching and blinded by mustard gas. Despite his agony, Rasoul slowly learned how to see once again. There are so many wounds that prevent Muslims and Christians from seeing one another today. The mysterious woman who had visited Rasoul told him that "the medicine will not help." I must disagree, at least when it comes to healing the blindness of religious believers. The medicine of deep and lasting friendships does help to heal our aching eyes. And working through this medicine, it is God and God alone that heals us.

Notes

1. "Rasoul" is Arabic for "prophet."
2. The city's normal spelling is Pune, though the university still goes by "Poona."
3. This is not to deny that God may also send difficult people into our lives for some greater good, such as deepening us spiritually or teaching us to be more attentive to the suffering of others.
4. In its discussion of various religions, *Nostra Aetate* gives more attention to Islam than to Hinduism or Buddhism, no doubt not only because the histories of Islam and Christianity are so closely intertwined, but also because the two religions hold so many beliefs in common: belief in one merciful and all-powerful Creator God, a place for Abraham, Mary, and Jesus, as well as the practices of prayer, almsgiving, and fasting.
5. *Nostra Aetate* (Vatican: October 28, 1965), 1, accessed June 17, 2014, http://www.vatican.va/archive/hist_councils/ii_vatican_council/documents/vat-ii_decl_19651028_nostra-aetate_en.html. It is, of course, a challenge to attribute the workings of divine providence to lives prematurely destroyed by senseless violence, not to mention the death of infants and small children.
6. Father Hesburgh was born on May 25, 1917.
7. Rasoul's younger brother, Majid Rasoulipour, was killed in 1986.

8. In Iraq, the battle is called Operation Ramadan Mubarak.

9. As is well known, the weapons were manufactured with the assistance of firms from many European countries and the United States.

10. *The Qur'an (Oxford World's Classics)*, trans. M. A. S. Abdel Haleem (Oxford: Oxford University Press, 2005), 234.

11. Most Iraqis are Shiites.

12. One of his teachers in the MA program was Abdolkarim Soroush, perhaps the most well-known Iranian intellectual in the world today. He now lives in the West.

13. Although Rasoul is a Shiite, his first teacher for Qur'anic recitation was a Sunni.

14. By contrast, it is never asserted in Christian theology that the very sound of the biblical words, whether in their original language or in translation, is of any particular importance, either aesthetically or spiritually. There is no theology of sacred sound in Christianity when it comes to scripture. It does not matter in what sound or language the Bible is transmitted; what is infinitely more important is the *meaning* of the Bible's message, the revelation it intends to convey. What the words of that message sound like is totally irrelevant to the Bible's importance. The words of the biblical text are quite ordinary, just as Jesus himself, the Word made flesh, was perhaps quite ordinary in appearance.

15. More than 80 percent of the world's Muslims do not understand Arabic. The population center of Islam is concentrated in South and Southeast Asia, not in the Middle East.

16. According to some Christian interpreters of Islam, there is a parallel to be found in the recitation of the Qur'an and the reception of Christian Holy Communion. In the receiving of bread and wine by Christians and in the recitation of the Qur'an by Muslims, one takes the Word of God into one's mouth for one's spiritual benefit. I thank my former colleague, David Burrell, for this important insight.

17. At a recent presentation at Notre Dame offered by Rasoul and other Muslims, we heard recitations from YouTube given by such Egyptian greats as Mostafa Ismaeil (1905–1978), Mohammad Siddiq Minshawi (1920–1969), Abdul Basit Muhammad Abdul Samad (1927–1988), and Shahhat Mohammad Anwar (1950–2009). Nevertheless, there is an Iranian saying that the Qur'an was revealed in Arabia, recited in Egypt, and most perfectly understood in Iran!

18. Fortunately, in addition to teaching in Tehran, he is able to teach two days a week, 60 kilometers away, in Karaj, a mountain city where the air is pure, unlike the heavily polluted capital city.

19. These children and their parents are all Sunni. Rasoul noticed very quickly the first time he visited the mosque, when the prayer began, that he was virtually the only Shiite present. Shiites begin the prayer with their hands at their side, whereas the Sunnis begin by crossing their arms.

20. In 2005 and 2006, Rasoul made visits to Oxford to study with Richard Swinburne; and in 2007 and 2008, he studied with Alvin Plantinga and

Thomas Flint at Notre Dame. Plantinga is regarded by some Iranian thinkers today as the world's greatest philosopher. This news came as a shock to me, since I had not expected that Muslims living outside the West would be aware of, much less hold in such high esteem, thinkers from outside their own tradition. But Plantinga's defense of theism in the face of the challenges of contemporary atheism and secularism made him a natural ally of Muslim thinkers—so long as the creator God was not further regarded as a Trinity, a teaching which is foundational to Christianity and which is anathema to the simple monotheism of Islam.

21. Rasoul revealed that he arranged a meeting one time in Tehran between American Christians and President Ahmadinejad. "He knows me well," said Rasoul. "We served in the same militia together during the war." When President Ahmadinejad saw Rasoul, he said to him, "You are working with the Americans, but you aren't working with your own government?" As I understand him, Rasoul tries to stay clear of politics and focuses his attention on academics and interreligious relations.

22. The address took place on September 12, 2006.

23. One of the final agreements reached by the participants was: "Christians and Muslims should go beyond tolerance, accepting differences, while remaining aware of commonalities and thanking God for them. They are called to mutual respect, thereby condemning derision of religious beliefs." Pontifical Council for Interreligious Dialogue, "Joint Declaration of the Pontifical Council for Inter-Religious Dialogue (Vatican) and the Centre for Inter-Religious Dialogue of the Islamic Culture and Relations Organisation (Tehran, Iran)" (Rome: April 28–30, 2008), 5, accessed June 23, 2014, http://www.vatican.va/roman_curia/pontifical_councils/interelg/documents/rc_pc_interelg_doc_20080430_rome-declaration_en.html.

24. Already on August 19, 1985, Pope John Paul II spoke the following words to thousands of young Muslims gathered in Casablanca, Morocco: "We believe in the same God, the one God, the living God, the God who created the worlds and brings his creatures to their perfection." The Pontiff had been invited to speak by Hassan II, King of Morocco. John Paul II, "Address of his Holiness John Paul II to Young Muslims" (Morocco: August 19, 1985), 1, accessed June 23, 2014, http://www.vatican.va/holy_father/john_paul_ii/speeches/1985/august/documents/hf_jp-ii_spe_19850819_giovani-stadio-casablanca_en.html.

25. The Supreme Leader of Iran is elected by a small number of Ayatollahs, just as a small number of men—Cardinals—elect the Pope.

26. Allamah Sayyid Muhammad Husayn Tabatabai, Shi'ah (Qum: Ansariyan, 2008, 14th reprint).

27. To read more about this, see my God's Other Children: Personal Encounters with Faith, Love, and Holiness in Sacred India (New York: HarperOne, 2013).

28. See the Internet Medieval Sourcebook, accessed July 16, 2014, http://www.fordham.edu/halsall/source/1250rumi-masnavi.asp.

29. *The Qur'an (Oxford World's Classics)*, 73. Rasoul also brought to my attention two other Qur'anic verses on God's love: "My Lord is merciful and most loving (11:90)" and "He is the most Forgiving, the most Loving (85:14)," in ibid., 142 and 416.

30. My colleague, John Cavadini, director of the ICL, was instrumental in extending invitations to Rasoul to work with both the ICL and with the Department of Theology. John immediately recognized Rasoul's academic credentials and personal qualities when he first learned of him in 2008 while serving as chair of our department.

31. I had worked with Turks in German factories during my days as a theology student, and I have come to know well many Muslims in India during the past 30 years. But all have been Sunni Muslims.

8

Study and Friendship: Intersections throughout an Academic Life

Francis X. Clooney, SJ

I welcome the opportunity to write this chapter, since it allows me to reflect on what are now a full 40 years of my encounter with Hindu religious traditions and study of Hinduism, and—inseparable from the preceding—my friendship with Hindus in Nepal, in India, and here in the West. As will become evident, my work is largely a matter of the study of texts; but around that study has been woven a rich circle of friendships without which the study would have been immeasurably poor. In turn, this study has created the possibilities for friendships that surely would not have been possible for me. The study and the friendships are not, for me, alternatives, but two dimensions of integral (interreligious) learning.

Some of the books I have studied have had a great impact on me as a scholar and person. Some classical and modern texts have been challenging, interactive conversation partners in the study of Hindu theologies, from which I have learned very much over the years. I am thinking of books such as the *Brhadaranyaka Upanisad* and the commentaries on it; the Srivaisnava *Tiruvaymoli* and the wonderful set of expositions of it known as the *Bhagavat Visayam*; and the formidable *Mimamsa Sutras* of Jaimini, with expansive commentaries from Sabara's *Bhasya* down to the one I am beginning to read closely at this writing, the *Jaiminiya Nyaya Mala Vistara* of Madhavacarya. Such books have guided me along the way, engaged and challenged me, and helped make me the person and scholar that I am today. Like good friends, they do not tell me merely what I want to hear. They are not passive instruments, safe in the hands of the scholar, as if merely convenient materials for the willful scholar, unchallenged by stubborn feedback or resistance. Like the best dialogue partners, when such books are taken seriously, they also resist my simplifications, raise more questions than they answer, and, from within their seemingly strict confines, push me to consider ideas and experiences I had not considered before.[1]

Over the years, and in the course of my studies, people I have met— often in academic settings and occasioned by a shared interest in texts— have given me a much richer sense of my books, their larger significance, and lived meaning. My Hindu friends in South Asia and here in the West give a name and a face to the ideas I have been studying and thinking though often on my own. This should be of no surprise. If we rightly expect that great texts live on in their cultures, then there are real connections of texts and persons, each illumining the other—texts forming our great religious cultures, and persons preserving texts for that purpose, but then also rereading them in new circumstances when they need to be brought back to life. Friends do not merely or mechanically live out what the texts say, any more than the texts themselves—rooted in human experience—say anything merely predictable. Christians find God in the Bible, tradition, community, and in innumerable persons who live out Christian faith today. It is no different when we meet Hindus, for in them, too, we see how the inspirations and sacred texts exist in the vagaries of human living, as words and persons together show us yet another living religious tradition.

In the following pages, I can mention only some of the friends who have enriched and deepened my life and my understanding of Hindu religious traditions, and highlight only a few instances in which those friendships have made a difference in my academic work; I ask the reader to imagine the still large circle of friends and interrelations that are woven around the words I write here. At the start, it will be useful to sort out instances of these bonds that make religious reading personal, even if they cannot all bear the name "friendship" in any univocal sense. I think here of my teachers, my students, my colleagues in the academic world, and many I have known in the broader community of Hindus who likewise live and think through the meaning of faith and our faiths in today's world.

Our best teachers bring to life the texts we study. Some of my most memorable teachers were Hindus, deeply immersed in the Hindu literary cultures I was learning. First I recall Sri Ramamurthy Sastry. He was a learned pandit, teacher of Mimamsa liturgical theology, and (retired) principal of the Sanskrit College in Mylapore, Madras (now Chennai). He was my teacher of Mimamsa when, for more than a year during 1982–1983, I studied Mimamsa in Mylapore, engaged in dissertation research. Elderly, he had never worked with a foreigner before, and spoke no English. He was a proper Brahmin, dressed in a prim, white *dhoti*, head shaved except for his tuft. At first, he was, not unusually, formal and a bit distant. He set the rules; he would do most of the talking, and teach me texts of his choosing; he stuck to the texts and to his way of teaching them. But as we read together nearly every day, our relationship warmed, little by little. By the end of the year, we were watching cricket on television together, and his dear wife was feeding me welcome snacks whenever I visited. Across gaps of age, culture, language, and religion, we connected, and, certainly, ours is a relationship I would never forget. Although he had died by my next visit to India, his teaching has always afforded a personal presence to go with the study of Hindu religious practices.

A decade later, again in Mylapore, Dr. Sampath Kumaran was my teacher, showing me how to read and understand more deeply the *Bhagavat Visayam* commentaries on *Tiruvaymoli*, one of the great devotional classics of south India, and the source of rich medieval commentaries. Since he had, for years, been teaching Western philosophy in an English-language college, our communication was easier from the start. He loved the text we were reading, and communicated to me his utter pleasure in teaching them. Conversely, over time, he became very eager to read with me, and insisted that I come more and not less often. It seems that he found me to be the student he was looking for, deeply interested in the texts he loved, asking very particular and intense questions about what we were reading. We never shared a meal—I think his sense of Brahmin proprieties, caste distinctions, and concern about his reputation prevented this—but during that year, the text brought us together as like-minded persons; I will always associate the *Bhagavad Visayam* with his love for the songs and his living out their truths. That same year, Dr. M. A. Venkatakrishnan, lecturer and now professor of Vaisnavism and department head at the University of Madras, was for a short time also a guide in reading *Tiruvaymoli*. But over the decades, he has rather more importantly been a welcoming friend, someone I am always glad to meet, usually at his home in the old Triplicane section of Madras. When I arrived in Madras in 1982, Venkatakrishnan went out of his way to help me obtain some hard-to-find books. Nearly 25 years later, when in 2005 some very conservative (and political) Hindus decided to portray me as an enemy of Hinduism—all the more dangerous because I knew what I was talking about and on the surface seemed quite sympathetic—he made it known in the community that he trusted me, and knew I was no enemy. I have no doubt that this was a great help in cutting short an unpleasant period of ill will.

One of the most memorable persons I met and studied with when I was a graduate student in Chicago was A. K. Ramanujan, longtime professor and, for some years, also chair of the department of South Asian Languages and Civilizations. He impressed me as a brilliant reader of literature; and the sensitivity and insight of his reading seemed grounded in the wholeness of a person who lived out the delicate balances and insights he found in the poetry he wrote or translated. He did not identify himself as a Hindu, but showed a way into the language and literature, the poetry, and the subtler tastes of life and religion in India. Ever the senior scholar, magisterial in his own inimitable way, he was nevertheless a friendly guide along the path of study of Hinduism.

Our students, too, teach us much, as the classroom brings old and large truths to life in people we like, and like to be with. Some of this has to do with a natural rapport that develops in the classroom at its best, and in the afterlife of classroom conversations on areas of common interest with students with whom we keep in touch with for years thereafter. In the beginning, it was my students in Kathmandu who made the religions come alive for me; over forty years they have meant very much to me, and it is wonderful to run into one or another of those I knew well, even after so many years. Three decades later, it was the students I worked with at Oxford's Centre for Hindu Studies between 2002 and 2004, largely though not exclusively Hindus, who breathed life and love into the study of Hindu texts. They were impressive young scholars, as well as believers, whose person and commitment infused their work, and who thereby also gave some personal face and voice to what being Hindu means in today's world. They have done well for themselves after finishing at Oxford, and I am always glad to see them again in academic meetings and at other venues. At Boston College and now at Harvard, I am happy to have Hindu students in my classes. By taking my courses, they were choosing to learn about Hinduism and Christianity from me, of course, and they have also kept me honest, reminding me of Hinduism lived and tested in ordinary life, and again, how the classic traditions both affect and are affected by the changing world around us. The classroom brings us together; for in that educational setting, the study of the text is the vehicle of rich personal interactions that grow from and around study. Neither the classroom context nor friendships stand independent of one another, and for me at least, one needn't choose between serious study and the bonds that teachers and students may form.

A still broader category is that of the "occasional" friends I have made in the course of my studies and teaching. I cannot but think of the many people who were simply friendly to me, in smaller and larger ways, for shorter and longer periods of time. I think of graced individuals, true Hindus, in Nepal and India, who welcomed me—the stranger and visitor—and made my life there so much more viable and enjoyable. There have been rickshaw drivers and shopkeepers and temple priests who have gone out of their way to be friendly (made all the more noticeable when, at some other temples, there were no such welcoming figures), and workers on campus I was happy to know. For example, I remember Krishna Bhagat, a cook at St. Xavier's School in Kathmandu, with whom I used to play handball during 1973–1975, and whose home I still visit when I go to Kathmandu. And though, unfortunately, I now cannot recall his name, I remember very well, too, a particular temple priest at the Madhava Perumal Temple in Mylapore, who always went out of his way to welcome me to the temple, engage me in conversation, patient with my very limited spoken Tamil. Elsewhere, too, my visits to temples in India, Australia, and the West have always been easier and happier due to the welcoming hospitality of devotees in the temples.

Some occasional contacts last more than a moment, and grow in significance over time. J. K. Bajaj, M. D. Srinivasan, and K. V. Varadarajan are scholars and leaders in the contemporary Hindu community whom I met almost by chance due to my interest in contemporary intellectual Hinduism, lived out in urban settings. Their *Center for Policy Studies* has, for over 20 years, been of interest to me as a place where thoughtful scholars try to bring India's history and traditions into conversation with urgent modern currents in Indian thought. I remember that early on they had introduced me to an important swami visiting the city, and thereafter I was interested in the series of books they have been publishing, on topics that link tradition and contemporary issues. Whenever I visit Madras, I visit their center, and look forward to a meal or tea with them if they have time. It has been those informal conversations that have meant much, giving flesh and blood, meaning and depth to the ideas that drew us together in the first place. They, too, once helped me in a difficult time. When a book of mine was under attack in 2005–2006, they went out of their way to arrange a public forum for a discussion on the book. While this well-attended public session did not end all debate, it did remove much of the vitriol in the air and enabled me to move beyond the dispute.

Hindu friends in the West, too, have brought Hinduism to life for me in all those places where I teach and write. Since many of these friends are themselves professors in American universities, the phenomenon of friends who are scholars of Hinduism, Hindus who study the texts of their tradition, melds all the more intensely the interpersonal and the intellectual. We are peers, and it is most obviously the case that such encounters are neither exotic nor a matter of "us" studying "them."

Here, too, I can only give several examples out of many. I first met Vasudha Narayanan, scholar of Srivaisnava Hinduism and longtime professor at the University of Florida, early on in her career, when she visited the University of Chicago, around 1980. Right from the start, I was impressed with her ability to speak eloquently on Srivaisnava Hinduism, from the tradition as well as about it. I enjoyed talking to her very much. We have been friends for more than 30 years now, and I immediately think of her when delving deeper into some particular Srivaisnava text that lives on in the community today. I was happy, too, to count as a friend the senior International Society for Krishna Consciousness (ISKCON) scholar, Tamal Krishna Goswami. We met at a Hindu-Christian dialogue meeting in 1996, and looked forward to our conversations and meals over the years; we finally met at Oxford in 2002 where he was living while writing his doctoral dissertation (at Cambridge), just before a car accident that cut short his life. Tamal Krishna radiated in a simple and pure way the meaning of being a Krishna devotee while being at the same time a scholar and an intellectual dedicated to exploring his faith in the modern university setting. I can only mention some of the other Hindu scholars who have embodied for me learning gained through study: Anantanand Rambachan and Chakravarthi Ramprasad, Anuttama Dasa and Graham Schweig, and from the younger generation, scholars such as Deepak Sarma, Sucharita Adluri, and Jonathan Edelmann. I never tire of conversation with any of these friends, and in the course of conversation we often delve deeper into, and have sort out, most enjoyably, the complexities of Hindu-Christian relations.

A cumulative effect of this chemistry of study and friendship has made it inevitable that I have formed as it were a deep personal connection with Hinduism, which is for me neither the abstract and deracinated content of books nor friendships unmoored in Hinduism's vast depths of learning. While one cannot literally befriend a religion, I find myself with a deep respect for, and a certain loyalty to, Hinduism as a whole, in part due to the books I have read and learned from all these years, and in part due to the many Hindus who have been and are part of my life,. Though I am neither a Hindu nor a hyphenated Hindu-Christian, Hinduism is not, for me, merely an object of academic study. I am reluctant to criticize Hindu ideas or practices when speaking to non-Hindus. I have known so many things Hindu in many ways for such a long time, and so I take it personally, and feel obliged to portray this religion—perhaps the least understood of the great religions in America—in a positive light—not denying that there are flaws or problems, but insisting in class, in writing, among Catholics and Jesuits, that this great religion not only is here to stay, but also brings many benefits and gifts to the world. The positive greatly outweighs the negative.

I often find myself among people who are not familiar with Hindu traditions, and in such circumstances I consciously emphasize the positive, what I like, and what has meant something to me, including elements that open into fruitful comparison with those of Christianity. I do not highlight ideas I find uninteresting and beliefs that are ill-defined or weakly presented; I do not write much about the social practices of which I do not approve. I yield little to those inclined to condemn Hinduism from afar or based on a visit or two to South Asia. To those wondering why I do not highlight the negative elements more sharply, I simply admit that my work is to build the bridges and stress common ground; others may have other missions. In any case, my role is to stress what is good and positive and beneficial, because such is obvious to me and because I feel a certain loyalty to the Hindu traditions I have studied for so long. This kind of loyalty, even if conscious and strategic, can puzzle or frustrate those who would prefer a more critical approach to religions in general, or specifically to religions other than Christianity. I do not criticize my friends in public, and will not slip into the too-easy stance of criticizing Hinduism among Western Christians. My study, my friendships, and my overall view of Hinduism cannot be entirely separated out.

Two members of the Ramakrishna Vedanta Society, Pravrajika Vrajaprana and Swami Tyagananda, have been my dear friends for decades. My first contact with Vrajaprana was by way of a kind note she sent to me regarding something I had written. We continued the correspondence, and found that we had much in common, from ideas to a love of literature to a sense of humor; I have always enjoyed wide-ranging conversations on spiritual matters, books, academic matters, and the like. When I went to India for a year in 1992, it was Vrajaprana who recommended that I seek out Tyagananda, and during 1992–1993 he and I shared many a long conversation on matters Hindu and Christian, the things I had studied and seen in India that year, and the more general state of intellectual and spiritual life today. Since we very much wanted to stay in contact, it was a pleasure for both of us when he was appointed assistant, and then head swami, at the Vedanta Society in Boston, where he has been residing now for some 15 years. It is a special, even if rare pleasure, when I can meet Vrajaprana and Tyagananda together.

In addition to being practitioners of monastic Hinduism and leaders in the Hindu community in the United States, Vrajaprana and Tyagananda are also religious intellectuals and authors. If the intersection of the academic and personal is inevitable and good, sometimes friendship also complicates my work as a scholar. This was the case when, in 2012, I was asked to review *Interpreting Ramakrishna: Kali's Child Revisited* (2010),[2] the book written by Tyagananda and Vrajaprana as a rejoinder to Jeffrey Kripal's *Kali's Child: The Mystical and the Erotic in the Life and Teachings of Ramakrishna* (1995).[3] For years before their book appeared, both were recognized as insistent, even if respectful, voices in disputing Kripal's interpretation of Ramakrishna, the nineteenth-century Hindu mystic and, many would say, the new appearance of God in the world. The dare of such a review was both dangerous and intriguing, given the long history of debate that had already risen around *Kali's Child*.[4] As I admit in the review itself, this was a writing assignment complicated not only by the ideas being argued—hard enough, and Bengali religion is not my specialty, despite my long familiarity with Ramakrishna—but also by the fact of my friendship with Vrajaprana and Tyagananda—and with Jeffrey Kripal as well, who I have known for some 20 years. Ordinarily, I would not have taken on such a review, but I did so partly because it was an inhouse task—or our own *Harvard Divinity Bulletin*—and partly because I thought it worthwhile to draw attention to these books and the important issues they raise, in common and in their disagreement.[5]

Having agreed to write, though, I had to be all the more cautious in seeking to respect both sides, while yet remaining critical regarding ideas and academic standards. Friendship and scholarship stand in tension here, and I needed to hear all views somewhat dispassionately. I did not want to be hard on my friends, but neither did I want to settle for the bland review that would offend no one. In the review, I insisted that even as I was recommending *Rethinking Ramakrishna*, *Kali's Child* remained an important book, rich in insights into Ramakrishna's life and times. I insisted that it serves as a useful (even if unnecessarily controversial) instigation for an important debate. *Rethinking Ramakrishna* is necessary reading, because its critiques need to be heard and brought into the academic discussion of Ramakrishna. Yet *Kali's Child* too needs to be read, because it brings to the fore issues about the flesh-and-blood Ramakrishna—the "historical Ramakrishna," one might say, rather than the "Ramakrishna of faith"—otherwise neglected. That is to say: both books written by my friends remain books that need to be read; and these friends are indeed friends, in part because of the books they write.

Eventually, I found ways to commend both books, even as I affirmed that *Rethinking Ramakrishna* offered necessary and unassailable criticisms of *Kali's Child*. Yes, but read *both* books. Was all of this a compromise, attenuating academic credibility by a fear of offending friends? I think not. I wrote what I thought needed to be written without compromising what I wanted to say, even as I tried to do so in a way that would bring out the best in both books. I seem to have succeeded, since Kripal, Tyagananda, and Vrajaprana—to whom I showed the review only after finishing it—professed appreciation of my balanced approach. We are still friends.

I could multiply examples in which scholarly work is inseparable from a web of friendships, complicated by the fact that we do not want to strictly separate personal relationships from the ideas we explore. Such complications, occasionally daunting, are, on the whole, a good thing. Friendships and scholarly work are not necessarily separate domains. In dialogue as an interactive conversation, as well as in the internal dialogue that constitutes the scholar's work, everything is critical, everything is personal, but interpersonal as well.[6]

I conclude simply by reiterating the key insight that governs this reflection: interreligious study and friendship have been, for me, natural partners, each making possible and enhancing the other, neither the surely better path able to displace the other entirely. Books mean a great deal in interreligious understanding, and so, too, the friendships that grow up in the course of and around our study. Friends are a valued gift, and so are books. One may feel at times the need to get out of the books and into more vital living community settings, just as at other times one may feel ready to put the dialogue aside, and return to study, to listening to the voices of great teachers of long past generations. But in my case at least, these two deeply human and challenging forms of knowing and loving flourish best in relation to one another, friendship and study, each making the other more possible. These realities can no more be separated than could heart and mind, body and soul.

Notes

1. That books matter and draw us into dialogue should not be surprising. My field, comparative theology, is a form of theology, and theology is a learning that most often proceeds by reading rather than by way of the direct exchanges of interreligious dialogue. Like most theologians, I work with texts, engaging the written word, great authors, and the communities of interpretation and practice that have preserved and passed down such texts for centuries, sometimes for millennia. Comparative study can hardly be expected to be less textual, at least if one has chosen strong and robust texts that teach us as we read them. On the connection and difference between comparative theological study and interreligious dialogue, see my essay, "Comparative Theology and Inter-Religious Dialogue," in *The Wiley-Blackwell Companion to Inter-Religious Dialogue*, ed. Catherine Cornille (Malden, MA: Wiley-Blackwell, 2013), 51–63.
2. Swami Tyagananda and Pravrajika Vrajaprana, *Interpreting Ramakrishna: Kali's Child Revisited* (Delhi: Motalil Banarsidass, 2010).
3. Jeffrey Kripal, *Kali's Child: The Mystical and the Erotic in the Life and Teachings of Ramakrishna* (Chicago: University of Chicago Press, 1995).

4. See Francis X. Clooney, SJ, "Swami Tyagananda and Pravrajika Vrajaprana's *Interpreting Ramakrishna: Kali's Child Revisited*," *Harvard Divinity Bulletin* 40.3–4 (Summer/Autumn 2012): 80–84. I admit in the review that I find *Interpreting Ramakrishna* to be a thoughtful book and also insightful regarding the nineteenth-century Hindu saint Ramakrishna (1836–1886) and a century-plus of scholarship about him. It was written after a decade-long debate about Jeffrey Kripal's *Kali's Child*, a book at odds with the traditional understanding of the saint, particularly in positing that the saint's complicated and troubling sexuality was a primary key to his mystical identity.

5. I must admit that I was also influenced by my long interest in Ramakrishna, a holy curiosity reaching back three decades. Perhaps reflecting my own Christian intuition of the irreplaceable centrality of Jesus, I have always seen in Ramakrishna a human place where the divine and the holy are manifest, whose intensity and love highlight the positive embrace of the other, the engagement and interaction with what was hitherto seemingly alien, in a way that serves well the scholar too, as she or he repeatedly learns from initially stubborn and puzzling texts. That a saint from a previous century and another religion might influence my attitudes toward study and friends today should not be surprising to any tradition's believers today.

6. In these pages I have not reflected on friendship as an independent good, good for its own sake, though in another context I could easily stress that friendship must be appreciated on its own terms, and not as an instrument of anything else. I have not mentioned at all the many friends I have who are not Hindu or Indian, and yet have helped me greatly in my study of Hinduism. I have sought only to show how my work as a scholar, primarily a form of study, is richly implicated in personal relationships, with teachers and students, colleagues and acquaintances made over many years, and all the better because what is written and what is lived are invariably connected.

9

Jivanmukti, Freedom, and a Cassette Recorder: Friendship beyond Friendship in the Tradition of Advaita Vedanta*

Reid B. Locklin

James Fredericks has proposed "interreligious friendship" as a "new theological virtue" for the twenty-first-century Church.[1] Such friendship, he suggests, is rooted not in the self-giving, disinterested love communicated by the Greek term *agape*, but precisely in self-interested love (*philia*): Christians become fascinated by other religious paths, become friends with the followers of these paths, and perhaps become convinced that they and their own religious traditions may gain from a continuing relationship. Such self-interested friendship would, at least at first glance, seem to presume the equality and mutuality that many contemporary Western thinkers have valorized as the ideal of any relationship. The Christian, according to this vision, would not interpret away the religious other or absorb the other tradition into her own; she enters into the give-and-take and mutual learning of authentic friendship.

A somewhat more nuanced portrait emerges when Fredericks recounts his interreligious friendship with his Buddhist teacher, Masao Abe. As his mentor, for starters, Abe is precisely *not* a peer. "In Japan at least," Fredericks writes, "calling us friends (*tomodachi*) would be presumptuous."[2] Yet, Fredericks is also reluctant to characterize their relationship as one of master and disciple, for he is clear that he does not stand in the same Buddhist path as his mentor and friend. Later in the essay, Fredericks suggests that their relationship is in fact based not primarily in anything they share, but in their strangeness to one another.

Invoking the philosopher Emmanuel Levinas, he emphasizes the ethical force of face-to-face, mutual encounter: "Otherness...forms the basis of our friendship."[3] We are back, it seems, in the language of mutuality. But the relationship is still asymmetrical in important ways. For example, Abe is perfectly comfortable offering a Buddhist interpretation of Christ and Christianity, of understanding Fredericks's tradition in terms of his own. Fredericks, on the other hand, characterizes his own position as one that does not strive for such "understanding," but remains committed to a practice of disciplined "listening," a practice that disposes Fredericks himself "to become one who is addressed by that face, not one who addresses."[4] Such a description, which places one partner in the role of speaker and the other in the role of listener, belies commonplace notions of friendship. Hence, presumably, the need to specify such inter-religious friendship as "*spiritual* friendship," akin to conventional friendship in some ways, but also possessed of its own distinctive character and integrity.[5]

The non-dualist Hindu tradition of Advaita Vedanta, I suggest, offers an even more forceful challenge to conventional notions of friendship. This tradition, which proclaims the ultimate non-duality (*advaita*) of self, world, and God, prescribes a spiritual path of radical renunciation. Its teachers and disciples have, historically, often been renunciants in a formal sense: they take vows of *samnyasa* and become wandering monks. But Advaita also prescribes a higher path of renunciation for monks and laypersons alike: renunciation of attachment to possessions, renunciation of ego, renunciation of any sense of "doership" or personal agency, renunciation of the objects of perception, and, with such objects, renunciation of binding relationships of any kind. Such renunciation would seem to exclude any disposition of mutuality on the part of the spiritual adept. The eighth-century CE Advaita text, *A Thousand Teachings*, for example, prescribes a practice of repetition (*parisamkhyana*) to be cultivated by spiritual seekers.[6] In this practice, disciples bring to mind the teaching of the sacred Upanisads on the true, divine self (*Atman*) of all beings as pure "seeing, non-object, unconnected, changeless, motionless, endless, fearless and absolutely subtle."[7] They go on to enumerate various experiences of sound, touch, sight, taste, and smell, and, at each step, proclaim their own ultimate freedom from such experiences, which have no power to affect this true self. "This being the case," such disciples conclude, "to me, a person of knowledge, nobody is foe, friend or neutral."[8]

In the remainder of this essay, I describe my friendship with precisely such a "person of knowledge," entirely beyond the bonds of human relationship: Swami Paramarthananda, an Advaita teacher in Chennai, India. I focus on two decisive moments in my relationship with "Swamiji": my initial period in Chennai, during the academic year 1999–2000,[9] and; a second period of study a bit less than a decade later, when I spent countless hours listening to Swamiji's tape recorded lectures. In both moments, my friendship with Swamiji well illustrated Fredericks's ideal of disciplined "listening." In one case, it was *all* listening! More than this, I believe it also reveals something of the complexity of interreligious friendship. Far from being a generic "friendship" that happens to cross the boundaries of religious difference, interreligious friendship is a friendship that is itself changed and transformed by religious difference. In the case of my friendship with Swamiji, the primacy of mutuality as such was largely displaced by another value that, at least arguably, has deeper roots in Advaita tradition: freedom from attachment. Rather than reducing the intimacy of the friendship, I suggest, such freedom has opened the space for a greater and wider intimacy, and one that necessarily opened our friendship to others—including that divine Other about whom Swamiji and I persistently disagree.

Is Friendship Possible with a Jivanmukta?

My friendship with Swamiji did not begin auspiciously.

Months before, I had written to him requesting instruction in the *Thousand Teachings* of the eighth-century Advaita teacher Adi Shankaracharya. A few days earlier, he and I had spoken briefly by telephone and set up a meeting time. A few hours earlier, I had made what seemed a perfectly reasonable decision to walk the short distance from the Jesuit seminary where I was lodging to his small apartment in the Mylapore district of Chennai. But I was ill-equipped for the driving October monsoon. By the time I arrived at his apartment, I was drenched from head to foot in rain and sweat.

Things sort of went downhill from there. I waited, dripping and miserable, with an older woman, a devotee, waiting to offer reverent salutations. I was, in the meantime, obsessing about finances: surely I should make some donation in return for instruction. What is an appropriate amount? Should I offer this at the beginning of instruction, or at the end? Would this be offensive to the teacher? By the time the young *brahmacarin* attendant invited me to meet with Swamiji, I had pretty much lost track of my purpose for coming in the first place.

I don't remember much of what *I* said at that first meeting, except that I am confident that much of it was gibberish. Swamiji asked a number of polite questions about my background and my research agenda, but then, perhaps sensing my discomfort and confusion, leaned forward in his small desk and made a dramatic announcement. "I am a Swami, a guru. I don't need anything from you. I have no expectations of you. So you should be completely free in my presence. You should ask of me whatever it is you wish to know, bring up any topic you wish to discuss." He leaned back and underscored the point: "You should be free."

Some 15 years have passed since Swamiji pronounced both of us free, and I have continually reflected on its meaning. On the one hand, it was a statement about Swamiji himself, as the kind of person described in the *Thousand Teachings*, free from attachment and thus ideally free from expectations of others. Later, entirely in passing, he would characterize this state in simple, yet truly extraordinary terms. "After all," he mentioned casually one day while explaining some other point, which I have long since forgotten, "I am a *jivanmukta*."

Some background may be helpful here. Few doctrines more clearly characterize Advaita Vedanta in its Indian context or have more consistently scandalized critics than its distinctive teaching on *jivanmukti*, "living liberation" or "liberation-in-life": the notion that final release from bondage and suffering can be attained here and now, without awaiting either physical death or some transformation of history. In the *Thousand Teachings*, for example, Shankara teaches:

> A person who has knowledge of *Atman*, which negates the notion that the body is *Atman* and is as [firm] as [ordinary people's] notion that the body is *Atman*, is released even without wishing.[10]

According to this vision, final liberation depends upon self-knowledge alone, not faith, will, or even divine intervention. It depends solely upon what is already the true, innermost nature of each and every conscious being. Lance Nelson explains: "Ontologically speaking, we are always liberated...To speak of attaining liberation is...figurative—accurate only from the epistemological point of view. The human experience of bondage—our sense of not being liberated—is a problem of our not being aware of what we already have."[11] Once the student of the teaching truly knows herself—identifying with *atman* as naturally as the rest of us identify with our bodies, minds, and personalities—liberation follows immediately.

This is a core teaching of Advaita Vedanta, but in my experience it is rather rare for teachers to declare that they have arrived at the goal, much less to do so in passing, while explaining some other point. Swamiji, however, felt entirely comfortable in his own skin, precisely as a *jivanmukta*. First of all, unlike some other Advaita traditions, his particular teaching tradition does not associate this highest form of freedom with extraordinary meditative states or yogic powers. Second, along with Shankara and other prominent Advaita teachers, Swamiji readily conceded that his empirical body, mind, and personality continue to exist in the world according to karmic patterns set long before his birth. He thus continues to react to phenomena with surprise, with delight, perhaps even with irritation or anger (though I never witnessed the latter), as one would expect from any embodied being. Finally, and most importantly, he was unshakably convinced that if he is liberated in this life, then, according to the Advaita teaching itself, so is every other conscious being. The difference is only that he has come to know this fact with a firm, spontaneous, and an unalterable conviction. The achievement of living liberation, he once said, confers nothing of ultimate significance, because it effects no actual change. It offers merely "incidental benefits to an unreal mind."

Jivanmukti is the highest goal of Advaita teaching, as well as one of the primary subjects of our shared study that year. Hence, as I attended Swamiji's public lectures and met with him one-on-one, he and the textual traditions we were studying began to interpret each other. When I encountered a characterization of *jivanmukti* in the text, I instinctively tested it against my experiences with Swamiji. When he spoke about his own daily life as a *samnyasin* and a teacher in the tradition, he helped me imagine the teachings and social settings described in these ancient treatises. From a critical-historical perspective, no doubt, this was a complete disaster, rife with the risk of anachronism. From the point of view of our friendship, however, it was perfectly natural. In becoming friends with Swamiji, I was becoming friends with the texts and teaching tradition of Advaita Vedanta. Or, perhaps better, they were becoming friends to me. According to the teaching of Advaita, I could become attached to Swamiji and regard him as a friend, but, as a *jivanmukta*, it was literally impossible for him to reciprocate in kind. So I was, strictly speaking, the sole beneficiary of the relationship.

Still, in Swamiji's dramatic statement on that first day of study, I too had been pronounced free. At one level, of course, this is simply the message of the whole tradition. One of the most famous Advaita "great sayings" (*mahavakya*) is the terse pronouncement, "*tat-tvam-asi*," "that is how you are,"[12] or, according to a more traditional English rendering, "Thou art That." That divine *atman*, one without a second, changeless, fearless, and absolutely free—that's who you are, in your most fundamental and innermost being. I have no doubt that this message was implied when Swamiji said, "you should be free," as it was implied in nearly everything he said or did. But he also intended something more concrete and practical: to set me at ease, to set me free of my concerns and expectations about *my relationship with him.* I could feel free to work with the text, even with my shaky Sanskrit. I could feel free to ask any question. I could feel free to challenge any particular argument. I could feel free to try out my own ideas. I could, finally, feel free to do all of these things as a Christian theologian, seeking instruction in a teaching tradition that firmly, gently, unpretentiously, and persuasively dismantles many Christian teachings on God, human selfhood, and salvation on which I have staked the entirety of my particular human life.

Of course, as one might expect, the context of freedom that Swamiji established for our relationship meant that, in fact, there was a good deal of friendly, back-and-forth dialogue. As we made progress on the *Thousand Teachings*, we opened up occasional sessions for open question and answer, about monastic life, about the relationships among different Advaita traditions, about the Hindu nationalist movement. At one point, relatively late in the period of study, Swamiji also began to ask *me* questions about Christian theology. On the one hand, he noted without hesitation the places where my tradition differed from his own, and never relented or nuanced the Advaita claim that final liberation follows from authentic self-knowledge alone, not from Christ, not from baptism or Eucharist, not from *puja* in a Hindu temple—though all of these may be useful and good in their own right. On the other hand, he actually invited me to offer an interpretation of him and his tradition from within a Christian framework. At his request, I hand copied important texts from Vatican II (1962–1965) dealing with the prospective salvation of non-Christians and offered him both "more progressive" and "more conservative" interpretations of these texts. Swamiji did not agree with the bishops of the Council on many matters, and he saw little use for the progressive interpretations in particular. Nevertheless, he seemed to judge, in some tension with Fredericks and not a few other comparative theologians, that it is basically a positive thing for Christians and Hindus to find ways of including one another in our respective visions of God and liberation. And he did all of this as a *jivanmukta*.

To adopt a well-traveled Advaita idiom, there is perhaps nothing unusual in this from the perspective of conventional understanding (*vyavaharika*). The complex of body, mind, and personality of a *jivanmukta* will, as I already briefly mentioned, continue to relate in ordinary ways with other such complexes, enlightened or not. Precisely, from such a conventional perspective, moreover, such interactions may look like, and rightly be referred to as, friendship.

This is fine as far as it goes. Over the years, however, I have increasingly located the distinctive character of *this* particular friendship in an Advaita ideal closely connected with both freedom in general and the highest freedom of the *jivanmukta*: *abhayatvam*, "fearlessness." Most of the desires that motivate and govern our relationships of all kinds can be translated into one or another form of fear: fear of vulnerability, fear of loneliness or isolation, fear of rejection, fear of losing one's identity in the other. With the Advaita teaching on *jivanmukti* in mind, I have come to perceive my friendship with Swamiji less in terms of negating relationship than in terms of their imaginative transformation. That is, I have increasingly felt myself invited to imagine something so remote from ordinary experience that it may look like pure negation: namely, a friendship without any basis in insecurity.

In the *Thousand Teachings*, the disciple undertaking a disciplined recollection and assimilation of the Advaita teaching proclaims, "to me, a person of knowledge, nobody is foe, friend or neutral." It is worth noting that it is not merely enmity and friendship that are here excluded from the life of the *jivanmukta*. Indifference (*udasa*) has also been ruled out of bounds. What remains? Perhaps we can imagine a friendship beyond friendship, a friendship beyond any trace of fear, a friendship founded on the absolute freedom of God, the divine self.

The Interiorization of Freedom

At the end of my study in Chennai, Swamiji sent me off with a closing pronouncement that echoed that first statement, months before: "If you write or visit, I will be happy. If you do not write or do not visit, I will take no notice. Please be free." We have indeed corresponded a bit, and I was able to go back and visit some seven years after my departure. Throughout these communications, Swamiji's unique disposition has continued to shine, unwavering: happy to make contact, untroubled by silence or delays, supportive, firm in his self-knowledge.

Such occasional communications do not, however, represent the primary way that our friendship has been maintained in the decade and a half since I studied with Swamiji. Instead, I retained my sense of connection with Swamiji by means of a device that, at least at first glance, further attenuated the mutuality of our friendship. That is, for at least a few of these years, I maintained our friendship by listening to a trunk full of cassette tapes.

When I initiated my study of the *Thousand Teachings* with Swamiji back in 1999, he and I agreed that it would be unrealistic to think that we could work through the complete text in the short five months I had allowed for my stay. Advaita study, in this tradition, moves slowly and meticulously, verse by verse, often dealing with only one or two such verses in a one-hour session. Swamiji noted, however, that he had been giving public lectures on most of the verse portion of the text for the past several summers. These lectures had been recorded and were available from his *sangam*, his community of disciples and devotees. So we focused our shared study almost exclusively on the prose portion of the text, and I put several boxes full of cassette tapes on an ocean freighter bound for the United States. Thus, a few weeks after my return, Swamiji followed me home, in the form of these cassettes. I wish I could claim that I initiated a disciplined regimen by, say, listening to a half-hour of teaching every day, or something like that. The truth is that I pulled a few tapes out, here and there, to clarify specific points as I completed my thesis, and then I packed them back up and shoved them under my office desk.

Some years later, the opportunity arose to write a Christian commentary on the *Thousand Teachings*.[13] In preparation, I decided to take the opportunity to reopen those boxes and to listen to those cassettes. For a few hours each day, for several consecutive summers, I would sit in my office, headphones in my ears, quietly listening and taking notes from Swamiji's lectures. Chapter by chapter, verse by verse, AA-battery by AA-battery, I listened to Swamiji's voice, unfolding the meanings of these chapters and, with them, his vision of the Advaita path. By the time I had the first draft of the book manuscript, this disciplined practice of listening to Swamiji's tapes had become, for me, a distinctive form of spiritual asceticism.

To say that I learned a lot from this discipline would be a bit of an understatement. I gained tremendous insight into the text of the *Thousand Teachings* more than I ever could have gained simply by reading the text. More importantly for the narrative in this essay, however, I also judged that the intimacy of my friendship with Swamiji was significantly deepened by the exercise. In many ways, I experienced a level of connection with Swamiji and with the teaching that was distinct from and more profound than when I had been in his physical presence.

As an inveterate radio listener, this experience of heightened intimacy should not have surprised me. More than a few media analysts have noted the resilience of radio in an era of new media and, in explaining its persistent appeal, have commented on the intimacy of the medium itself. Though the signal reaches a wide area, radio tends to produce the psychological effect of personal connection: a single host whispering into the ear of a single listener. A generation ago, the Jesuit theorist Walter J. Ong generalized still further, noting the close affinity between experiences of intimacy and interiority and what he called the "oral sensorium" constituted by sound rather than sight. Whereas, he proposed, sight renders space an empty void between the eye and any particular object, sound renders space a vast interior filled with voices, music, or other noises.[14] Sight reaches only to surfaces; sound penetrates objects without violation, such as when one taps on a box to find out if it is full or rings "a coin to learn whether it is silver or lead."[15] Most importantly for my purposes, the interiors thus penetrated included the existential "interiors" of human selves.[16] "You can immerse yourself in hearing, in sound," Ong wrote in 1982. "There is no way to immerse yourself similarly in sight."[17]

The Upanisads similarly testify to the special relationship between hearing and intimacy. In a famous dialogue with the sage Yajnavalkya in the *Brhadaranyaka Upanisad*, for example, the fabled King Janaka initiates an inquiry with the question, "What is the source of light for a person here?"[18] "The Sun," replies Yajnavalkya, for "it is by the light of the sun that a person sits down, goes about, does his work, and returns."[19]

"What about when the sun has set?"
"Then the moon is the source of light."
"When the moon has set?"
"Then the fire."
"When the fire has died out?"
The sage answers:

The voice is…his source of light. It is by the light of the voice that a person sits down, goes about, does his work, and returns. Therefore, your Majesty, when someone cannot make out even his own hand [with his eyes], he goes straightaway towards the spot from where he hears a voice.[20]

And what about when the voice falls silent? Then the light for a person is *atman*.[21] A lengthy discourse on *atman* follows, punctuated by the declaration, "this is the immense and unborn self, unageing, undying, immortal, free from fear—the *brahman*. Brahman, surely, is free from fear, and a person who knows this undoubtedly becomes that *brahman* that is free from fear."[22]

Jacqueline G. Suthren Hirst refers to the kind of pattern followed in this discourse as a "method of interiorisation."[23] For Suthren Hirst, the primary focus of such interiorization is the content of the teaching itself, as Advaita teachers like Shankara initiate many inquiries with concrete, tangible objects and steadily shifts disciples' attention toward more subtle realities, beyond the scope of perception. But the *Brhadaranyaka Upanisad* also suggests the importance of the medium itself. The shift from a more to less objectified experience, and toward greater subtlety and interiorization, ideally proceeds by means of a medium particularly suited to subtlety and interiorization. That is, it proceeds by means of sound.[24]

Whether this rings true for Advaita teaching as a whole—which could, I think, be contested—it certainly resonates with my own experience and friendship with Swamiji. No doubt, the intimacy fostered by listening to his lectures depended upon our prior friendship in a number of important respects. I would have less reason to trust Swamiji's wisdom and less admiration for his character, for instance, had I never had the opportunity to witness his spontaneous interactions with me and with members of his *sangam*, years before. Yet, in the process of listening to his voice, with headphones, in the quiet solitude of my office, this friendship became interiorized in a new way. Swamiji became, in a way, available for deeper intimacy in the reduction of his presence to pure sound. As I reflected on individual verses, I naturally brought Swamiji's analogies and explanations to mind, rather than needing continually to consult my notebooks. My spouse noted that I began to sound like Swamiji when I read portions of my book manuscript out loud. I might venture to say that Swamiji and the teaching of Advaita Vedanta began, for perhaps the first time in earnest, to coexist in me, to co-inhabit my own body, mind, and personality.

Now, it is important to note that I am describing an *experience* of intimacy, without necessarily claiming much about the content of that experience. Obviously, first and foremost, this was an experience of intimacy entirely devoid of any sense of mutuality or reciprocity: Swamiji had given these lectures years ago and since moved on to other things. He was quite literally indifferent and unaffected by this dimension of our friendship, insofar as he had no direct experience of it. More than this, I am sure that I misunderstood some or much of Swamiji's teaching in these recorded lectures, and the experience of intimacy itself was always quite limited. It came and went, particularly as I was more or less engaged in the interpretation of the *Thousand Teachings*. My listening to the tapes was also rather selective, according to the material I was working with at any given point in time; no doubt, my interiorization of the Vedanta was still more selective, according to some biases I could openly acknowledge and others unknown even to myself. Nevertheless, at some profound level, I judged that my friendship with Swamiji had become an interior aspect of my own consciousness. With his friendship, moreover, followed some affinity with his fearlessness and freedom, precisely as a *jivanmukta*. And with his freedom, in turn, followed new insight into the source of this freedom: the co-presence of *atman*, the divine self, "that *brahman* that is free from fear," in the life and mind of the Advaita disciple.

As a Christian hearer of the Advaita teaching, such insight necessarily led me back to the sources of my own faith in the Christian scripture.

Thus, I noted, the Apostle Paul also speaks of freedom in terms of the co-presence of God in the disciple. In his letter to the Galatians, for example, he offers a famous allegory that contrasts the slavery of the children of Hagar against the freedom of the children of Sarah—that is, the freedom of those who have received the promise and the Spirit of Christ. He announces:

> For you were called to freedom, brothers and sisters, only do not use your freedom as an opportunity for self-indulgence, but through love become slaves to one another. For the whole law is summed up in the commandment, "You shall love your neighbor as yourself."[25]

Here freedom is spoken of as a freedom from self-care in order to take up the command to love, a freedom from a life bound by slavery that opens a new existence as a different kind of slave. More than this, the freedom that fulfills the whole law is, at its root, the freedom of God the divine self, the Spirit of God in the person of that Christian disciple who brings forth such fruit as "love, joy, peace, patience, kindness, generosity, faithfulness, gentleness, and self-control."[26]

At one level, I now encounter passages such as this and note that it was precisely those virtues that Paul associates with the Spirit that seemed, in my experience, most manifest in the disposition and character of Swamiji. As I ever-further interiorized Swamiji's presence in my own life and consciousness, I was also striving to become more like him in precisely these qualities. During this time, I judge that I did indeed become at least somewhat more inclined to love and to joy, more peaceful, more kind and generous with my time and energy, and perhaps more gentle in my dealings with others. At a deeper level, my experience of Swamiji's friendship and, beyond this, his co-presence in my own life and consciousness, sensitized me in a new way to the friendship and co-presence of God the Spirit as the sole true author of such virtues in me. According to Advaita Vedanta, every finite consciousness includes the trace or reflection, the *abhasa*, of the divine *atman*. Though itself beyond the reach of empirical perception, *atman* remains copresent with and in every perceived experience by means of this reflection.[27] The Advaita discipline is, at one level, simply a discipline of attending to this co-presence, identifying ever more fully with it and thereby allowing the freedom of *atman*, the divine self, to reshape one's empirical life, consciousness, and worldly activity. And this is also, increasingly, how I have come to regard my own path of Christian discipleship.

I would not say that, as a result of my friendship with Swamiji, I have begun to seek my own freedom in the co-presence of *atman* in my consciousness, though I find this teaching persuasive in many ways—not least, in Swamiji's own example. Differences between my tradition and his remain and have, in some ways, become even more intractable the longer I have persisted in my studies. Instead, I have come to perceive in this friendship a reflection (*abhasa*) of the life of grace, a life of divine freedom, a life defined by ever-greater attentiveness to the liberating co-presence of God the Holy Spirit. I would say that Swamiji became a sacrament of the Spirit for me, and thus also a sacrament of Christ.

Fruit of the Spirit

When Apostle Paul addressed the Galatians, he addressed a community, and when he called them to freedom, he called them to mutual love. Christians have generally understood that personal, intimate friendship with Christ and his Spirit opens naturally into still further relationships of friendship and love.

Advaita tradition does not typically speak in this way, but this has nevertheless also characterized my experience with Vedanta. That is, my friendship with Swamiji has opened the door to other friendships in the tradition. I have continued to remain connected with the teaching tradition whenever I can, receiving instruction in Swamiji's own Arsha Vidya lineage, in the Chinmaya Mission from which both Swamiji and his own guru received their first instruction, or in the Ramakrishna Mission. I have come to know one of Swamiji's peers who became a lay teacher, academic, and prominent scholar of Advaita, as well as a lay Vedantin eager to pursue ordination in a mainstream Christian tradition. I have attended Advaita youth groups, visited Advaita research institutes, and met a range of delightful men and women committed both to their spiritual instruction in the tradition and to political and economic justice in the wider world. Some of these relationships are close ones, most are passing acquaintances, but all of them are rich in affection.

Perhaps the most profound such relationship opened by my studies with Swamiji has been with a student who traveled from India to complete his doctoral studies in Canada. We initiated our correspondence via email, when he first shared his research project with me, and we continued our conversation for years thereafter, debating historical reconstructions of the earliest layers of the tradition, its relationship with early Vaisnavism, and the complex interplay between critical scholarship and traditional study. In his personal dispositions, he revealed many of the same qualities that I had always admired in Swamiji: gentleness, kindness, intellectual acuity, and a personal freedom that revealed itself as self-gift. He was, indeed, one of the freest and most sincere persons I have ever known. Much later, I would discover that this was no coincidence. Unbeknownst to me at the time, this student had previously studied with Swamiji in Chennai, and still considered Swamiji his personal guru. He and one of his friends in Toronto regularly listened to podcasts and watched streaming videos of Swamiji's public lectures in India. Swamiji had, in a way, created a space for our mutual learning and friendship.

Long before I learned of this connection, however, this student asked me to serve on his thesis committee. I carefully explained that I am neither a proper South Asianist nor a proper Advaitin, but a Christian theologian, and that there were plenty of other scholars on the campus who would bring far more expertise to his project. But he persisted. When I finally signed the form, the student offered me a winning smile. "This is what I wanted to finish my committee," he pronounced. "A real Vedantin!" At some level, I think, this student did not see me, but saw the reflection of my friend Swamiji, his abiding co-presence in my life, my consciousness and, most relevant to the student in question, my scholarship.

I could not have been more delighted.

Notes

* This essay is dedicated to the memory of Devanathan Jagannathan.

1. James L. Fredericks, "Interreligious Friendship: A New Theological Virtue," *Journal of Ecumenical Studies* 35 (1988): 159–74; and James L. Fredericks, *Faith among Faiths: Christian Theology and Non-Christian Religions* (New York/Mahwah: Paulist Press, 1999), 173–177.
2. James L. Fredericks, "Masao Abe: A Spiritual Friendship," *Spiritus* 3.2 (2003): 219–230, 219.
3. Ibid., 224.
4. Ibid., 225.
5. Ibid., 219.
6. *Upadesasahasri Gadyabanda* 3, following, with small modifications, the translation in Sengaku Mayeda, trans., *A Thousand Teachings: The Upadesasahasri of Sankara* (Albany: State University of New York Press, 1992). Please note that standard diacritical marks for Sanskrit terms and texts have been omitted. Names have been spelled phonetically.
7. *Gadyabanda* 3.115, in Mayeda, *A Thousand Teachings*, 252.
8. *Gadyabanda* 3.116, in ibid., 253.
9. I have detailed this relationship in greater depth in my earlier work, *Spiritual but Not Religious? An Oar Stroke Closer to the Farther Shore* (Collegeville: Liturgical Press, 2005), esp. chs. 2 and 3.
10. *Padyabanda* 4.5, in Mayeda, *A Thousand Teachings*, 112.

11. Lance E. Nelson, "Living Liberation in Sankara and Classical Advaita: Sharing the Holy Waiting of God," in *Living Liberation in Hindu Thought*, ed. Andrew Fort and Patricia Mumme (Albany: State University of New York Press, 1996), 19.

12. *Chandogya Upanisad* 6.8.7, here following the English rendering by Patrick Olivelle, trans., *Upanisads* (Oxford and New York: Oxford University Press, 1996), 152.

13. Reid B. Locklin, *Liturgy of Liberation: A Christian Commentary on Shankara's Upadesasahasri* (Leuven: Peeters, 2011).

14. Walter J. Ong, SJ, *The Presence of the Word: Some Prolegomena for a Cultural and Religious History* (New Haven, CT: Yale University Press, 1967; Binghamton, NY: Global, 2000), 163–165. This paragraph, and the two following, draw from and depend upon the fuller discussion in Reid B. Locklin, "Sacred Orality, Sacred Dialogue: Walter J. Ong and the Practice of Hindu-Christian Studies," *Journal of Hindu-Christian Studies* 26 (2013): 80–90.

15. Walter J. Ong, *Orality and Literacy: The Technologizing of the Word* (London and New York: Routledge, 1982), 71–72, quotation at 72; Ong, *Presence of the Word*, 117–22.

16. Ong, *Orality and Literacy*, 72–73; Ong, *Presence of the Word*, 118–22,

17. Ong, *Orality and Literacy*, 72.

18. *Brhadaranyaka Upanisad* (*BU*) 4.3.1, in Olivelle, *Upanisads*, 58.

19. *BU* 4.3.2, in ibid.

20. *BU* 4.3.5, in ibid.

21. *BU* 4.3.6, in ibid.

22. *BU* 4.4.25, in ibid., 68.

23. J. G. Suthren Hirst, *Sankara's Advaita Vedanta: A Way of Teaching*, RoutledgeCurzon Hindu Studies Series (London and New York: RoutledgeCurzon, 2005), 83–85.

24. On this point, see especially Harold G. Coward and David J. Goa, *Mantra: Hearing the Divine in India and America*, 2d ed. (New York: Columbia University Press, 2004).

25. Galatians 5:13, NRSV.

26. Galatians 5:22–23.

27. This theme is developed further in Locklin, *Liturgy of Liberation*, esp. 159–178.

10

Toddlers and Teas: Parenting in a Multireligious World

Tracy Sayuki Tiemeier and Mugdha Yeolekar

We met several years ago through a colleague. Mugdha was working on her PhD at Arizona State University, but living in Los Angeles because of her husband's job. We got to know each other a little through our participation in the Los Angeles Hindu-Catholic Dialogue. When Mugdha presented her ethnographic findings to the group after a major research trip to India, we realized that we had some shared scholarly interests. Later, Mugdha would teach part-time at Loyola Marymount University (LMU), inhabiting an office across from Tracy. As colleagues and interreligious dialoguers, our relationship was cordial.

What really grew our friendship was the fact that we both had daughters the same age. The girls grew from infancy to toddlerhood before our unbelieving eyes. Conversation about teething and sleep morphed into strategies for potty training and managing the terrible twos and threes. The children are now enrolled in the same preschool, though different classes. Now, we discuss curricula, learning development, and how to address their increasingly complex and difficult questions.

Our friendship has far less to do with structured interreligious dialogues between experts than it has to do with the "dialogue of life," sharing the day-to-day celebrations and concerns of raising our children (now that Tracy has a son as well, conversations have morphed and doubled back to infant care, sleepless nights, and gender development). Indeed, we have learned more about each other and our faiths through our "toddlers and teas" discussions than we have learned though any structured interreligious dialogues in academic settings.

Here, we reflect on our recent conversations about parenting in an interreligious world. Tracy's work in comparative theology and Mugdha's work in religious studies make us highly aware of the religious and interreligious realities of the contemporary world. We are acutely aware that we cannot ignore the religions of the world, particularly as our Los Angeles-raised children are surrounded by religious diversity. More than building interreligious knowledge for the sake of tolerance, we strive to build in our children a true appreciation for the religious peoples of the world and the religions of their friends. We struggle with how to do this in developmentally appropriate ways, and we are also cognizant of the power dynamics inherent in teaching other religious traditions. In the end, we take our cue from our toddlers, who model interreligious learning through concrete relationships and imaginative play. Our daughters' examples of imaginative interreligious play give us hope and a renewed purpose: the encouragement and formation of an integrated and interreligious—even multireligious—spirituality.

Diwali 2012

Neither of us knew that we had each decided to create a short lesson for our daughters' classes in celebration of Diwali in 2012. It wasn't until afterwards, in fact, that we discovered what each of us had done. Although we would have certainly benefited from a discussion before we planned our classes, we had great follow-up "toddlers and teas" going over our strategies and own sense of how to educate preschool age children about Diwali in particular, and intercultural (and interreligious) appreciation in general.

The Lizard Lounge

The Lizard Lounge is a class of 22 three- and four-year-olds at the Loyola Marymount University Children's Center (LMUCC). As a part of the social studies curriculum, the class visited the parents who work at LMU and learned about what people do for their work. Tracy was excited for kids to visit the Department of Theological Studies, but unsure how to present her work to them. She was worried that visiting her office wasn't as exciting to children as visiting the Biology Department, where the "Lizards" were able to do a plant experiment and see a human skeleton. An additional concern for her was whether other parents would be nervous about their children learning about religion. The teacher in charge of the social studies curriculum expressed some anxiety about what the children would be learning, as well. Were they going to learn about God? The Bible? (LMUCC does not provide any religious instruction in its curriculum. It maintains an unstated secular humanist approach to early childhood education.)

Tracy ended up sending an email to all the parents to allay any of their possible fears about visiting our Department. Her email assured parents that "I COMPLETELY understand and share parental concerns about whether/how religion is taught and introduced to children. I...will discuss Diwali as a cultural holiday." None of the parents objected; a number of parents responded with appreciation for the notification and support for intercultural learning.

Purely by coincidence, there was a student art and religion show on display in the Theology Village the day the children visited. As part of their final project, students produced an original piece of art. One of the projects was a Tibetan Buddhist *mandala* (geometric sand design), created meticulously over the weekend by several students. Initially concerned that her energetic and enthusiastic "students" would not be able to help themselves and would play in the sand, Tracy decided to try to incorporate the *mandala* into the lesson for the Lizard Lounge.

As the children entered the Theology Village, Tracy told them that she taught big kids at college, and that the children were going to go to college with her that day. They each got a small canvas backpack and markers to decorate their backpack. After the children decorated their backpacks, they each received a children's book about Diwali—their "textbook"—to place in their backpack. Tracy introduced Diwali as a festival and read the book to them, pausing over the parts of the book that discussed fireworks and treats. When the book discussed *rangolis* (decorative floor designs made during special times), Tracy brought the children to the big *mandala* in the Village. They got to walk around it and look at the sand. The children left with their backpacks on, excited to learn about a new festival to celebrate. (They did leave a little disappointed, however, that they didn't get to eat any Diwali treats during their class trip!)

The Mixed-Age Classroom

The Mixed-Age Classroom (MAC) is a class of 21 children. It has a mix of three-, four-, and five-year-olds. Inspired by the Reggio Emilia approach to early childhood education, the teachers build the curricula of the classroom by taking cues from the everyday discussions of the children. During one such discussion, a Chinese American child said, "China is a far, far away land." This developed into a full-fledged social studies learning module about "faraway" places in the world, ways to commute to the "faraway" places, familiarity with a world map, and so forth. Since Diwali was approaching soon, the MAC teachers asked Mugdha if she were willing to do something for them as a part of this learning module. Mugdha's strategy for presenting Diwali was inspired by her experience a year before, when she attended a storytelling session with her daughter at a public library in Los Angeles. As Hanukkah was approaching, the topic for that particular day was the celebrations associated with it. The Hanukkah book that the storyteller used had pictures of the Hanukkah menorah (candelabrum) and latkes. Latkes were explained to the two-year-olds as "potato pancakes." There was no reference to the religious framework of Hanukkah. Mugdha's two-year-old daughter was most impressed with the latkes and wanted to eat latkes as soon as she got home. Mugdha realized that material culture was a perfect way to introduce Diwali to the toddlers. She decided to focus on the *rangoli*.

Mugdha brought stamps from India and colored sand to make *rangoli* designs. She spread large sheets of paper all over the ground in the outside playground of the MAC. She asked the children, "What are the different ways of decorating your home?" Kids answered various things, such as stickers and flowers. Taking a cue from their answers, she introduced the *rangoli* as a material to decorate homes in a "faraway" land. She left the kids with the colors, stamps, and paper for an hour. Then, Mugdha asked the children when they decorate their homes. Some of them came up with the idea of decoration during a "special time." This was Mugdha's way of introducing Diwali as a "special time" for some people in India.

Our Diwali Discussions

In our follow-up conversations over tea, we discussed our strategies and wondered if we took the right approaches. As good friends, we both reassured and challenged each other. Tracy questioned her motives and wondered if her choices were ultimately essentialistic and imperialistic. Did she choose to talk about Hinduism just because she knew that parents were less likely to have a problem with that than if she taught about Christianity, therefore playing off of parents' possible romantic Orientalism or fears of Christian proselytization? Second, by emphasizing cultural components of Diwali, such as fireworks, treats, and sand designs, did she lay a developmentally appropriate foundation for later interreligious knowledge and appreciation; or did she reinforce (in parents and children) the idea that there's a clear difference between religion and culture that can be separated and navigated easily? Finally, she wondered about her misrepresentation of the *mandala*. There is no doubt that there are important connections between *rangolis* and *mandalas* (and, indeed, the line between is not so clear); but the LMU students had intentionally produced a Tibetan Buddhist *mandala*, while Tracy presented it as a Hindu *rangoli*. Here, the "co-optation" was outright and conscious. Was there such a thing as positive—or at least neutral—co-optation?

Mugdha was much less worried about such concerns. As an ethnographer investigating people's behavior as "texts," and analyzing written scriptures as only one of many sources of meaning-making in everyday life, Mugdha argued that we were bound to tailor our approaches in light of the audience and the materials available to us. She saw us taking very similar approaches that privileged the cultural elements of Diwali in ways developmentally appropriate to young children. Moreover, she reminded Tracy, "religion" was much more than beliefs and ritual practices. To present religion only through religious narratives, theologies, or rituals would also be problematic and assume a Western model of religion. An emphasis on treats, gifts, and the visuals/feel of colorful *rangoli* was not just appropriate for teaching young children; it was very much true to the overall celebration of Diwali.

Mugdha's approach not only helped affirm Tracy, it also challenged her in important ways. First, Mugdha emphasized *material* culture in the educational process itself. The children didn't just learn about *rangolis* or look at them: they *made* them. This seemed to be very powerful for our tactilely oriented preschool children. They will remember the feel of the *rangolis* long after any specifics about why they are made. Second, although she talked about Diwali as something "far, far away," Mugdha and her daughter were there to bridge the distance between exotic, faraway places and the children. This, also seemed important in light of Tracy's concerns; for not only did the children learn about what people faraway do, they learned about what their *friends right here* do. The tactile focus and the personal element were both missing in Tracy's own lesson about Diwali. That made the event less interactive, concrete, and relational for the children. The framing of the lesson as something our friends, near and far, do seemed very important for personalizing Diwali and resisting romantic essentialism.

Interreligious Play

Mugdha's broader concern was whether the presentation of Diwali as a cultural festival really did serve to develop an interreligious sensibility in our children. She worried that the children wouldn't make the connection between their cultural "game" and an appreciation for religions. After all, we both realized after the Diwali lessons that the children never asked any follow up questions on our allusions to religious narratives, beliefs, or practices (the story of Diwali, going to the temple, various deities, etc.). Thus, while we agreed that an emphasis on cultural elements of religious traditions was a developmentally appropriate place to begin, the children's lack of questioning could mean that the strategy didn't necessarily lay a foundation for interreligious appreciation. Perhaps we were missing something essential.

Tracy noted that young children take things in and learn over time, according to their own readiness. Questions emerge piecemeal, as they learn, digest, and relearn; this is why parents and teachers have to listen very carefully to children's actual questions (and not what our panicky minds might think is being asked). Tracy jokingly compared this to our daughters' inevitable questions about "where babies come from." As with many of the "hot button" issues, like sex and death, (inter)religious education had to be child-led. When our children were ready, they would ask. And we should be careful to proceed according to their readiness and line of questioning.

As we reflected on how cultural lessons might lead to religious ones, we laughed over how our daughters' questions frequently emerged in surprising ways. This, again, both affirmed and challenged our parenting approaches. Tracy related, in typical comparative theological fashion, her own daughter's love of fairies and Tracy's use of fairies to explain Hindu goddesses. In this way, the theological nature of Tracy's work helped Mugdha to think about times when her daughter did inevitably bring up the "religious questions" and could be connected to past experiences and knowledge (such as, hopefully, our cultural presentations of Diwali).

Fairies and Goddesses

Tracy's daughter inexplicably adores her mother's office. She finds great joy coming to the office and puttering around. The office is full of Christian and Hindu images and objects—photographs, paintings, posters, statues, and other religious items. For a long time, Tracy's daughter paid little attention to them unless they could be used in whatever game she was playing. Recently, she has wondered who the images and statues are that are displayed so prominently in her mother's office.

When she first started asking questions, Tracy's daughter was interested only in the name of the deity and the animal depicted with the god/

goddess. She was most fascinated with Ganesha and his mouse. This wasn't so surprising. She loved animals, and she wanted to play with the "elephant" on Mommy's desk. She thought it was hilarious that an elephant would ride a mouse. But then she became much more interested in gender, focusing on her own "girl-ness." She wanted to know all about the "girls" in the office. What are they holding? Why? Why do they have more arms than her? Who are they? What do they "do"? Where do they live? Are they "real" or "pretend"? Names did not satisfy her anymore. She had Bigger Questions.

Tracy was caught completely off guard when her daughter first started asking substantive questions about Hindu goddesses. The first analogy that came to her mind was one that would make the most sense to her daughter: fairies. Her daughter had become obsessed with fairies. While the princess phenomenon had come to the house a bit (despite all efforts to the contrary), Tracy's daughter was most consumed with fairies. She looked for their houses wherever she goes. She wanted to watch and read every fairy-related product. She played fairies, dressed fairies, talked fairies, and waited an hour and a half to meet "real" ones at Disneyland. She was comforted by, inspired by, and taken care of by fairies. In Christian theological terms, Tracy's daughter had a "high" theology of fairies. So, caught off guard and in the moment, Tracy compared Hindu goddesses to fairies. And it worked in remarkable ways. While Tracy's daughter noticed that Hindu goddesses didn't have wings or fairy dust, she also noticed other things about fairies (and goddesses) that she hadn't articulated before: they (fairies/Hindu goddesses) were caretakers and healers; they were protectors, rescuers, and fighters; they were many-colored and beautiful (even though they sometimes seemed scary); they were ever-present Mommies and Big Sisters (another obsession now that there was a baby brother in the picture); they were sometimes funny, angry, or sad. So, her daughter's love of fairies served as a bridge for Tracy to address evolving questions about Hindu goddesses, and in a way that allowed for a certain appreciation of their power and complexity.

But even though the comparison seemed to work, Tracy worried to Mugdha that she may have ultimately contributed to the mythologization of Hindu goddesses (as her daughter would grow up and learn that so many of her childhood loves, like fairies, weren't "real"). Nevertheless, Tracy hoped that precisely the opposite would happen: hopefully, her daughter would instead learn to appreciate the very real strength and power of Hindu goddesses and the female divine (something desperately needed for her little girl to navigate her future religious and social life in very patriarchal worlds).

Playing Jesus

Mugdha connected to the value of comparing Hindu goddesses with fairies and saw the comparison as a kind of interreligious experiment or play. She explained to Tracy that her own daughter had become enamored with "pretend play" over the past few months. She adopted different roles ranging from *Dora the Explorer*, to Mom, to "big sister" of the house. In her pretend play, she involved others (persons and toys), assigning them roles as well. Mugdha's daughter constructed elaborate settings and engaged in amazingly involved conversations with her toys and friends in her imaginative games. She used surprising words and phrases (such as "weird," "wacky," and "you know something"). She would teach a pretend class the importance of eating vegetables or give instruction on good manners. She would relate events or conversations from school to her dolls. Among all her collection of toys and dolls, she was especially attached to Pitu, whom she assumed to be her daughter. Pitu had to be a part of each and every conversation in the house.

Recently, Mugdha arranged a few playdates with schoolmates during the winter vacation. These playdates at people's homes became the perfect occasions for the children's pretend play. One afternoon, when Mugdha hosted a child and her mother, the girls immediately began their games. They dressed up as Indian princesses at first and took lots of (pretend) photographs of each other. Mugdha's daughter carried around Pitu, as usual. Suddenly, the friend came to Mugdha and asked if she could "be Mary." Mugdha didn't immediately understand the reference. The girl explained, "Mary, Jesus's Mom. And you know what? Pitu can be baby Jesus." Mugdha responded, "Absolutely!" The girls were both thrilled by the idea. They started arranging a crib for baby Jesus. The girl's mother explained that she was Catholic, and that her daughter had become obsessed with reenacting the story of Christmas. Mugdha's daughter was excited to play the Nativity game. But, as they were playing, she asked the innocent (but profoundly difficult to answer) question, "Mama, who is Jesus?"

The question was profoundly difficult to answer for more than one reason. First, Mugdha was taken by surprise and had seconds to respond. Second, she didn't want to disturb the light, playful mood of the girls with a heavy-handed theological response. Third, Christians themselves have argued about this question for two thousand years. How (Who) was she to answer the question? Here, Mugdha's own concerns over how to introduce the "other" without "othering" the "other" emerged.

After saying that Jesus was a god to some people, Mugdha further elaborated, "[He was] someone who always helped others and shared everything he had. You know, his birthday is coming up next week." She thought that "sharing" and "birthday" were key, relatable terms for a three-year-old. Mugdha's daughter seemed satisfied, but Mugdha was not. She wondered to Tracy whether she had oversimplified things. And yet, the girls had a wonderful time together; and through the game, Mugdha's daughter learned a bit about Jesus while her friend learned that not everyone knew of (or worshipped) Jesus. Thus, while our explanations to our children were bound to be incomplete, they were imaginative bridges into new ways of understanding.

Religion and Interreligious Play

As we discussed Mugdha's daughter's interreligious play and questioning about baby Jesus, what struck Tracy wasn't Mugdha's particular answers. What she noticed was the way in which religious questions emerged spontaneously through play. Like her daughter's questioning after over a year of playing with Hindu images and statues, Mugdha's daughter raised questions that occurred to her and were natural to the Christian Nativity game and her developmental pace. We marveled that the interreligious game itself highlighted the extent to which interreligious learning could be an imaginative process. Mugdha's daughter was *playing* interreligiously before she understood anything cognitively about Christianity. Play led to interreligious questions and learning, not the other way around.

This insight led us to explore the significance of play for theological and religious life, which has been the subject of scholarly attention for some time now. Of course, play is an important theological category for both Hinduism and Christianity. Divine play, or *lila*, is employed in Hinduism to articulate divine freedom, spontaneity, and mystery in the creation, sustenance, and destruction of the cosmos. *Lila* is imagined diversely among the various Hindu philosophical and theological traditions, from the erotic (as with Krishna's love play), to chance and chaos (as with Shiva and Parvati's dice game),[1] to the terrifying and beautiful (as with Kali's battlefield). *Lila* is multivalent and ambiguous, as is the divine and the cosmos.[2] It is also something *we* participate in through its dramatic and ritual staging.[3] While not as prominent in Christianity, the concept of play has been theologically fruitful for many Christians who strive to follow Jesus's directive to become like children.[4] For a Christian theologian such as Jürgen Moltmann, the ultimate *purposelessness* that, in part, defines play highlights the *meaningfulness* of "true" play *and* God as fundamentally free, relational, and liberative.[5] But even more than the theological significance of play, we were intrigued by the growing number of religionists exploring the ludic in religious thought and practice. For these scholars, the ludic, or playful, can be seen as both a method for approaching religion (as scholars adopt multiple, shifting strategies to approach the complexity of religion) and as a fundamental dimension of religion (for example, in the creativity and imagination of rituals).[6]

Perhaps, then, we *were* on the right track. As we reflected back on our cultural approaches to Diwali, we noticed another key element that we both highlighted: the *fun* of Diwali. Drawing *rangolis*, eating treats, and fireworks are all ways of engaging the play of Diwali. What we were really doing at an intuitive level was leading the children in an interreligious game, inviting them to explore and inhabit a new imaginative space. This new imaginative space for play doesn't just lead to questions about other cultures, religions, or peoples; it is the offering of an entirely new worldview and horizon of being. The "magic" of playing Hindu "fairies" or baby Jesus isn't a magic of mythologization, romanticization, or colonialism. It is much more simple, a pure act of joy with others that will become a part of their bodily memory long after they forget the specific games they played.

A Multiple Religious Spirituality

We both have complicated relationships with our own Hindu and Christian backgrounds, relationships that have led us to maintain some distance from our traditions in the early years of our children's spiritual formation. Though Tracy's children were both baptized Catholic, she has avoided joining a parish. She has many hopes for a truly egalitarian Catholic Church, but she has many fears about its entrenched patriarchy and clericalism. The spiritual damage done to her when she was a devoted young Catholic who felt called to the priesthood has led her to be more than a little skittish about committing fully to a Catholic upbringing for her daughter and son.

Mugdha was brought up in a community that celebrated religious identities through cultural expressions more than through congregational practices. Growing up, she would visit Hindu temples from time to time without officially "belonging" to any one temple or specific tradition. Similarly, Mugdha's family does not "belong" to any one Hindu temple, though they visit some occasionally. Even when they do attend temple functions, it is more important to Mugdha that her daughter imbibe and enjoy the diasporic Hindu social context in the United States rather than for her daughter to associate with any specific Hindu tradition or community. But this does not mean that the "religious" is absent from their family life. Indeed, while there are plenty of Hindus who are deeply engaged with temple life and a particular sectarian community, there are many others who are not. And even for the temple observant, home rituals and cultural practices are at least as important for "religious" identity as temple practice. It is therefore tricky to discuss Hindu religious identity, particularly in a Western context that seeks easily identifiable analogues like institutional membership. Mugdha resists raising her daughter in such reductive ways.

But as much as we worry about raising our daughters religiously, their interreligious play offers a different possibility: an integrated multireligious education and even spirituality. Over another "toddlers and teas," Mugdha reflected on some of the personal and unstated goals in her anthropological approach to teaching at LMU. As a part of her "World Religions" class, Mugdha organizes field visits to places of worship of various religions, including Hinduism, Buddhism, Sikhism, Judaism, Christianity, and Islam. Typically, students are required to observe these religious places for over an hour and take notes on ritual space, hierarchies, ritual time, ritual process, and ritual objects. Similar projects are required in many World Religions courses. But what we want to highlight here is the inclusion of her daughter. Since most of these field visits are scheduled over weekends, Mugdha's daughter accompanies her on the field visits. Of course, Mugdha's three-year-old makes age-appropriate associations with these places. Thus, she gets excited when going to a *Gurdwara* (Sikh place of worship) saying, "Oh, I know where we are going! I get to wear a purple bandana and eat lots of *halwa* (sweets) there." For Mugdha, these encounters are a way to personalize a wider interreligious and multireligious education. Of course, she reads a variety of narratives from world religions in bedtime stories. These stories feature Krishna, Rama, African rivers that give gifts, characters such as Angulimal from Buddhist and Pali sources, and more. It is through these stories that Mugdha aims to weave a fabric of interreligious world in her daughter's mind. But in also bringing her daughter to religious rituals and celebrations, Mugdha brings the imaginative world of religious stories to life. Far from disregarding her Hindu heritage, Mugdha integrates it into an interrelated web of multiple religious thought and practice. In this way, she hopes to form, in her students and her daughter, fearless minds that are capable of grasping manifold realities and acknowledging different ways of being. In the context of a university classroom, explicit learning outcomes may be focused on intellectual understanding and interreligious appreciation in service of a more collaborative, just world. But implicitly, and for her daughter, Mugdha also hopes to foster a multireligious identity and spirituality. As Mugdha's daughter both reads about, and experiences, Hindu and non-Hindu beliefs and practice, she understands how "others" live and, with Mugdha's support, learns to navigate the tensions and even contradictions between (and within!) religious worlds. Mugdha's intentional multireligious spiritual hopes for her daughter make Tracy—a cradle Catholic—nervous. Although born in the years after the Second Vatican Council (1962–1965), Tracy was told that her non-Christian family members were going to hell. Her discovery of a more inclusive theology rooted in Vatican II's *Nostra Aetate* was a revelation and a relief. Yet, even as Catholic inclusivity "rejects nothing that is true and holy" in other religions, it maintains a unique and universal place for Christ.[7] She wonders whether a genuine multireligious spirituality is proper, or even possible, when Christ is so central to Catholic teaching and faith.

But while Tracy's Vatican II Catholicity is unnerved by Mugdha's celebration of multireligiosity, her own racial/ethnic and religious multiplicity gives her pause. A Japanese-German American woman, she grew up "between" Asia and America, ever reminded by those in her mostly white Catholic parish that to be "properly" white was to be best, and to be "properly" Christian was to be white. But her spirituality was nourished by Japanese Buddhist practices and beliefs, which led to a good deal of religious and racial/ethnic anxiety in her youth. The ability to embrace multiplicity, tensions, and even contradictions became essential to her psychological and spiritual health. Thus, while there are any number of good reasons to highlight the borders between cultures and religions— including concerns over superficiality and imperialistic "plundering" of marginalized traditions/peoples—her struggles to embrace her own multiraciality and Japanese Buddhist family have convinced Tracy that multiplicity need not be facile nor fragmenting: it can be deeply life-giving for oneself, for others, and for building relationships in the search for a better world. And the joyous interreligious play of her daughter and Mugdha's daughter gives her profound hope for them and the world.

Learning from Each Other, Learning from Our Children

Our daughters will likely not remember their interreligious games or the specific answers we gave to their questions emerging through these games. But their minds, bodies, and spirits have nevertheless created— even if only for a brief time—imaginative, multireligious spaces that will stay with them. They have begun to internalize a whole way of approaching other religious and cultural worlds that crosses borders into the creative space of play, a space that does not engage religious others because they are "useful" or simply important to know because they are neighbors. Instead, it is to be shared space with friends of mutual enjoyment and love.

Through our "toddlers and teas" conversations, we have also been playful as we found ourselves pulling our choices apart and putting them together again in spontaneous, new, and fun ways. Through these "playful" discussions, we imagined ways of raising our daughters as well as rethought our own orientations to our disciplines. Imaginative play allows us to see the positive place of multiple religious identity, as well as the importance for multiple, imaginative approaches to anthropology/religious studies and theology. Our work together has been relational and playful, celebrating the imaginative and complex—and yes, ambiguous—spaces between traditions, texts, and people.

The biggest lesson is this: while we have spent so much time talking about how to teach our children, it is our children who are teaching us.

Notes

1. See Don Handelman and David Shulman, *God Inside Out: Siva's Game of Dice* (New York: Oxford University Press, 1997).
2. See Selva J. Raj and Corinne G. Dempsey, eds., *Sacred Play: Ritual Levity and Humor in South Asian Religions* (Albany: State University of New York Press, 2010).
3. William S. Sax, "Introduction," in *The Gods at Play: Lila in South Asia*, ed. William S. Sax (New York: Oxford University Press, 1995), 3.
4. Matthew 18:1–5. An example of this is the Child Theology Movement. See Vivienne Mountain, "Four Links between Child Theology and Children's Spirituality," *International Journal of Children's Spirituality* 16.3 (August 2011): 261–269; Keith J. White, "Insights into Child Theology through the Life and Work of Pandita Ramabai," *Transformation* 14.2 (April 2007): 95–102.
5. Jürgen Moltmann, *Theology of Play*, trans. Reinhard Ulrich (New York: Harper & Row, 1972), 70–71.
6. See André Droogers, Peter B. Clarke, Grace Davie, Sidney M. Greenfield, and Peter Versteeg, *Playful Religion: Challenges for the Study of Religion*, ed. Anton van Harskamp, Miranda Klaver, Johan Roeland, and Peter Versteeg (Delft: Eburon Academic Publishers, 2006).
7. *Nostra Aetate* (Vatican: October 28, 1965), accessed May 23, 2013, http://www.vatican.va/archive/hist_councils/ii_vatican_council/documents/vat-ii_decl_19651028_nostra-aetate_en.html.

11

With New Eyes to See: Changing the Perception of Self and Other through Interreligious Friendship

Karen B. Enriquez

Changing the Perception of the Other: Making Friends with the Other

In the fifth year of my doctoral program, I became a teaching fellow assigned to a course on the comparison of Buddhist and Christian doctrines and practices. One day, as I was entering the building where my class was held, I encountered John just as he was leaving the same building. From a distance, I saw him, but did not recognize him at first. It was only as we both neared the door that we finally recognized each other. In that moment, we both stopped, smiled, and chatted a little bit. Then, in what I realize now was a moment of teaching, he asked me to notice how our reactions changed the moment we recognized each other. He talked about how, from a distance when we did not yet recognize each other, we were strangers. Right then, we did not have anything to do with each other's lives so we kept walking, lost in our own thoughts and concerns. Then as we walked closer to each other, something changed. As the perception of the other changed from "stranger" to "friend," our attitude became different. From indifference, we moved to the surprise and pleasure of bumping into a friend. He asked me to notice how my attitude and emotion changed within those few seconds of moving into recognition.

In that moment, standing at the threshold of McGuinn Hall, John taught me about how our perception of another affects our attitude toward them, that our recognition and labeling of others as "friends," "strangers," or "enemies," direct the way we act toward the other, and how quickly that perception can change. In a matter of moments, with each step closer to each other, he quickly moved from stranger to friend, and my attitude changed from indifference to happiness. As I've thought about this moment more, I realized that strangers are just friends that we do not yet recognize, because they are still too far to be seen and heard; and, sometimes, I am too busy to take the time to know them. The challenge is how to take that one step closer to recognition, and therefore see that the "stranger" can indeed be a "friend." How do I move out of my bubble of indifference, of the busyness of my life that leads me to walking past others who can then only be strangers to me? How can I find those moments of slowing down, so that I can recognize that there may be friends all around me, if I just take the time to see, to listen, to know others? In many ways, this story of me and John walking closer to each other at McGuinn, moving from strangers to friends, epitomizes the journey toward our interreligious friendship, and my journey toward a greater interest and appreciation of Buddhism.

Coming from Asia, many have assumed that my interest in other religious traditions was a natural outcome of living in a region of the world filled with religious diversity. However, to be honest, my interest in other religious traditions only started as I began my graduate work in theology, when I moved to the United States. In some ways, it seems ironic that it was in moving away from home that I somehow discovered it a little more fully.

I come from the Philippines, a predominantly Catholic country, and I grew up in a very Catholic household and attended Catholic schools until college. Though many of my friends were Filipino-Chinese, they were still all Christian (again, mostly Catholic). They would not have been able to explain the religious grounding for many of the Chinese practices that their families continued. Moreover, living in Manila, the Muslim-Christian conflict in the southern part of the Philippines was as remote to me as conflicts in other parts of the world. In other words, I was living in a very Catholic bubble. Traveling to other parts of Asia was more foreign to me than traveling to Disneyland or other parts of the United States.

It was not until I came to the United States to start my Masters program that I realized, first, that "Christian" meant more than just being Catholic, and, second, that there were other great religions out there. I became interested in trying to understand the relationship between Christ and other religions. Much later, during my doctoral program, I realized that religious pluralism was indeed one of the contemporary issues of the day that I wanted to understand better. In the beginning,

I thought I would study "Theology of Religions"; that is, the theological attempt to understand the role of other religions in light of the Christian understanding of Christ and salvation. However, as Francis X. Clooney, SJ, I was developing a new area in comparative theology, I realized that this was the area that truly interested me. I thought it would be apt to study Islam, in light of both interest in the United States after the terrorist attacks of 9/11 and Muslim-Christian conflicts in the Philippines. I took a class in Islamic Theology and Philosophy at Harvard during my first year, but that first year was to bring many surprises.

It was also in that first year that I decided to take a class on Buddhism because a friend of mine needed a second doctoral student in order to request a graduate level course on Buddhist ethics. It was in this very first course on Buddhism that I met John Makransky, a professor of Buddhism and Comparative Theology at Boston College, who also happened to be a Tibetan Buddhist meditation teacher and a lama in the lineage of Dzogchen master Nyoshul Khen Rinpoche. In this first class, I experienced what many others who practice Buddhism have described: that the teachings somehow rang true, that there was some kind of resonance with its worldview or practices that made sense on a deeper level than could be easily explained. It was then that I knew that I had found my teacher in the deepest sense of that word, a mentor and spiritual friend.

In that class on Buddhist ethics, one of the lessons that made a huge impact on me was how ethical action had its foundation in one's change of perception of self and other. This is why wisdom and compassion are seen as the two wings of a bird. Without wisdom, the "pure perception" that sees the true Buddha-nature of all sentient beings, universal compassion cannot be fully realized. Without the practice of compassion, wisdom cannot fully develop either. In his book, *Awakening through Love*, John quotes Dilgo Khyentse Rinpoche's definition of pure perception: "To recognize the Buddha-nature in all sentient beings and to see primordial purity and perfection in all phenomena."[1] With such perception, we are able to get beyond our dualistic frames of reference—of seeing "self" and "other," and of labeling others as "friends," "strangers," or "enemies"— that become the basis for our attitude and actions toward them. As I look back at my experiences with John, I realize that so many of our interactions have been moments of training me, of teaching me and his other students to develop pure perception, which becomes the basis of true universal compassion in the world. This is no surprise, given John's lineage, and how pure perception is one of the central practices of the Vajrayana tradition, of which Dzogchen is understood as its very essence.

For example, I remember the ways that he would engage the students with their questions, taking them seriously, and helping them feel that their questions and their insights were truly worth something. One of the ways that he did this was in his very manner of being with the students. Whenever I or another student would ask a question, he would look directly at the student and pause for quite a bit. For many of the students who were not used to this kind of silence, and what seemed like intense scrutiny, it was a very awkward encounter. Sometimes, you felt the need to speak more, to fill that silence with more words to explain or to clarify. However, the more I saw this method, the more I realized that this was his way of taking the questions seriously, of taking them to heart and pondering them deeply. It was his way of showing how important those questions were. Then, before he would answer, he would clarify the question by restating it in order to make sure that he understood it. After that, he would then proceed to answer the question.

It was only later, as I delved more deeply into Buddhism, that I realized that what he was doing was the practice of deep listening in order to truly hear and understand the students. Part of that practice is making room for silence, as uncomfortable as it may seem. These pauses, through the years, have made me reflect upon the unending noise all around me: of gadgets that keep me plugged in with the outside world tuned out. I see this in my students now. They come to my class with headphones, big and small, walking in the hallways not looking at each other, but at their smartphones; and I wonder how we can be so disconnected, despite being so "connected" through technology. We do not live in a world that is comfortable with silence; and with all the noise, how do we filter out what matters? How do we begin to truly hear each other, or even begin to notice each other, and in so doing truly know one another, no longer strangers but friends in the process? This, I began to see, was why deep listening and silence were so important. This was what John had been demonstrating for us: teaching us to pause in order to be able to listen deeply before we spoke, instead of wanting to immediately respond without truly listening to the other. Only in this way can we truly hear, and therefore see and know the other better. Only in this way can a class of strangers become a group of friends. As a teacher now myself, I try to practice this in my classroom, in hopes of understanding my students better, and in hopes that they recognize my respect for them and their questions, perspectives, and experiences.

I also saw how his respect for his students, shown in his wanting to truly hear them and understand them, was mirrored in his attitude toward Christianity. One of my first memories of John was when he would ask me and a fellow doctoral student about certain teachings in Christianity, asking us to explain it to him. I saw his seriousness in wanting to learn about and from Christianity. I saw his humility and willingness to learn from others in asking his doctoral students about it. Whenever he would discuss these doctrines with us, I always came away with the impression of his deep understanding of the concepts at hand and his respect for Christianity.

One time, John was teaching us to cultivate pure perception by going beyond labels through meditation on the sameness of all beings—particularly in how we are all the same in our suffering and in our wanting to be free from suffering. To do this, he discussed the three layers of suffering, and then, after his explanation and our practice, we had one of our more difficult discussions focusing around this question: If we are all the same in our suffering, and therefore love and compassion must be extended to all, what about those who have committed great atrocities, such as Hitler? Do they truly deserve the same kind of love and compassion? Does it mean that there is no justice for the victims and that they are just forgiven? It became one of our more interesting, though very challenging, discussions in class.

John led us through a very thoughtful discussion and meditation on the topic. He talked about developing compassion for that enemy by trying to imagine the depths of their suffering and ignorance that have led to the suffering of others. In the years to come, I would read a poem by Thich Nhat Hanh titled *Call Me By My True Names*, and I would come to more fully appreciate what John had been trying to instill in us.[2] In that poem, Hanh writes about how we are all both victims and victimizers. In explaining the inspiration behind it, Hanh writes how he had read about the story of a young girl who took her own life because she was raped by a pirate. In meditating upon this situation, he realized that he "could not take sides against the pirate. I saw that if I had been born in his village and brought up under the same conditions, I would be exactly like him."[3] Here, we see his coming to the sense of the sameness of all beings and, consequently, the non-condemnation of the pirate, by cultivating the wisdom that sees the causes and conditions that led to the suffering of the pirate, and thereby the pirate's actions that led to suffering for the girl. This, I later realized, was what John was trying to get at: a deeper empathy, understanding, and insight into what may be the invisible suffering of the other, and therefore a greater attempt on our part to understand the other better—even the enemy.

Yet, the dilemma remains: Do they just get away with it? As John explained to us, love and compassion do not mean allowing injustice and harm to continue. Rather, the loving and compassionate way is to stop that harm and actually confront that person with their actions. As he writes, "that requires forceful confrontation; one that holds the person *responsible* for his actions. But that means we are holding him responsible to his innate capacity to do *other* than evil—his capacity to do good."⁴ In this way, John was trying to train us in pure perception, of holding ourselves and others to our capacity to do good; in this case being judged in our actions by such capability. Therefore, those who are seen as "evil" are only judged to be evil in light of their capacity for good. This, for him, is cause for compassion, a compassion that leads to confrontation in order to stop that person from inflicting suffering on another and themselves. It is a challenge to confront that other in their "wholeness"—not just their capacity for goodness, but also in the inability to live up to that capacity. In other words, pure perception is not just rose-colored glasses and seeing the best in people while ignoring the harm they do, but the ability to see things as they are: not just in our great capacity for goodness, but also in the ways that we are lost, caught in the deep net of ignorance that leads to the frustration of that goodness.

These discussions brought me back to my own tradition, and reminded me of how challenging it could be. In order to follow Christ and be like Christ, I am asked not just to "love my neighbor," but also to "love my enemy." In light of our conversations on Buddhist compassion and pure perception, I started thinking not just about what it means to love one's enemies, but how one cultivates love for the enemy. What Christian worldview and practices would allow for the development of such love, since the mere command to love the enemy does not automatically mean that one is able to practice it?

Francis X. Clooney, SJ, a pioneer in comparative theology, wrote that theology today needs to be dialogical; that is, "believers learn to speak to one another across religious boundaries…they learn to write in a way that speaks and responds to people in other traditions as well."⁵ In these first conversations with John, in trying to answer his questions about Christianity and in the questions raised by our comparative conversations, I realized some of the challenges and difficulties of interreligious dialogue: of making one's own faith intelligible to others, and of becoming responsible and accountable not just to one's tradition, but to that of another. One of the first things I realized, having grown up in a very Catholic environment, was how challenging it was to explain certain Christian concepts without reverting to other Christian concepts, and therefore, how difficult it was to explain Christianity to an outsider and how impenetrable the language can be. This demonstrated for me how easy misunderstanding can happen, if the right attitude toward the religious other is not there. If there is no sense of wanting to truly listen and understand, how do we truly learn about the other, especially when they seem very alien, very different? How does a perceived stranger, even an enemy, become a friend? How do we not let our suspicions and preconceived notions of the religious other guide our understanding, but let the other speak and to hear the truth of the other and receive that other's truth? Here again, I saw the importance of deep listening, as embodied in John's questions and his attitude toward our imperfect, sometimes fumbling conversations about Christ, justice and compassion, salvation, etc. It was in this exercise of dialogue, though stumbling and awkward at first, that the beginnings of a friendship blossomed, supported by the patient work of deep listening, the careful use of words to explain, debunk, challenge, and then retreat into silence when words became an obstacle.

It was this same kind of attitude that I saw him trying to instill in his students in his class "Religious Quest," a comparative investigation of Buddhism and Christianity. As his teaching assistant in that class, I learned a lot from his own attitude toward Christianity and learning through comparison. Most of the time, we got students who did not want to study Christianity, and thought that taking a class on Buddhism or other comparative classes would be a good way to "escape" it. Given this attitude, it was not difficult for many students to have the perspective that "Buddhism is better than Christianity." Many of them saw Buddhism as a very peaceful religion, and much easier to follow, since one does not have to believe in a God, and meditation seems like a very helpful practice in their lives. For all these reasons, when they were asked to compare certain concepts, it was very easy to fall into the conclusion that Buddhism is better, or that Christianity is lacking. However, John never let the students become lazy or too biased in their comparison. In the same way that he paid attention to his students' questions, he also trained them to pay better attention to the religions they were studying, and to not let their preconceived notions of Christianity and Buddhism become stumbling blocks in truly understanding and appreciating both traditions more deeply. There have been so many instances where I remember him patiently explaining to students certain Christian doctrines or practices in order to clarify their comparison, and I was always impressed at the depth of his understanding and appreciation of Christianity.

Through all this, I saw that he was indirectly training us all in cultivating pure perception for the religious other by teaching us to listen deeply and to listen generously for what is good in these religions, and not allowing our labels or prejudices about these religions to become obstacles to true understanding. This did not mean lumping them together and concluding that they were all the same. Rather, with deep listening, one learns to truly respect and appreciate, not only the similarities, but also the differences between traditions, without necessarily making judgments that one is better than the other.

Changing the Perception of the Self: Making Friends
with Oneself through the Other

John writes that, in meditation, "we are not just *wishing* for others to
have well-being and joy, we are actually *communing* with the primordial
well-being that already abides in the nature of their minds. Our buddha
nature is *communicating* with theirs, below the radar of self-centered
understanding."[6] As I read these words in his book a few months later,
I remembered that fortuitous meeting at McGuinn and I realized that
this dynamic was what was going on. In that moment of recognition, as
short and seemingly mundane as it was, in the enjoyment of each other's
company, we were communing and communicating with each other. This
was what friendship was about: communing and communicating on this
deeper level that not only recognizes the preciousness and value of the
other, but also wishes them well-being and joy. This, I have always felt
from John—as teacher, mentor, and friend.

One time, John shared with me about how he felt that we had a shared
karma, that we were somehow meant to meet and have our lives woven
together. John spent some time in the Philippines as part of the US Peace
Corps program. He talked about how it was partly his experience there
that led to his exploration of Buddhist practice in Asia.[7] For this reason,
and probably more, he has fond memories of the Philippines, and I believe
this was one factor that contributed to our friendship. He talked about
how he felt connected to me through his own experience and memories
of being in the Philippines, and I felt connected to him, hearing his stories
about the Philippines. Here I was, from the Philippines, led to the pursuit
of Buddhist studies because of John, who went to the Philippines, which
led him to Buddhism. It felt like coming full circle. Coincidence? Shared
karma? I do not know, but I know that it felt right to pursue Buddhism
and to study with John.

However, more than just communing and communicating with the
deepest well-being of the other, John also says that "pure perception not
only perceives and communicates with others' inmost goodness and well-
being, but also *evokes* it by calling it forth from them."[8] As an example,
John recalls that, as a graduate student, he had to arrange housing for
high-ranking lamas during an important talk given by the Dalai Lama at
the University of Wisconsin in Madison. He had to place many of them in
the low-cost dorm rooms the university provided. As he and his wife were
about to say good-bye to one of them, he remembers how they were welcomed "as if they were honored dignitaries" and the shabby dorm room
was described as a pure realm. John recounts, "That dingy place was
heaven for him [the lama], and the people all around were divine beings

in his eyes. In spite of our initial bewilderment, his pure view became infectious. Suddenly, we too felt totally blessed to be right there, as if it truly were a holy realm, and we, with him, were pure and holy beings."[9]

As I read about this encounter with the lama, I could not help but reflect upon how my own encounters with John have also helped me to begin to see a holier realm and to begin to see myself and others as "pure and holy beings." In particular, I experienced this in his mentorship, and in the ways that he supported my scholarship, helping me find my own voice, and to believe in my capabilities and strengths as a teacher and scholar. When I was his teaching assistant, he asked me to teach a few of his classes. He informed me that he would be present and observing some of the classes that I taught. To be honest, I was scared and nervous to be teaching in front of my mentor. I felt vulnerable, wanting to impress, to demonstrate that I knew my stuff, but worried that deep down, I didn't really know anything. So I prepared (probably overprepared!) for my lectures. I had my outline and handouts for the students. I taught and he observed. Sometimes, he would raise his hand like the other students to make comments or add to what I was saying, and sometimes he was silent, listening, observing. After his classes, we would usually walk back together to the department, discussing and unpacking what happened in the class. One day, after one of my lectures, he looked me in the eye and mentioned that he thought that I was a natural teacher. I was absolutely surprised by it. Though I have felt such great affinity for teaching, the challenges of teaching undergraduate students had made me question my skills. When he said this statement to me, I wasn't sure how to receive it, let alone how to begin to believe it. However, as we continued to work together, I began to feel the change in my own perception of myself. He would ask me about the examples I used, and would give feedback and suggestions. In these discussions, he always made me feel like he had learned something from me, and he showed his appreciation of what I was trying to do in class. I remember discussions about liberation theology, his questions about justice, and his objection that divisions of victim and victimizer deepened our dualistic thinking that causes greater suffering. I remember being challenged to think more deeply about these issues of justice, forgiveness, universal love, and compassion. How is a universal love for all compatible with the preferential option for the poor and suffering? How does one obey the commandment to love one's enemies, yet seek justice for the victims? Is he right that victim/victimizer is just another dichotomy that is more a problem than a solution? But if so, what's the alternative? In these discussions, he made me feel like we were two equals on a quest toward an answer, or at least, searching to deepen the conversation and understanding of such serious issues. It was in these kinds of conversations that I felt myself becoming more confident with my own voice, my own point of view. I felt as he felt in front of his lama, that I was a "pure and holy being" with great capacities. All this was evoked through our conversations, and I couldn't have been more affirmed in my vocation. This, I realized, was what his mentorship was about: helping another see their potential, to evoke seeing oneself as a "pure and holy being." It was this kind of perception and recognition that allowed me to begin to accept my own capability and sustained me through the difficult road of finishing my dissertation. It is the kind of mentorship that I seek to emulate today: to be able to evoke the goodness and potential of my own students by cultivating my ability to see them clearly; to turn them from strangers into friends with something of great value to offer to each other; and to turn all our encounters into hallowed ground.

Expanding Friendships: Making Friends with Many Others

In his mentorship, John also showed me the importance of building a community of colleagues, and how such a community would support all of us as we went through the program together. Since the comparative theology doctoral degree was new, there were only three of us in the program doing Buddhist-Christian studies. There was also another student, a Buddhist practitioner, at the School of Theology and Ministry. John was her mentor as well, and he would talk about how the two of us needed to meet because we had similar research interests, particularly in the area of feminist studies. By chance, we both attended the same lecture, and at the end of it we both introduced ourselves to each other. We talked about how John had encouraged us to meet and decided that we should meet up later that week. In that second meeting, we also invited one of the other doctoral students. The three of us had a wonderful time talking about research and the demands of scholarly life. During my next meeting with John, I mentioned how the three of us had finally gotten together, and how we were thinking about making it a regular event. As John and I kept talking, he gave one suggestion for our group. He said to try to make it not just a social event but a professional one, helping each other with our papers or whatever work we were doing. He also said to try and be serious about meeting weekly instead of trying to just meet whenever we were all free. I relayed the suggestion to the other two and also invited the other doctoral student in Buddhist-Christian studies. What started was, in many ways, a support group and more that has continued in some form or other until today. In those beginning days, we decided to meet once a week for a couple of hours, booking one of the conference rooms in our department. During those days, we would bring our work that we wanted some feedback on. We shared our syllabi and lectures, drafts of papers and proposals, and ideas for dissertation and other projects. We kept John's suggestion in mind and took seriously meeting every week without any excuses. Beyond our work, we also shared about our joys and struggles, our triumphs and setbacks, both in our personal as well as professional lives.

In my last year of dissertation writing, I went back home to the Philippines to finish. It became very difficult because I felt very disconnected from academic life. I did not have the resources I needed and colleagues with whom I could converse and share this experience with. In light of this geographical shift, I reached out to the various members of that group and asked if they would be willing to continue our work online instead. I experienced their generosity as, despite the time difference and the hectic pace of their lives, they made time to read my chapters, to make comments, and to make time to chat via Skype or e-mail their suggestions. It was through their encouragement, suggestions, and conversations that I was able to continue and, ultimately, finish my dissertation. It was a gift to have my Buddhist friend correct or deepen my chapters on Buddhist emptiness and compassion, and to have conversations about our shared research on feminist studies, and the status of women in Buddhism and Christianity. It reminded me of what I had learned from John about learning to listen and learning to write for another audience, of becoming accountable to not only one's own community, but that of another also. My dissertation was strengthened because of their perspective, of our dialogue, of our willingness to listen and speak the truth with one another, all of which would not have been possible without the friendship that we had built over those weekly meetings in Boston.

In one of our doctoral seminars, John expounded on the *Vimalakirti Sutra*, a beloved sutra in the Mahayana tradition that focused on the example of a layman as a *bodhisattva* (enlightened being). The first chapter was a discussion on the purification of Buddha-fields. A Buddha-field (*buddhaksetra*) is the sphere of Buddha's influence and activity in the Mahayana tradition. Each world has one Buddha. However, John also explained that the Buddha-field can also be understood as an individual's particular network of connections or relationships. Though each one strives to develop universal compassion, the cultivation and practice of this compassion usually grows out of one's own context, of one's own set of relationships, which becomes one's Buddha-field. It is in this set of relationships that one practices purification. As the *Vimalakirti Sutra* states:

> A bodhisattva embraces a buddha-field to the same extent that he causes the development of living beings. He embraces a buddha-field to the same extent that living beings become disciplined. He embraces a buddha-field

to the same extent that, through entrance into a buddha-field, living beings are introduced to the buddha-gnosis. He embraces a buddha-field to the same extent that, through entrance into that buddha-field, living beings increase their holy spiritual faculties.[10]

As I read these words and listened to John's explanation, I slowly began to realize the implications of this and our conversations about shared karma and our connection, as well as his encouragement to form a community of colleagues. It was in this community of colleagues and friends that my "purification," described in the quote above as "development," or "increase in holy spiritual faculties" would happen. In telling me about our shared karma, he was saying that I was part of his Buddha-field, and as my mentor, he was devoted to my development and the increase of my wisdom and spiritual faculties. Of course, he said none of this explicitly. But I felt that this was what I had been experiencing with him. At the same time, in the Buddhist-Christian group that I had formed, I had identified my other Buddha-field where, as we continued to deepen our personal and professional ties, we were becoming spiritual friends whose lives were tied together, our development, success, and progress somehow dependent on each other. They would be spiritual friends on my journey toward purification and liberation. We were all connected by John, our mentor, who was the core and foundation of our Buddha-field.

As I continued to reflect on this, I could not help but think about the idea of the communion of saints as well as the social nature of salvation. I thought about the practice of the litany, of singing or chanting the names of the saints who have come before us, joining us in that moment as we prayed for those who were being baptized, confirmed, or ordained. This vision of the Buddha-field and of pure perception, however, gave me a richer understanding of this kind of communion: of the communing and evoking of each other's goodness, of the support and encouragement that we give to each other, of the ties we currently have and the ties we have yet to make. We are all implicated in each others' well-being and joy; but in particular, the specific network of friendships and relationships that we have and make can lead us to greater wisdom, development, and spiritual faculties. It is only through the help of one another, in communing with each other, in finding ourselves as the Body of Christ, the communion of friends, that we are saved, as that one body, and not just as individual parts. In that moment, I suddenly had a greater appreciation for this tradition of the communion and litany of saints. It felt more alive and relevant to me—all evoked by John's discussion of Buddha-fields. Such spiritual friendships, and the understanding of their value and role in Buddhism, have helped me to rethink the value and role of the communion of saints as friendship. It also helped me to rethink how salvation is never just a personal or individual matter, but includes the whole community, working together, living and sharing their lives in friendships that ever reveal to us our preciousness and value as individuals and as a community. Moreover, it reminds me of the value of such interreligious friendship and mentorship, of truly learning from the other and sharing one's world with the other that opens our eyes to a greater reality, a new way of perceiving oneself and one's relationships. In the face of so much misunderstanding, suspicion, and the challenge of religious pluralism today, I hold it as even more precious, the shared karma that has brought me and John Makransky into each other's lives, transforming us from strangers to spiritual friends, and finding that network of spiritual friends that leads to our mutual development and purification.

Final Thoughts

The Second Vatican Council's *Nostra Aetate* promotes unity with other religious traditions by looking at what all people, and by the same token, all religions, "have in common and what draws them to fellowship."[11] It looks to the shared beliefs with the other Abrahamic traditions, and promotes reverence and respect for other religions who "often reflect a ray of that Truth which enlightens all men."[12] In the end, it concludes that "no foundation therefore remains for any theory or practice that leads to discrimination between man and man or people and people, so far as their human dignity and the rights flowing from it are concerned."[13]

As I reflect upon these words in light of my interreligious friendship, I think about the truth of these words and how such a foundation can be for interreligious friendship and dialogue. In many ways, my friendship with John grew out of certain commonalities, not least of which, as I mentioned, was a certain shared experience of the Philippines, as well as the ways that the Buddhism he introduced to me "rang true" with my own Catholic upbringing. To focus on unity and commonality, then, is a good starting point for friendship. However, in my friendship with John, I have also experienced the challenges of talking across differences. There were many moments when I did not fully understand what he was trying to convey, and when I was challenged to convey my own beliefs. It was in these gaps, in the differences, and not just in the seamlessness of our relationship, that I think my true learning and a deepening friendship happened. In the moments when I was challenged to think from his Buddhist perspective, to use categories that I was not familiar with, to inhabit that world that was so alien from my own—those were the moments that had the biggest impact on me and my friendship with John. Our attempt to bridge the differences in language and worldviews, in finding and respecting the limits of such, of staying in the moments of painful silence and awkward pauses because we had reached the limits of our language and worldviews, and realized that it was okay to stay in this space—these became the strong building blocks and foundation of deeper friendship. This is also what helped me realize what true friendship was: not unity through commonality, but a true unity-in-difference, of a real respect for the other by respecting not just what we have in common, but what it is that continues to be different, and the ways we can mutually enrich each other through dialogue not only about our similarities but also our differences.

Nostra Aetate acknowledges the need for respecting difference by stating that "she regards with sincere reverence those ways of conduct and of life, those precepts and teachings"[14] that differ in many aspects from what the Catholic Church holds. However, it also does not state how to truly respect that other, especially when their perspective is different from one's own. Here, I think I learned most from John's discussions and example about deep listening: not just a listening and understanding of what is familiar, but a true attentiveness to otherness; not necessarily needing to smooth things over or resolve the differences, and learning when to stop speaking to just commune in silence when words and commonality have reached their limit.

In the end, reflecting upon my friendship with John, I see the promise and the limits of what the declaration was trying to promote: unity through commonality, respect and tolerance for the religious other. However, to truly learn about and learn from the other requires more than just respect and tolerance, it requires a friendship that goes beyond these and listens attentively to the other, giving them space to be themselves: a true dialogue of equals where equality does not dissolve into unity through commonality. And friendships, at least the ones that endure, are ones that are not just rooted in commonality, but are the ones who respect difference and distance, leading us more and more deeply into ourselves as we are more deeply led into the life of the other.

Notes

1. Dilgo Khyentse Rinpoche and Mattieu Ricard, *The Spirit of Tibet: The Life and World of Khyentse Rinpoche, Spiritual Teacher* (New York: Aperture Foundation, 2000), 52, as quoted in John Makransky, *Awakening through Love: Unveiling Your Deepest Goodness* (Boston, MA: Wisdom Publication, 2007), 133.

2. Thich Nhat Hanh, *Love in Action: Writings on Nonviolent Social Change* (Berkeley, CA: Parallax Press, 1993), 107–109.
3. Ibid., 107.
4. Makransky, *Awakening through Love*, 130.
5. Francis X. Clooney, SJ, *Hindu God, Christian God: How Reason Helps Break Down the Boundaries between Religions* (New York: Oxford University Press, 2001), 10.
6. Makransky, *Awakening through Love*, 134.
7. Ibid., 5.
8. Ibid., 135.
9. Ibid., 136.
10. Robert A. F. Thurman, trans., *The Holy Teaching of Vimalakirti: A Mahayana Scripture* (University Park: Pennsylvania State University Press, 2006), 15–16.
11. *Nostra Aetate* (Vatican: October 28, 1965), 1, accessed June 24, 2014, http://www.vatican.va/archive/hist_councils/ii_vatican_council/documents/vat-ii_decl_19651028_nostra-aetate_en.html.
12. Ibid., 2
13. Ibid., 5.
14. Ibid., 2.

12

Masao Abe: A Spiritual Friendship

James L. Fredericks

Some years ago, I enjoyed a fine Japanese lunch with my friend and teacher, Masao Abe, the great exponent of Zen Buddhism and leader in the dialogue among Buddhists and Christians.[1] Professor Abe has taught me wonderful things about Buddhism for some 20 years now. I gathered with him and his wife, Ikuko Abe, in a traditional restaurant in Kyoto. We had a private room with a low table and sat on *tatami* mats. Abe Sensei ("Sensei" is a term of endearment and respect for a teacher used in Japan) had been somewhat pensive and withdrawn for most of the meal. Mrs. Abe and I had been bantering about how late the *tsuyu* rains had been that year and the effect it was having on Kyoto's hydrangea. Suddenly Sensei began to speak with an unusual tone of voice, as if saying something of great importance to no one in particular. "It is not enough," he said. Mrs. Abe and I fell silent and attentive. He repeated himself in the same voice: "It is not enough." I knew immediately what my teacher was talking about. In his old age and after a long and distinguished career of teaching and lecturing about Zen in the West, Abe Sensei was talking about a Buddhist teaching dear to his heart, "the standpoint of emptiness." Out of politeness, I did not want to indicate that I understood his meaning so directly and sat, wondering what I should say in response. Finally, I settled on something like this: "I will continue to study; Sensei, please continue to teach." I spoke in the most formal Japanese I could muster, out of respect for my teacher, but also out of friendship.

I am not sure how I should describe my relationship with Masao Abe. To call us colleagues in the dialogue among Buddhists and Christians hardly does justice to how dear he is to me. To call me his *deshi* (disciple) does not fit the expectations this word conjures in Japan. He and I disagree professionally over many important matters. Besides, Sensei is a Buddhist and I am not. Is Masao Abe my friend? He is 35 years my senior and a distinguished scholar. In Japan at least, calling us friends *(tomodachi)* would be presumptuous. I will stick with friendship, however, and will try to justify the term by qualifying it. My friendship with Abe Sensei is a *spiritual* friendship. I want to write about this spiritual friendship and reflect on what my teacher meant that day in Kyoto when he said, "It is not enough."

Friendship is a familiar theme in Christian spirituality. This is hardly surprising. Friendships humanize. Friendships must therefore be related in basic ways to our spiritual lives. The one who is without friends is poor indeed. More specifically, I am interested in spiritual friendships with those who follow other religious paths. I think we should look on these "interreligious friendships"[2] as a form of Christian spiritual practice. Friendships that reach across the boundaries of community, doctrine, scripture, asceticism, and liturgy that separate religious believers should rightly be recognized as new opportunities for exploring Christian spirituality. Certainly this is the case with my friendship with Masao Abe. Sensei's Buddhist path is central, not incidental, to our friendship. Interreligious friendships are not common. They are not unheard of either. Gustav Weigel's friendship with Rabbi Abraham Heschel and Thomas Merton's friendship with D. T. Suzuki (one of Abe Sensei's mentors) come readily to mind.

Friendships with those who follow other religious paths contribute to human flourishing. They are a way of building up new forms of solidarity between religious communities. The virtue of interreligious friendship also helps us to resist vices, like our propensity to fear those who are different. In our sinfulness, fear leads us to demonize, caricature, or simply ignore the other. A spiritual friendship with someone who follows another religious path helps us to resist not only intolerance, but also our penchant for developing elaborate theological schemes that reduce the other to what David Tracy calls "simply more of the same."[3] Spiritual friendships with those who follow other religious paths help us to resist vices such as these.

Every friendship, no matter how good or how old, once involved making a hospitable place in our lives for a stranger. After all, every friend, no matter how good or how old a friend, was once a stranger. This practice has spiritual value. Welcoming a stranger entails a decentering of the self. We are moved off our home ground. The sovereignty of the ego is undermined. In welcoming a stranger, we have to make room for another way of imagining the world and acting within it. Sartre was unable to see the advent of the stranger as anything but a threat. Emmanuel Levinas, reflecting Jewish tradition, saw the stranger not only as threat, but also as beatitude.[4] Welcoming the stranger brings a loss of security, but also a loss of hopelessness; the ruination of autonomy, but also a liberation from self-absorption.[5]

Every friend was once a stranger. Less obviously, friendships of lasting value and depth retain a sense of the stranger in the friend. This is very true of my friendship with Masao Abe. Years ago, I spent an evening with Professor and Mrs. Abe in their home in Kyoto. Sensei was unusually gregarious and informal that evening. He wore a summer kimono. In July, the taste of cold noodles goes nicely with the drone of cicadas in the garden and the clean smell of the *tatami*. Not knowing any good Japanese word for what I was trying to say, I told Mrs. Abe that everything was *gemütlich* (cozy). Sensei laughed as he tried to translate it into Japanese for us. In the alcove was a very simple flower arrangement and a hanging scroll with Chinese characters painted in a spontaneous hand. I asked Sensei about the calligraphy. The scroll contained the characters: form, emptiness, emptiness, form. Now able to read the scroll, I was left with a sudden sense of what a stranger Masao Abe remains for me.

"Form is emptiness, emptiness is form." This famous teaching comes from the Heart Sutra and tells much about why my cherished teacher and friend is still a stranger to me. According to this teaching, sensible forms, the objects we fashion out of our passions and obsessions and call "reality," are in fact "empty." They are illusions fashioned by what the Buddha called "the mind on fire." All our pretensions to selfhood—our construction of racial and national identity, our preoccupation with status, our obsession with autonomy—are but fleeting forms without substance, founded on nothing. They do not endure. They are empty. Clinging to such forms as if they were real and enduring only entangles us in a world that will never be satisfactory. This is *samsara*, what the Lotus Sutra calls the "burning house" of sorrow. The path of wisdom, the path that leads to an extinguishing of the fires that inflame the mind, entails renunciation. Clinging to empty forms will never be satisfactory. When clinging ends, empty forms no longer constitute a prison of our own construction. The forms become just transient manifestations of the emptiness that characterizes everything. Wisdom, for a Buddhist like Masao Abe, means finding freedom in the realization of the emptiness of all things through nonattachment.

Form is emptiness, but according to the Heart Sutra, the reverse is also the case. Emptiness itself is merely a form and has no existence apart from the fleeting and ever-changing shapes taken by the world. This means that emptiness is not a transcendent realm beyond this world. Awakening to the emptiness of all things does not entail an "ascent" of the soul into a realm beyond the world. Form is emptiness—and emptiness is simply the myriad forms themselves. Therefore, in speaking of emptiness, Sensei likes to use phrases strange to me like, "the original naturalness of all" (*jinen*) and the "true suchness of things" (*shin-nyo*). For my friend, things have no "beyond." Visible forms are not symbols that speak of what is "higher." In a way that would have been utterly foreign to the Pseudo-Dionysius, my friend does not live in a world in which appearances open up into a redeeming transcendence. Form is emptiness and emptiness is form—nothing more. There is nothing beyond empty forms because there is no beyond.

For many years, in our discussions, Masao Abe and I have tried to find a place for my God in those Chinese characters. Neither one of us has succeeded to the degree we had hoped. Form is emptiness. Emptiness is nothing other than form itself. In the asymmetrical grace of a flower arrangement, in the play of textures, tastes, and sounds of the tea ceremony, in the spontaneous hand of the calligrapher—there is the suggestion of a kind of intimacy of all things. In the "true suchness of things" and the "original naturalness of all," the perfectly ordinary finally becomes numinous in itself, without bearing the burden of pointing to a transcendence beyond it. Zen is witness to an immanence so radical and uncompromised that the otherness of the Christian God is overcome.

At the dedication of the Temple in Jerusalem, Solomon had to deal with the unimaginable otherness of God: "Even heaven and the highest heaven cannot contain you, much less this house that I have built!"[6] The "true suchness of things" negates the unimaginable otherness of Solomon's God. The "original naturalness of all" deconstructs the transcendence of the God of Zion.[7] In my friend's Buddhist world, there is neither a Creator nor a creation that witnesses to the Creator. The heavens do not declare the glory of God. There is only the drone of cicadas, the clean smell of *tatami*, and the taste of cold noodles, in Kyoto, in July, underneath the hanging scroll. Form is emptiness—but emptiness does not lie beyond form. Nothing lies beyond the intimacy of forms. But unlike my friend and teacher, I cannot abide contentedly in this "original naturalness" that is without transcendence. The hound of heaven will not allow me to rest in this intimacy with the ordinary. In this, Sensei is not like me. He does not know what it means to be pursued by such a hound. For all our friendship over the years, there still are times when we look at one another in what only can be called an appalling bewilderment. This friend of mine remains a stranger.

So, as I began to discern the shape of those Chinese characters on the hanging scroll with Sensei's help, a poorly alloyed mixture of regret and gratitude began to arise within me. My dear friend and teacher, Masao Abe, for all his erudition about my God (he studied theology with Tillich and Niebuhr), does not know a God beyond the world of forms. He does not know the subjectivity that arises by being addressed by the Holy One of Israel, as Abraham was. Beyond the "true suchness of things," there is no transcendent One who creates and redeems, who judges but relents also. The regret arises because I recognize the goodness of the Buddhist path but cannot embrace that path as a believer and practitioner. I am not a Buddhist. To say so would be not only pretense, but harmful to Buddhism. I will not hurt my Buddhist friend. The gratitude arises in the fact that my Buddhist friend has been such a patient and generous teacher. I cannot be a Buddhist. I can, however, be a friend to Masao Abe. My spiritual friendship with this Buddhist is a way to embrace and honor what I cannot become.[8]

There is something paradoxical in my friendship with Masao Abe. In no small way, our strangeness to one another is the bond that holds our friendship together. Sensei, I think, would agree. I have other friends who manage to inhabit the world of Zen and the world of Christian theism with little difficulty. No doubt, this is a grace and should be accepted as such by those to whom this grace is given. I have never prayed for such a grace. On reflection, I suppose the reason I do not pray for such grace is the fear that this might corrode my friendship with Sensei. Our strangeness to one another has brought a depth of spiritual purpose to our friendship. This depth of purpose, however, has been a pearl purchased at a great price. My friendship with Masao Abe has required me to find my way in a territory uncharted by my own religious tradition. This calls for some explanation.

My faith, tutored by the Catholic sacramental imagination, teaches me to watch for epiphanies. We should live life always ready to take off our shoes. In a world where the Word is always becoming flesh, my deepest spiritual instincts beg me to recognize in Sensei's otherness yet another wondrous trace of the divine. Do I not see in the face of my friend the presence of a Mystery that both summons and beatifies? Is not this Mystery the same otherness that led Anthony into the desert and Juan de la Cruz to an ascent into *Nada*? As a child, I was taught that the redwood trees prayed to their Creator—and that I could hear them pray if only I would quit the trail and listen hard enough. If this is true of redwood trees, how much more must this be true of my Buddhist friend? Sensei certainly invites me to quit the trail. If only I could listen hard enough, I would hear in Sensei's voice a hymn to the Creator.

Absorbing Masao Abe's Buddhist life into the encompassing Mystery of God, however, would be a betrayal of our friendship. The betrayal would not lie in the fact that my teacher has repeatedly told me that Buddhist emptiness cannot be identified with the God of Christian faith. Sensei and I have plenty of theological disagreements. The betrayal would lie in the loss of the otherness that forms the basis of our friendship. The great Jewish thinker, Emmanuel Levinas, has taught me much in this regard. Levinas speaks of the other as a "face" (*le visage*) that is "defaced" by incorporating it comfortably into our preexisting view of the world.[9] By defacing the other, we render the "face" harmless, pressed into service of the self and the world it has constructed for itself. For my friendship with Masao Abe, this would constitute a monumental loss. Appeasing my need to make theological sense of the world would come at the expense of an enriching, if troubling, friendship. This is too high a price to pay by far.

My Buddhist friend has run me off my theological roadmap. The greatness of Buddhism, which comes to me not in any book, but in the concrete form of my devoted friend, must be the work of God. And yet, this very friend assures me that this is not the case. Learning to live off the roadmap is what makes this interreligious friendship such good, if difficult, spiritual practice. A friendship with someone who follows another religious path calls for a spirituality that resists the attempt to overcome differences and to incorporate the other into "simply more of the same." The strangeness of my Buddhist friend is not merely provisional. His otherness is not something to be overcome. My friend's Buddhist life cannot be situated comfortably within my Christian understanding of the world without doing violence to Buddhism and to our friendship. My spiritual practice of interreligious friendship, therefore, is not so much a quest for understanding as a disciplined practice of listening. By "understanding," I mean here the attempt to assimilate the other into my Christian grand narrative. "Listening," in contrast, means to let the other appear as a "face," to resist my need to deface, and above all, to dispose myself to become one who is addressed by that face, not one who addresses.

What I speak of here is something more than Christian humility before another religious tradition. Like humility, honoring my friendship—even at the expense of theological coherence—is a form of spiritual practice. In this respect, I have been changed by a great Buddhist truth, and Masao Abe has been a great teacher of this truth. But to tell of this, I must tell more about my Buddhist friend.

Sitting on the *tatami* mats in that Kyoto restaurant was not the only time that Sensei has ever said "It is not enough." In April 1942, four months after the beginning of the Pacific War, Masao Abe entered Kyoto Imperial University (now Kyoto University) to study the philosophy of religion. He was 27 years old, buffeted by criticism for not enlisting in the army, and fearful of the power of nihilism at work in his militarized society. In Kyoto, he was much attracted by the lectures of Hajime Tanabe, who was already filled with foreboding over Japan's impending defeat and looking to Pure Land Buddhism for guidance. Zen is focused on unflagging effort on the meditation pillow and sudden *satori* (awakening). The Pure Land path, in contrast, is a Buddhism of repentance and faith in the compassion of Amida Buddha who rescues us from our egocentricity. Tanabe's comment, "Amida is not far from here," brought Abe to weep inconsolably in the realization that it was he who was moving away from Amida even as Amida was moving toward him. Even still, Sensei would eventually find the Pure Land path "not enough" for resisting the forces of nihilism in the world and in himself.

After the war, Abe joined a Zen meditation group that met at Reiun-ji within the great temple complex of Myoshin-ji in Kyoto. The group was directed by Shin'ichi Hisamatsu, a Zen layman and lecturer on Buddhism at the university. In December 1951, Abe had a violent encounter with Hisamatsu that people still talk about. Zen had begun to erode Abe's Pure Land faith and, in the resulting personal crisis, the threat of nihilism had returned to him in force. One evening, in great agitation, Abe rose from his meditation pillow and lunged toward Hisamatsu screaming, "Is this the true self?" He was restrained briefly and then left the room. Later, Abe recalled the anguish of that dark night. "It's all a lie!" he told Hisamatsu. Still later, Abe said in despair, "I cannot find any place where I can stand." Hisamatsu answered: "Stand right at that place where there is no place to stand." Zen calls this the standpoint of emptiness.

This "place where there is no place to stand" is where my friend has stood for more than half a century. Hisamatsu introduced Masao Abe to D. T. Suzuki who was already corresponding with Thomas Merton about Zen and Christian contemplation. Abe would eventually teach at great universities in the United States and Europe and become one of the leading figures in the dialogue among Buddhists and Christians. At the heart of all of this has been Abe Sensei's unwavering commitment to expounding the standpoint of emptiness.

In honoring my friendship with Masao Abe—even at the expense of theological coherence—I too have had to learn how to stand in "the place where there is no place to stand." Without ceasing to be a Christian believer, my friendship with Masao Abe has required me to move off my Christian theological roadmap. In doing so, I have not become a Buddhist. Nevertheless, I have been changed profoundly by the Buddhist truth of emptiness. My Christian friends have little understanding, and in some cases, little patience, with my attempt to stand in this "place where there is no place to stand." Christianity, they remind me, is an encompassing vision that interprets the world completely. How could anything lie beyond the roadmap? Abe's Buddhism must be the work of the Holy Spirit. Even though Buddhists do not realize it, they too give praise to the Creator of heaven and earth. In this, of course, my Christian friends speak a great Christian truth. Nothing created by God has been abandoned. No corner of reality is God-forsaken. While I stand within this Christian theological roadmap, however, the face of my friend and teacher is no longer recognizable. Looking on Masao Abe as an "anonymous Christian" does violence to our friendship. The sacramental instincts of my Catholic spirituality pose a great temptation to redraw the lines of my friend's face into my own image and likeness.

I cannot abandon my Christian faith and I will not abandon my Buddhist friend. Therefore, in my own way, I have had to learn how to stand in the "place where there is no place to stand." This has not meant forsaking my trust in God and replacing it with the "original naturalness of all" and the "true suchness" of things. The practice of my faith, however, has been changed profoundly by the truth of Buddhist emptiness. This brings me to a final reflection on what my friend meant when he spoke in that restaurant in Kyoto and said, "It is not enough."

Sensei's favorite passage from the New Testament is the *carmen Christi* (Philippians 2:6–11). Singing of the savior, the hymn begins, "though he was in the form of God, did not regard equality with God as something to be exploited, but emptied himself, taking the form of a slave..." Abe Sensei and I discussed this passage one afternoon, drinking green tea in his office. He wanted to know what "emptied himself" meant to me. I must have said something about the Incarnation of the Word in reply—I no longer remember. Sensei spoke even more softly than usual that day. "I think it means," he began, "that Christ is a kind of *bodhisattva*." I was deeply touched and, after a respectful moment, I said, "Sensei, please understand that this *bodhisattva*-Christ who takes the form of a slave is the only God that Christians know anything about." Abe Sensei closed his eyes and made the whole room very quiet.

Of Buddhism's many impressive teachings, the *bodhisattva* ideal must be one of the most wondrous. A *bodhisattva* is one who, in the quest for enlightenment, has come to the threshold of *nirvana* itself. Ready to enter into bliss, the *bodhisattva* renounces *nirvana* and turns back to *samsara*. This return to *samsara* takes the form of a vow to work skillfully for the benefit of every sentient being. In the *bodhisattva's* vow, Buddhism teaches a great and paradoxical truth. Since attachment is the birthplace of sorrow, wisdom requires that attachment be renounced. In the quest for liberation from sorrow, however, the *bodhisattva* is the one who has overcome every attachment save one, the attachment to *nirvana* itself. If the *bodhisattva* is to attain enlightenment, all attachment must be renounced, even the attachment to *nirvana*. Herein lies the paradox: only in renouncing this last attachment, our desire to abide in *nirvana*, can *nirvana* be attained. According to the *bodhisattva* ideal, true enlightenment involves not an escape from *samsara*, but rather a return to it in order to work skillfully and compassionately for the benefit of all sentient beings. Therefore, only by turning away from *nirvana* does the *bodhisattva* become fully enlightened. In living the vow, the *bodhisattva* uproots the last taint of egocentricity, the desire to find personal bliss by escaping *samsara*.

Sensei sees in Christ this paradoxical truth of the *bodhisattva*. Christ renounces divinity and takes on the form of a slave in order to benefit sentient beings. Because of this great renunciation, Christ is raised up and exalted. The *bodhisattva* is truly enlightened only by renouncing *nirvana*. Christ is truly divine only by abandoning divinity. By entering the world of form, the transcendent monarch becomes the living God of Christian faith. According to the epigram from the Heart Sutra on Sensei's hanging scroll, emptiness is truly emptiness only when it empties itself and becomes the world of form. According to the *carmen*, Christ is truly Christ only by renouncing his divinity and entering the world of form.

In the *bodhisattva* teaching, emptiness becomes a spiritual practice, not merely a metaphysical assertion about the nature of things. In fact, when it is merely an assertion about the nature of things, emptiness is no longer empty. The *bodhisattva's* practice of emptiness is what Buddhists call "hard practice." Only by renouncing *nirvana*, understood as an escape from *samsara* and the suffering of sentient beings, is *nirvana* attained. Only in renouncing emptiness as a metaphysical belief is emptiness truly realized as a spiritual practice. Therefore, *bodhisattva* practice means standing neither in *samsara* nor *nirvana*, but rather in the "place where there is no place to stand." This takes the concrete form of selfless compassion.

In the restaurant in Kyoto, when my friend and teacher said "It is not enough," and I realized that he was talking about his life's work in spreading the Buddhist teaching about emptiness, that feeling of gratitude and regret came over me again. The regret flowed from the pathos of an old man as he realizes that this life will end before the quest is over. Masao Abe knows that he has been more creative in imagining Christianity anew with Buddhist insight than in his quest to renew Buddhism with Christian insight. The doctrine of emptiness, the place where Sensei has stood for so many years, cannot encompass the God of Abraham, Isaac, and Jacob. It is not enough.

I felt gratitude as well—the gratitude every Christian should feel before a *bodhisattva*. My teacher has had to do much renouncing over his almost 90 years of life. In his youth, the threat of nihilism drove Masao Abe to the Pure Land path of faith. But this was not enough. Only with much anguish and at great personal cost, my friend renounced his attempt to live by faith. Later, in the confrontation with Shin'ichi Hisamatsu, Masao Abe began to stand in the "place where there is no place to stand"—the standpoint of emptiness embraced by the Zen path. By standing "where there is no place to stand," Sensei has lived a Zen life that has taken him to classrooms and lecterns in the West and to friends, like myself, who follow the path of Christ. But now, in his old age, my wonderful friend has realized that even the standpoint of emptiness is "not enough." In the paradoxical wisdom of the *bodhisattva*, this last attachment must be renounced. The quest to become truly empty demands it. I do not presume that Sensei will stop being a Zen Buddhist. On the contrary, his words came to me as a kind of promise that he will continue to be a good Buddhist for my benefit. I am so grateful for this. "It is not enough" was the vow of a *bodhisattva*, the voice of a true Buddhist, struggling to realize the truth of emptiness as compassion.

Sensei wants me to be a good Christian. Anything less would do violence to our interreligious friendship. My friendship with Masao Abe, however, requires me to stand where there is no place to stand. Let me then take the path of Christ, as Sensei has taken the path of the *bodhisattva*. I will empty myself and take the form of one who has no place to stand—the form of a believer and a friend.

In Kyoto, sitting on the *tatami* mats, halfway through lunch, while his wife and I bantered about *tsuyu* rains and hydrangeas, my teacher took the *bodhisattva* path, vowing to work for the benefit of all sentient beings, including his Christian friend. Sensei is now very old—too old for dialogue meetings. His life of formal dialogue has come to an end. But his vow of compassion continues. In this, Masao Abe is a true friend, a skillful teacher, and a stranger to be welcomed. What is to be said in the face of such compassion? "I will continue to study; Sensei, please continue to teach."

Los Angeles, 2003

Abe Masao Sensei died in Kyoto in 2006.
He was 91 years old.

Notes

1. Originally published as James L. Fredericks, "Masao Abe: A Spiritual Friendship," *Spiritus* 3.2 (2003): 219–230. © 2003 Johns Hopkins University Press. Reprinted with permission of Johns Hopkins University Press.

2. For a reflection on interreligious friendship as a new theological virtue, see my "Inter-religious Friendship: A New Theological Virtue," *Journal of Ecumenical Studies* 35.2 (Spring 1998): 159–174.
3. David Tracy, *Plurality and Ambiguity: Hermeneutics, Religion, Hope* (New York: Harper and Row, 1987), 82–114, esp. 111.
4. Jean-Paul Sartre, *Being and Nothingness*, trans. Hazel E. Barnes (New York: Philosophical Library, 1956), 259–273; Immanuel Levinas, *Totality and Infinity: An Essay on Exteriority*, trans. Alphonso Lingis (Pittsburgh, PA: Duquesne University Press, 1969).
5. Feminist thinkers have noted that the drama of losing a false self in order to gain a "true self" is a male narrative that does not serve the needs of women very well. Women do not need to be moved off their "home ground" or lose their "autonomy." Rather, "home ground" is what patriarchy has taken from women. Befriending the stranger is less *agon* (struggle) than a recovery of *koinonia* (communion). Therefore, interreligious friends like Rita Gross (a Tibetan Buddhist) and Rosemary Radford Reuther may look on their spiritual friendship differently than I look on my friendship with Masao Abe. See Rosemary Radford Reuther and Rita Gross, *Religious Feminism and the Future of the Planet: A Buddhist-Christian Conversation* (New York: Continuum, 2001). For examples of feminist thinkers critical of the loss-of-autonomy narrative, see Judith Plaskow, *Sex, Sin and Grace: Women's Experience and the Theologies of Reinhold Niebuhr and Paul Tillich* (Washington, DC: University Press of America, 1980), and the classic article by Valerie Saiving, "The Human Situation: A Feminine View," which is reprinted in *Womanspirit Rising: A Feminist Reader in Religion*, ed. Carol Chirst and Judith Plaskow (San Francisco, CA: Harper and Row, 1979), 25–42.
6. 1 Kings 8:27, NRSV.
7. See the essay by Abe's teacher Shin'ichi Hisamatsu, "Zen as the Negation of Holiness," in *The Buddha Eye: An Anthology of the Kyoto School*, ed. Frederick Frank (New York: Crossroad, 1982).
8. For a reflection on the notion of "spiritual regret," see Lee Yearly, "New Religious Virtues and the Study of Religion" (Fifteenth Annual University Lecture in Religion, Arizona State University, February 10, 1994), 6–10, 14.
9. Levinas, *Totality and Infinity*, 197.

13

A Friend and Scholar:
A Guide on the Way to
Understanding Buddhism

Peter C. Phan

I came to the study of East Asian religions rather late in life, by hap-
penstance, and not by a deliberate change of the focus of my scholarly
research. By training, I am what the academic guild calls a systematic
or constructive theologian, whose task is to seek a deeper understanding of the doctrines of one's religious community and to reformulate
them in ways appropriate to contemporary cultures. My first doctoral
dissertation studies the theology of the icon in the Russian Orthodox
theologian Paul Evdokimov.[1] My second examines the eschatology of the
German Jesuit theologian Karl Rahner.[2] For my third doctorate in the
1980s, I researched the history of Catholic missions in Asia and related
theological issues, such as liberation, inculturation, and interreligious
dialogue.[3]

During my research on seventeenth-century Catholic missions in
Vietnam, I stumbled upon the French Jesuit Alexandre de Rhodes
(1593–1660), whose missiological method and impact on Vietnamese
Christianity rival those of other fellow Jesuits, such as Matteo Ricci in
China and Roberto de Nobili in India. Born in Avignon, then a papal
state, de Rhodes joined the Society of Jesus in 1612, and after his ordination to priesthood, requested to be sent to the missions in China and
Japan. Due to the persecutions of Christians in Japan by the shoguns of
the Tokugawa family, Ieyasu (1598–1616) and Hidetaka (1605–1623), de
Rhodes was sent to Cochinchina (the southern part of Vietnam) in 1624
and to Tonkin (the northern part of Vietnam) in 1627. In 1630, expelled
from Tonkin, de Rhodes went back to Macau; and in 1640 he returned

to Cochinchina, where he worked off and on until 1645, when he was finally expelled and forbidden to come back under the pain of death. In 1645, de Rhodes returned to Rome, where he arrived in 1649, to carry out his plan of establishing dioceses in Vietnam, with the Vietnamese clergy as leaders. As the result of his efforts, in 1659, two bishops, albeit French and not Vietnamese, François Pallu and Pierre Lambert de la Motte, were appointed for Tonkin and Cochinchina, respectively. De Rhodes himself was sent to Isfahan, Persia, in 1654, as superior of the Jesuit missions there, where he died in 1660.[4]

De Rhodes on Vietnamese Religions

De Rhodes left behind a Vietnamese-Portuguese-Latin dictionary, a Vietnamese-Latin catechism, two travelogues, and several reports on the Jesuit missions in Vietnam.[5] This literary corpus is a rich treasure trove of information on Vietnamese history, culture, and religions, all the more rare and precious as they are derived from protracted firsthand experiences rather than from others' reports and books. Like many of his missionary confreres who lived for years among the indigenous peoples they evangelized, acquiring fluency in their languages (even, in de Rhodes's case, inventing their alphabetic scripts) and adopting their ways of life, de Rhodes was an anthropologist avant la lettre. Admittedly, de Rhodes's primary concern was to convert the Vietnamese to the Christian faith from their religions which, following the theology of religions of his time, he terms "superstitions" or "superstitious sects."

Quintessentially a missionary, de Rhodes was interested in the Vietnamese religions only to the extent that they could be used, after being purged of their errors, as a means for evangelization. Needless to say, such an apologetic approach does not lend itself to the kind of scholarly objectivity that is *de rigueur* in the academy today. However, apart from de Rhodes's exposition and critique of the doctrinal teachings of the Vietnamese religions and his evaluation of their moral codes and religious practices, his descriptions of the ways in which these religions were *practiced* among common people are unique and priceless, giving us a trove of detailed information, without which we would be left in the dark about the religious practices of seventeenth-century Vietnamese common people.

Following a long-standing tradition among his fellow missionaries, de Rhodes refers to the religions of China and Vietnam as consisting of three main "ways," that is, Confucianism, Daoism, and Buddhism: "The Chinese were divided into three main false ways, without counting other less important but equally false one. The first religion is that of the literati called *Nho*; the second is that of those who worship demons and perform sorcery, called *Dao*; the third is that of idolaters, called *But*."[6] In addition to these three religions, he also reports at length on the cult of Heaven and the spirits, including the worship of ancestors.

My interest here is not to discuss de Rhodes's description and critical evaluation of the three Chinese/Vietnamese religions as such, which I have done elsewhere.[7] Rather, it is to show how the grace and blessing of friendship with Nguyen Tu Cuong, one of the most respected scholars of Vietnamese Buddhism, himself a Vietnamese and a Buddhist, has enriched my understanding of Vietnamese Buddhism and of inter-religious dialogue in general, subsequent to the publication of my book on de Rhodes in 1998. But first, a few words on de Rhodes's report on Vietnamese Buddhism as the context for my friendship with Nguyen Tu Cuong.[8]

De Rhodes on Vietnamese Buddhism

When de Rhodes came to Tonkin in 1627, he wished that when the Vietnamese threw off the yoke of Chinese domination it had also rejected the religious "superstitions" imported from China. Unfortunately, these religions continued to flourish, in particular Buddhism, which enjoyed, de Rhodes noted, a greater prestige in Vietnam than in China. He remarks, "There are today in the kingdom of Tonkin innumerable pagodas and idols. There is not a small village that does not have a pagoda with idols where people come to practice their superstitious devotion. However, these pagodas are filthy and badly kept; the monks who serve there are greedy, appropriating all the offerings for their own use and for their wives and children, and not taking care of the decorations of the pagoda and the statues of their gods."[9]

While de Rhodes had little esteem for the Buddhist monks, he greatly admired the devotion of the Buddhist faithful. Twice a month, he notes, they would come to the pagodas to pray and make their offerings: "They perform these practices with great piety; there is hardly anyone among them, however financially deprived, who would not bring offerings on those occasions and place them reverently at the feet of these dusty statues."[10]

For Buddhist teachings, however, de Rhodes had nothing but condemnation. According him, Buddhism teaches two fundamental errors. The first is the worship of idols, and the second, which is worse, advocates atheism, that is, the teaching that "nothingness is the origin of all things, and that at death all things return to nothingness as to their ultimate end."[11]

That de Rhodes misunderstands the Buddhist teaching on no-self (*anatta*) or emptiness (*sunyata*) and the final release from suffering (*moksha*) or liberation (*nirvana*) needs no elaboration; misrepresentations of such highly complex doctrines are not rare even today, despite abundant literature on these matters. Fortunately, my study of Buddhism has spared me of de Rhodes's errors, but a serendipitous acquaintance with Nguyen Tu Cuong's first published book deepens my knowledge of Buddhism in general and of Vietnamese Buddhism in particular.

Nguyen Tu Cuong and Zen Buddhism in Vietnam

In 1997, the *Journal of Buddhist Ethics* asked me to review Nguyen Tu Cuong's book, *Zen in Medieval Vietnam: A Study and Translation of the Thien Uyen Tap Anh.*[12] Neither a Buddhologist nor an ethicist, I complied with the request with fear and trembling. But I saw that a close reading of this book would provide me with an opportunity to learn something new about Vietnamese Buddhism (not to mention a free copy of an expensive book!). Also, the fact that the author is a fellow Vietnamese helped me overcome the remaining scruples over my lack of mastery of the field dealt with by the book. In retrospect, I am deeply gratified, not only by the acquisition of the rich information on Vietnamese Buddhism the book imparts, but also by the blessing of a lifelong friendship with its author.

The length allowed by the journal for the review was quite limited, and I could not do justice to *Zen in Medieval Vietnam.*[13] Before expanding what I wrote there, allow me to say something about Nguyen Tu Cuong. He was born in Vietnam and received his BA degree in Buddhist Studies in 1969 from Van Hanh Buddhist University, which was founded in 1964 by the celebrated monk Thich Nhat Hanh, under the aegis of the Unified Buddhist Sangha of Vietnam. After the fall of South Vietnam in April 1975, Cuong and his family emigrated to the United States, where he began graduate studies. In 1979, he received his MA in Religious Studies from the University of California at Santa Barbara. He then went to Harvard University to pursue another MA in 1982 and PhD in 1990.

Cuong's primary field includes South and Southeast Asian religions, Buddhism, and Hinduism. His secondary field includes East Asian religions; religious literature in Sanskrit, Tibetan, and Chinese; and Vietnamese religions and culture. His linguistic abilities are formidable: Sanskrit, Tibetan, Pali, Chinese, Japanese, German, French, and Vietnamese. I have been told that Cuong once had the habit of taking

with him religious texts in ancient Asian languages to parties to read if
he became bored.

Cuong's doctoral dissertation studies Sthiramati's sixth-century commentary on Chapter IX of the *Mahayanasutralamkara*, a major text of
the Mahayana Buddhism. The root verses of the *Mahayanasutralamkara*
are attributed to Maitreyanatha, the founder of the Yogacara school and
the prose commentary is composed by Vasabandhu. The dissertation
consists of a study and translation of Chapter IX (on Omniscience) that
includes the root verses and the prose commentary in Sanskrit together
with the sub-commentary composed by Sthiramati, which is extant only
in Tibetan. In 1992, Cuong began his teaching career at George Mason
University, Fairfax, Virginia, and has remained there until today.

Until the publication of Cuong's magnum opus in 1997, there had been
no serious and critical study of Vietnamese Buddhism. Part of this dearth
of scholarly production lies in the fact that there exists very few ancient
Buddhist texts from which to draw historical information on Buddhism
in Vietnam and to formulate its distinctive teachings. Buddhism does not
have the kind of literary classic and historical documentation, in terms of
both quantity and quality, in Vietnam as it has in China, Japan, and Tibet.
Indeed, the most important source is the relatively short text studied by
Cuong, the *Thien Uyen Tap Anh* (*Compendium of Outstanding Figures of
the Zen Garden*, henceforth *TUTA*).[14] There have been several Vietnamese
translations of, and commentaries on, the text by Vietnamese scholars,
notably Tran Van Giap, who first discovered this text in 1927. All of these
studies uncritically assume that *TUTA* is a historically accurate history
of Zen Buddhism in Vietnam, in the literary genre called *chuandeng lu*
(transmission of the lamp, or lamp history) that is popular in Chinese
Zen Buddhism. They then proceed to use it to reconstruct the history
of Vietnamese Zen Buddhism. Cuong finds these interpretations of the
TUTA unsatisfactory.[15]

In his book, Cuong sets out to demolish this uncritical, albeit wide-
spread, reading of the *TUTA* and its consequent history of Vietnamese
Buddhism. Through a painstaking and thorough textual and historical
analysis of the text,[16] Cuong convincingly shows that the *TUTA* is not a
"transmission of the lamp" text, as it claims to be, and therefore cannot
be read as such. His conclusion deserves full quotation:

> My conclusion is that through the outset of the Ly dynasty (1010–1225),
> Buddhism in Vietnam was of a composite nature. It was a mixture of some
> Buddhist elements from India and China and the beliefs and practices
> characteristic of the indigenous people's religious sensibilities and popular
> cults. This Buddhism emphasized magic, ritual, and thaumaturgy. From

the middle of the tenth century on, Chinese Zen literature and probably a number of Zen adherents made their way to Vietnam. Zen literature began to appeal to the Buddhist elite at the capital. It was this newly introduced (Zen) Buddhism that influences medieval Vietnamese Buddhist intellectuals in forming their conception of Buddhist history and Vietnamese Buddhist history in particular...A thorough textual and historical analysis of the *Thien Uyen* in light of other available sources and the contemporary social and institutional background brings me to the conclusion that Zen in medieval Vietnam was only a limited presence. Whatever our understanding of the term "Zen school" might be, Zen in Vietnam was never what it was in China, Japan, and Korea.[17]

With these findings, Cuong has established a new foundation and a new method for the study of Vietnamese Buddhism. This discipline will never be the same after Cuong's work.

A Friend and a Guide

Needless to say, my earlier understanding of Vietnamese Buddhism, though spared from the crass and tendentious representations of missionary apologetics, was immensely enriched by Cuong's scholarship. But more than intellectual enlightenment, there is something much deeper and more transformative, namely, my subsequent friendship with him. In the 1990s, I organized a series of summer workshops for Vietnamese Catholics in the United States on Vietnamese history, culture, and religion. I invited Cuong to lecture on Buddhism in general and Vietnamese Buddhism in particular. With characteristic generosity and kindness, he accepted my invitation, even though the financial remuneration was meager. The students, mostly adults, admired his lucid expositions and his precise answers to their questions.

But what impressed me most was Cuong's intellectual humility and kindness of heart. Despite his immense learning, Cuong never made a display of it to intimidate anyone. His tone is always soft and kind, his demeanor ever gentle, even withdrawn, befitting a genuine Buddhist scholar. Not only did he teach me the intricate history of Vietnamese Buddhism; but above all, he shows me how to lead the life of a teacher and scholar. I well remember the day we went out to lunch together after the condemnation of my book *Being Religious Interreligiously* by the Congregation for the Doctrine of the Faith and the Committee on Doctrine of the National Conference of Catholic Bishops. Cuong showed me his firm support and gently encouraged me to seek the truth no matter the consequences.

Once, in one of his lectures for our summer institute, Cuong told us that when he was young in Vietnam he attended a Catholic school. One day the priest in the catechism class said that only those who belong to the Catholic Church can go to heaven: the rest would go to hell. Cuong was much disturbed by this. During recess, he asked his classmates whether what the priest taught was true. They told him that, yes, only Catholics could go to heaven, and that Buddhists would go to hell. But his classmates told Cuong not to worry and said that he, though a Buddhist, could go to heaven because he was their friend!

Friends don't let friends go to hell. And, of course, friends don't reach *nirvana* without their friends, either.

Notes

1. See Peter C. Phan, *Culture and Eschatology: The Iconographical Vision of Paul Evdokimmov* (New York: Peter Lang, 1985).
2. See Peter C. Phan, *Eternity in Time: A Study of Karl Rahner's Eschatology* (Selinsgrove, PA: Susquehanna University Press, 1988).
3. See Peter C. Phan, *Christianity with an Asian Face: Asian American Theology in the Making* (Maryknoll: Orbis Books, 2003); *In Our Own Tongues: Perspectives from Asia on Mission and Inculturation* (Maryknoll: Orbis Books, 2003); and *Being Religious Interreligiously: Asian Perspectives on Interfaith Dialogue* (Maryknoll: Orbis Books, 2004).
4. See Peter C. Phan, *Mission and Catechesis: Alexandre de Rhodes and Inculturation in Seventeenth-Century Vietnam* (Maryknoll: Orbis Books, 1998).
5. For a detailed bibliography of de Rhodes, see Phan, *Mission and Catechesis*, 206–207.
6. Phan, *Mission and Catechesis*, 249.
7. On this point, see ibid., 13–28, 82–96.
8. I am giving here the name of Nguyen Tu Cuong in the Vietnamese order (family name, middle name, and personal name). Furthermore, a person is always addressed by the first name, even formally. Thus, Professor Cuong, not Professor Nguyen. In the West, the order is reversed: personal name first, middle name, and family name last. This is how Professor Cuong is officially known in the United States.
9. Alexandre de Rhodes, *Histoire du Royaume de Tunquin et des grands progrez que la prédication de l'Evangile y a faits en la conversion des infidelles* (Lyon: Jean Baptiste Devenet, 1651), 69. All English translations of de Rhodes's works are mine.
10. Ibid., 70.
11. Alexandre de Rhodes, *Cathechismus pro iis, qui volunt suscipere Baptismum, in Octo dies divisus* (Rome: Propaganda Fide Press, 1651), 47.

12. Cuong Tu Nguyen, *Zen in Medieval Vietnam: A Study and Translation of the Thien Uyen Tap Anh* (Honolulu: University of Hawai'i Press, 1997).
13. See Peter C. Phan, "Review of *Zen in Medieval Vietnam*," accessed June 24, 2914, http://www.buddhismtoday.com/english/book/003-zen.htm.
14. This text seems to have been written in 1337. There are two extant editions of this text: the Le edition, published in 1715, titled *Thien Uyen Tap Anh* [Compendium of Outstanding Figures in the Zen Garden] and the Nguyen edition, published in 1858, titled *Dai Nam Thien Uyen Truyen Dang Tap Luc* [A Record of the Transmission of the Lamp in the Zen Garden of Great Viet Nam]. There are insignificant variations between the two editions. The original Chinese text is 148 pages long (or 74 pages in two columns), and the English translation is 102 pages long. The original text is reproduced in *Zen in Medieval Vietnam*, 253–330, and the English translation, 103–205.
15. For Cuong's evaluation of these scholarly studies, see his "Rethinking Vietnamese Buddhist History: Is the *Thien Uyen Tap Anh* a 'Transmission of the Lamp' Text?" in *Essays into Vietnamese Pasts*, ed. K. W. Taylor and John K. Whitmore (Ithaca, NY: Cornell University, 1995), 88–84.
16. Nguyen, *Zen in Medieval Vietnam*, 24–55.
17. Ibid., 7.

14

My Friendship With Rita Gross

Rosemary Radford Ruether

It is with great pleasure that I write on my friendship with Rita Gross, and particularly, what that has meant in terms of our Buddhist-Christian conversation. Let me begin by saying that interreligious relations come fairly easily to me. My family background was somewhat diverse religiously, and that made me feel early on that community across religious lines was normal and enriching. My mother came from an English and Austrian Roman Catholic family, but one open to cultural and religious diversity. My father was from a staunchly Anglican background, although he himself was not a regular church attendant. My mother was committed to her church and saw that my three sisters went to Mass regularly, but was open to having me attend church with my father on the occasions when he went.

My uncle, the husband of my father's younger sister, was from a New York Jewish family. Trained as an opera singer and skilled as an artist, Uncle David was a surrogate father when my own father was away in the Second World War and then died in 1949. Having no children of his own, my two sisters and myself became his children whom he tutored in art and music. Although he did not go to synagogue, he was deeply committed to the Jewish tradition and cultivated images of Judaism in Western art. Thus, I grew up with a strong sense of having family relations across religious lines—Catholic, Episcopalian, and Jewish. Although Catholicism was central to our core family, the other two identities were very much a part of my family, which I cherished.

This pluralism of religious identity expanded as I grew up. After my father died, my mother found the opportunity to move us (herself and her daughters) back to Southern California, where she had grown up (having been born and spent her early years in Mexico). A close friend visited us in Washington and offered my mother the option of renting her house in La Jolla, California, which Mother seized with pleasure. In La Jolla, I was invited by this friend to teach art to Mexican American children at the local Friends meeting. I was soon drawn to attending the Sunday Friend's meeting (along with attending Mass with my mother). I found these two worship experiences, so different in liturgical style, very compatible. I remember thinking of Catholic Mass and Quaker meeting as having the same deep spirituality, the one expressed in liturgical externality and the other in meditational silence.

I attended Scripps College in Claremont, California, from 1954 to 1958, and there I became drawn into an immersion in the pre-Christian, Near Eastern, and classical worlds through the study of the background to the development of Christianity. Traditionally, Christianity has dismissed these "pagan" worlds as having no lasting value. But my professor, Robert Palmer, taught the classics in a way that deeply appreciated these earlier religious cultures, and indeed preferred them to Christianity. Through him, I came to appreciate these other religious worlds. This opened my sense of religious meaning to these worlds before and beyond Christianity. I was then ready to look at the religious traditions in the Asian world—Hinduism, Jainism, Buddhism, and others. But I did not quickly move in this direction, feeling deeply preoccupied with the religious traditions I had already encountered.

The International Buddhist-Christian Theological Encounter

In 1980, there was a conference on Buddhism and Christianity. Rita Gross was there and gave a paper on Buddhism and Feminism. The next meeting was in 1983 at the University of Hawaii. There, John Cobb, from the Claremont School of Theology, with Masao Abe, from Japan, announced the formation of the International Buddhist-Christian Theological Encounter. The hope was to have about 30–40 members, divided equally between Buddhists and Christians, who would engage in a dialogue. Each group would be deeply informed and committed to their own traditions, but not experts in the other tradition. The purpose was not conversion to the other side, but mutual understanding. I had been asked by John Cobb to join this group, but had turned down the invitation, feeling overwhelmed with the work I was already doing.

Members of the projected dialogue group met on a stage before an audience of auditors. It was an all-male group, and there was an outcry from the floor. John Cobb approached Rita Gross who was in the audience and asked her to join. But she said she would not come if she were the only woman. There had to be at least two Christian and two Buddhist women. This impelled John Cobb to come back to me and to ask me to join the group, which I then accepted.

The third meeting took place in Vancouver in 1985, and Rita and I were there, as well as other women. After that, there was a meeting in Purdue in 1986, and a fifth in Berkeley in 1987. At the Berkeley meeting, plans developed for a Society of Buddhist-Christian Studies (independent of the Cobb-Abe group), and Rita Gross was asked to be the Vice-President.

In the Cobb-Abe Dialogue group, Rita Gross and myself were quickly singled out as the two scholars who had done feminist work in our respective traditions. We soon became the spokespersons for issues of women in Buddhism and Christianity. This brought the two of us together as a dialogue team.

Dialogue with Rita

In 1989, the Grail, a Catholic feminist religious community in Ohio with whom I had worked many times before, invited Rita and me to do a dialogue on feminism in our two traditions. This brought us to a new stage of dialogue with each other. We worked out a series of topics for mutual conversation. First, we would each trace our personal autobiographical route to intellectual development and dialogue on religion. Then each of us would engage in a discussion of the oppressive and sexist aspects of our respective traditions, with a response by the other partner. We would turn to what we found liberating in our own traditions, again with a response by the other. We would then discuss what each of us had learned from the other tradition; that is, what Rita had learned from Christianity and what I have learned from Buddhism. Again, there was a response by the other partner to these topics, I to Rita's paper and Rita to mine. We concluded with reflections on how each tradition has contributed or not to the ecological crisis and the future of the planet, again with a response by the other partner.

This format proved very stimulating to our audience at the Grail, which was fascinated by the conversation, particularly that from Rita, whose life and development in the Buddhist tradition was less familiar to the Grail members and friends. This brought Rita and myself to the recognition that we had the makings of a book that could be helpful to many readers. In the next months, we translated our discussion into a book manuscript, which was published by Continuum in 2001.[1] This work brought Rita Gross and myself to a new level of friendship, rooted in having entered very deeply into each other's lives, and the roots and hopes of each of our journeys into interreligious conversation.

Each of us realized that we had something unique to give to audiences interested in women and the interreligious journey. Rita has, several times, expressed a wish that we might continue with this kind of joint presentation. Although I would also like to do this, each of our involvements in our own work has not lent itself to a similar occasion, although several times since then we have been members of additional conferences. I will delve into our joint conversation primarily by drawing on the ideas we developed at the Grail and in our 2001 book.

Rita's Academic Story

One of the things that particularly moved me in our interchange was Rita Gross's autobiographical account of her childhood struggle for education and ongoing recognition of her scholarship, particularly in the area of women's studies in religion. Rita grew up on a farm in Northern Wisconsin in a log cabin built by her own parents. She spent much of her childhood and teenage years doing major tasks as a farmworker to help her mother and father; milking cows twice a day, preparing and feeding them hay. This heavy farm work, which she nevertheless enjoyed, was carried on while also struggling for an education in religious and public schools that did not much value education, and with local libraries that were not helpful to a girl on a farm desiring to read books. Neither of her parents had gone to high school. Books were absent from the house and hard to come by at schools and libraries. Her mother wanted Rita to marry a farmer and continue the life in which she had been nurtured in the family. There was little expectation of college education, much less graduate school.

Thus Rita spent her childhood struggling to move beyond the limits of the farm and cultural expectations that girls have no prospect of a future beyond marriage and reproduction. To get books to read was a continual struggle in grade school and even in high school, although high school did open up some sense of the larger world. Expensive private colleges were beyond the family means, but Rita was able to move into a somewhat more urban world at the University of Wisconsin in Milwaukee. Even here, there was little expectation of graduate education, especially for women.

After graduating from college, she moved on to graduate work in religion at the University of Chicago. Here the expectations of higher education were much higher, but then Rita ran into another roadblock. The study of religion brought her into the unusual area of the study of the religious lives of Australian aboriginal women. Scholarship at the time claimed that these women had no religious lives, that religion was entirely the sphere of males. But Rita discovered that, in fact, these aboriginal women had their own spheres and understanding of religion that were highly distinctive. Some of her professors encouraged her to do her doctoral dissertation on this subject. But other professors were alarmed and hostile to her discovery—that not only these women had a distinctive religious culture, but also this and other religions could not be understood unless one also studies the traditions and practices of the females. Religious studies, which up to then had only studied male traditions, was truncated and inadequate. This was a highly unwelcome idea for many at the University of Chicago. Controversy enveloped her work, despite her success in defending her dissertation.

In 1973, Rita won a teaching position at the University of Wisconsin at Eau Claire, where she would teach for the next 35 years or more. This teaching position was vital to her economic survival, yet also put her back in some of the limited intellectual environment of her Wisconsin background. The University of Wisconsin at Eau Claire did not open up opportunities to teach graduate students or even many upper division students who might actually be interested in scholarly work. Her main teaching through the years was a freshman introductory course in world religions, which was of marginal interest to her students. Her increasing success as a published scholar, whose work was read internationally, brought little recognition from her local colleagues. It was only the occasional escape to national or international conferences that brought her into dialogue with appreciative colleagues.

Rita Gross continues to live in the large house she was able to buy in Eau Claire, with the richly planted garden of plants and flowers, many of which were rescued from the farm on which she had grown up as a child. But only with her retirement in recent years, in which she has been able to move into a new kind of teaching as a recognized Dharma teacher in the Buddhist community, has she been able to bring her religious and intellectual life more into union.

Rita's Spiritual Story

Rita Gross's movement into Buddhism is also a moving story. Having grown up in rural Northern Wisconsin as a Wisconsin Synod Lutheran, she became attracted to a progressive Jewish community. For several years, she identified as a Jew and wrote some of her first published works in the feminist development of Judaism. This brought about an extraordinary confrontation with the Lutheran pastor of her home church.

This occurred when her mother died in 1965. At her mother's funeral, the Lutheran pastor engaged in a polemic against several members of her family, but particularly against her. This then led the pastor to come over to her house after the funeral to confront her for daring to attend a synagogue. The pastor interrogated her on her religious beliefs, and when Rita replied with a courageous defense, he became increasingly angry. When he asked her if she still held completely to the doctrines of her Confirmation, she retorted that this is what the Catholic Church asked of Luther at the Diet of Worms (1521). The pastor turned and left, slamming the door. A few days later she got a letter from him excommunicating her and threatening her with Hell if she didn't apologize.

Needless to say, this letter did not draw Rita back into the local Lutheran church. She continued to attend and be nurtured in the Jewish community, but when she moved from Chicago to Eau Clair there was no such progressive Jewish synagogue available. She also began to struggle with the Buddhist tradition and wonder whether what she was teaching about this tradition in her classes was actually manifest in her own experience. In 1973, when she was walking across the campus to teach her class on Buddhism, having recently returned from visiting her lover who was dying of an inoperable brain cancer, it dawned on her that the four noble truths of Buddhism really articulated the misery and struggle that she was experiencing in her life.

This recognition brought Rita to the realization that she needed to do more than teach about these noble truths in theory. She needed to live them. The practice of meditation, which is called for in the fourth noble truth, needed to be incorporated into her own practice. She began to attend workshops on Buddhist meditation and to learn to practice meditation. She then moved on to sessions at the Naropa Institute in Boulder, Colorado, yet she was still reluctant to commit herself as a member of the Buddhist religion. It was her experience there of the creativity and nurturing attitude of the Buddhist community that finally brought Rita to a decision. In the summer of 1977, she "took refuge" and became a committed Buddhist. While Rita continued for many years to teach as a world religion scholar, in her personal life she entered a new relation with Buddhism and has become recognized in United States and international Buddhism as a teacher within the community. She is now a senior teacher at the Jetsun Khandro Rinpoche Lotus Garden Center.

Learning through Friendship

My relationship with Rita Gross did not develop, of course, in the context of her role as a teacher of the Buddhist tradition. It developed in the context of the International Buddhist-Christian Theological Encounter. This encounter went on for over 20 years, meeting about every two years for several days. Thus, we had the great privilege of really getting to know each other as friends over a considerable period of time. Rita speaks of her relationship with the colleagues in this group as having "become one of my closest collegial communities, a community in which I can express myself fully and be received as a friend and colleague for doing so."

Our friendship was also broader than two Buddhist and Christian colleagues in dialogue. It was an exploration of each of our lives as a whole, as we each looked at our biographical roots and our ongoing search for intellectual understanding and ethical meaning over more than 60 years. Thus, what I came to understand about Buddhism was only one aspect of this conversation, although a very important one. Moreover, the Buddhist aspect of the conversation was more as Rita had succeeded in understanding and making the Buddhist tradition meaningful for her in her life context.

Rita was a committed feminist and activist for women's human rights years before she became a Buddhist, and she became a Buddhist very much as one who intended to be a *feminist Buddhist*. She did not understand Buddhism as superseding her feminism, but rather feminism was a commitment that she intended to bring into her Buddhism. She realized that this meant that she would have to write critiquing Buddhist misogyny and sexism, as she had already written as a feminist critic and reformer in Judaism. This realization indeed made her at first hesitate to become a Buddhist as her primary religious identity. Once she made that commitment, Rita soon became the major spokesperson and writer for feminist reform of Buddhism, arguing that such reform is essential to the authentic expression of the Buddhist tradition itself. Rita's 1993 volume, *Buddhism after Patriarchy: A Feminist History, Analysis and Reconstruction of Buddhism*,[2] is the foundational study on this question. In my own classes on feminism across world religions, this is the book I assign to my students on feminist reform of Buddhism. Rita's 2009 book, *A Garland of Feminist Reflections: Forty Years of Religious Explorations*,[3] surveys her key contributions across her life, including her early critique of androcentrism in religious studies at the University of Chicago, her feminist critiques of Hinduism and Judaism, and her major articles on Buddhist feminism.[4]

In the book we wrote together, Rita's major chapter under the topic of "What is most problematic in my tradition" focuses on the problem of male domination in the Buddhist teaching tradition. For Rita, Buddhism has a key advantage over the monotheisms of the West. Lacking a concept of God, it is not burdened with a male God as the central figure that biases the tradition toward androcentrism. However, it does suffer from the problem that most of the teaching lineage is male; and this is particularly true of her own Tibetan tradition. The teacher-student relation is key to passing on the tradition, and so this pervasive lineage of male teachers has something of the same effect as the male God in monotheism; it creates a dominant androcentrism at the center of the heritage.

Why are the teachers almost all male in this tradition? The tradition does not teach that only men can be teachers. There are traditions of leading and creative nuns in the early history of Buddhism, but this is biased by the rules set up for nuns that dictated that the oldest and most experienced nun must nevertheless be subordinate to the youngest monk. Moreover, donating to female monastic communities brings little honor to a layperson, compared to the prestige of giving to a male monastic community. Consequently, female orders tended to be impoverished and die out.

Buddhism arrived in the United States in the 1960s, at a time when feminism was also developing. Consequently, women teachers have been much more common in American Buddhism. This is beginning to have an effect. Rita sees this as a fortunate karmic reality for American Buddhism. Yet, the heritage of male teachers as the dominant historical lineage still weighs heavily on the tradition. These women in the ancient past of Buddhism, as well as its present reality in North America, are only beginning to be referenced as part of the heritage of the tradition. Rita's own contribution to Buddhism includes not only a theoretical feminist critique and reform; she has also been engaged in research to uncover female teachers in Buddhist history who can be lifted up in present life.

In the section of our book titled "What is most liberating about my tradition," Rita addresses the topic of "What keeps me in the Buddhist orbit?" She lifts up three key ideas: silence, contemplation, and the Dharma. In her decision to identify with Buddhism as her religion, Rita focused particularly on her realization that she must learn how to engage in Buddhist meditation and to practice this on a regular basis. Meditation or contemplation is key to the practice of Buddhism. This does not mean focusing on some key religious or spiritual "idea," as it might in the Christian tradition. Rather, the method of meditation is central to overcoming clinging to the "ego" and to putting aside the desire for ego possession as the central tendency of the self. Meditation is fundamental to actually becoming Buddhist, in the sense of dissolving egoism, thereby actualizing the core of the Buddhist understanding of reality.

Rita found the practice of mediation, in this sense of dissolving ego-possession, to be personally transformative. For many years as a feminist, she had been accustomed to experience deep anger and rage in response to the reality of sexist oppression by society and its dominant social ideologies. This sense of anger often debilitated her and gave her an aggressive style of response that was not helpful in communicating her concerns to others. Meditation gradually helped her put aside this experience of rage and its distressing side effects. This did not mean that she put aside being a feminist and her critique of systems of male domination. Rather, it meant overcoming an accompanying anger and rage that was hurtful to her and blocked communication with others. As she became freed from this side effect of anger and rage, she actually found herself much more effective in communicating with others the basis of her critique of sexism and the need to overcome this social distortion of our system of life. This has been enormously liberating for her.

Rita's discussion of the importance of meditation and its liberating effects on her life emphasized for me one of the limitations I found in our Buddhist-Christian theological encounter: the dialogue had been constructed by its founders as an intellectual process. We started out with a series of dialogues on parallel themes in Buddhism and Christianity, such as "Ultimate Reality: God or Nirvana," "Material Existence: Creation or Maya," "The Path of Transformation: Conversion or Enlightenment," "The Founder: Buddha or Christ," and "Religious Community: Church or Sangha." In each three-day meeting, there would be four primary papers on the topic, two by Christians and two by Buddhists, and then response papers, Buddhists to the Christian papers and Christians to the Buddhist papers. This method allowed for a comprehensive interchange on the topic.

But this method was highly intellectual. Our style of communication was the academic one of the university. There was little sense of what the Buddhist or the Christian religious or spiritual experience might be about. To actually have some experience of meditation in the Buddhist tradition or prayer in Christianity was never a part of the discussion, much less of the practice. Thus, the transforming experience of meditation that has become so important to Rita and central to her Buddhist practice was never discussed, much less touched upon in our dialogue. For me, this has been a major lack in my own experience of Buddhism. It is very helpful for me that Rita has written about how important meditation has been in transforming her life. I feel the need to go farther in experiencing this practice myself.

In her essay in our book on "What Buddhists could learn from Christians," Rita talks about the importance of the "prophetic voice" in the monotheistic traditions and the need for Buddhists to deepen their own social justice commitments though learning from the prophetic religions. She herself discovered the prophetic voice primarily through Judaism, rather than from Christianity, since the conservative Lutheranism she grew up in Northern Wisconsin did not emphasize prophetic social critique.

The progressive Jewish community she belonged to in Milwaukee, and its social justice-minded rabbinic teachers, were strong on the prophetic voice, and this became important to Rita's worldview.

Buddhism is not without a concern for justice. Enlightenment in Buddhism is not just self-development. It calls for concern for others, for "compassion for all sentient beings." This tradition is notable in its concern for justice to animals, not just for other humans. Thus, it goes beyond the anthropocentrism that tends to limit the emphasis on justice in monotheistic religions. But Buddhism also tends to think of suffering and social ills primarily on an individual level. There is little analysis of social systems as oppressive, and working to overcome unjust social systems is not much recognized. Social justice work and the overcoming of unjust social systems for more just societies have not been included in what it means to be "enlightened" in Buddhism. Thus, Buddhism's ways of coping with suffering can easily lead to passivity. Rita sees the Buddhist tradition of social ethics as needing a prophetic critique of unjust and oppressive social systems. But it needs to be brought into Buddhism in a way that builds on Buddhist social ethics, and does not appear to be just a borrowing from the West, or a critique of Buddhism as lacking social ethics.

This emphasis on social ethics became central to the International Buddhist-Christian Theological Encounter in its second phase in the late twentieth and early twenty-first centuries. Having focused, in its first phase, on comparative theological and doctrinal aspects of the two religions, the group decided to continue, during the second phase, with a discussion of social questions. This led to a somewhat different kind of discussion. The group started out with a focus on ecology, a topic suggested by the Buddhists, although important to the Christians as well. We then went on in a second gathering to discuss war and peace, how Christians and Buddhists have each dealt with the issues of militarism and the quest for peace. Here, Christians were more involved in the critique of theories of just war and religious justifications of war, while Buddhists were more concerned about how to develop inward peace and bring this into social relations.

Poverty and social justice was chosen as the subject for our third gathering, a topic that allowed for a rich discussion of each tradition's gifts and deficiencies on this topic. Our final gathering, as we realized that lack of financial support was forcing the group to terminate, decided to focus on sexuality. This led to very different kinds of discussion on both the Christian and the Buddhist side, and brought out issues in both religions that had never been discussed before. It is interesting that we got around to discussing sexuality in the two traditions only at the end of our history!

All of these issues are, of course, of great interest to both Rita and myself. Our own book closed with the discussion of ecology and the "future of the planet." In Rita's discussion of this topic, she developed particularly the way in which traditional Buddhist ethics could foster ecological sustainability by teaching people to put aside their consumer demands and to live simply. Of particular importance to Rita is the question of population explosion and the need for religious traditions to back off demands for large families. Christianity particularly has had a negative outlook toward sex pleasure as evil, and has rejected contraception, views that have not been a part of Buddhism. Buddhism needs to add to its teaching on limits to consumption, an encouragement of birth control, and a recognition of the way in which human population expansion is threatening the sustainability of the planet.

In my own chapter on what I have learned from Buddhism, I drew on my valuable learning from my Buddhist colleagues in the Buddhist-Christian Theological Encounter, and from Rita in particular. I have found the basic understanding of reality in Buddhism to be very helpful. At its core, Buddhism critiques the desires of consumerism and the clinging to the ego as immortal. These mistakes are the root of frustration and suffering. Overcoming this frustration and suffering brings a meditational equanimity as one lets go of ego-clinging. I find this critique and worldview convincing. I have never been convinced or much interested in the Christian focus on personal immortality and the view of the soul as eternal and everlasting. Giving up this view of the self in the Buddhist analysis of spirituality makes sense to me.

My explorations of Buddhism have also led me to explore Engaged Buddhism, as that has developed in the teaching of Sulak Sivaraksa in Thailand, and to attend a major conference there organized by him. Sulak makes a social interpretation of the Buddhist call to overcome greed, hatred, and delusion. He sees the global capitalist system, and its militarist and ideological defenses, as greed, hatred, and delusion writ large on a global socioeconomic level. Social justice means overcoming these systems. Engaged Buddhism has emerged globally as the Buddhist counterpart to liberation theology in Christianity. I find the union of these two movements very central for my own life and for global culture.

Conclusion

In conclusion, my dialogue with Buddhists worldwide, and my friendship with Rita Gross in particular, have been, and continue to be, very important in my personal development. Rita's and my dialogues together at the

Theological Encounter, and in our Grail presentations and book, were profoundly enriching for both of us. Again and again, in our dialogue and writing, we found each of our processes of development as a Christian and as a Buddhist paralleling one another, each reaching out to affirm realities that the other found important. We have become soul mates, and that is a rare and wonderful thing.

Notes

1. Rita M. Gross and Rosemary Radford Ruether, *Religious Feminism and the Future of the Planet: A Buddhist-Christian Conversation* (New York: Continuum, 2001).
2. Rita M. Gross, *Buddhism after Patriarchy: A Feminist History, Analysis, and Reconstruction of Buddhism* (Albany: State University of New York Press, 1992).
3. Rita M. Gross, *A Garland of Feminist Reflections: Forty Years of Religious Exploration* (Oakland: University of California Press, 2009).
4. See also Rita's newest book, which offers a Buddhist view for appreciating religious diversity: Rita M. Gross, *Religious Diversity – What's the Problem? Buddhist Advice for Flourishing with Religious Diversity* (Eugene, OR: Cascade Books, 2014).

15

Interreligious Friendship: A Path to Conversion for a Catholic Theologian

SimonMary Asese Aihiokhai

I was born into a religiously diverse family; my paternal family is Catholic, and my maternal family is Muslim. I was raised in both worlds. However, as a young boy, I deliberately opted to become a Catholic. I followed the Catholic faith assiduously and even decided to become a Catholic priest. I joined the missionary community of the Holy Ghost Congregation (Spiritans), Province of Nigeria, in 1992, and took temporary vows in 1994. I left in 2000. I had thought that I fully understood the path the Lord was leading me to—I was called to preach Christ to all nations, especially to Muslims and worshippers of the Indigenous Religions in Nigeria. Little did I know that my faith journey was about to begin.

I focus here on a transformative encounter that continues to shape my outlook on non-Christian religions. I reflect on the salient aspects of the encounter that can serve as points of reflection for those who continue to hold on to exclusivist views in the Christian religion. I call this encounter "the event" because it is one of the singular moments of my life, when I lost the ability to articulate a theological response to justify the Christian narrative to which I was introduced. It was a moment of grace for me: a moment of listening to the strange voice of God who encounters us in foreign places and shows us new perspectives of being.

As much as possible, this chapter will be a reflection on my story and not an abstract reflection on what interreligious friendship is about. I believe much has already been written on that subject. I come from a culture where the wisdom of living is shrouded in storytelling. By tell-ing one's story, one reveals one's vulnerability and an honesty of heart. Interreligious friendship can only be fruitful if people of faith are willing to share their stories of how they have encountered God in the religious other. There is no shame in this process. It is only the brave who can share their vulnerability. I hope that, by sharing my story, I can truly say I am one of the brave.

The Event

As part of the formative process of the Spiritans of the Province of Nigeria, those in temporary vows are sent to parishes and missions run by Spiritans in the summer to gain missionary experiences. In 1995, I was sent to work under the guidance of the Spiritans ministering in Saint Michael's Parish in the town of Ezinifite-Nnewi, which was within the Archdiocese of Onitsha.[1] When I arrived at the parish, the pastor sent me to be in charge of the mission in Umudiala village, one of the mission churches that make up the parish of Saint Michael. Umudiala village is also one of the four major villages that make up the town of Ezinifite-Nnewi.

My responsibilities included conducting daily services and facilitating the growth of the Catholic faith in the village, with the hope that the mis-sion church would one day become a parish of its own. As a missionary strategy, I decided to visit all the families in the village, Catholics and non-Catholics alike, with the agenda of making converts to the Catholic faith. The catechist of the mission assigned one of the youths to be my companion. He served as my interpreter. During the course of my pas-toral presence in the village, I noticed that the shrines dedicated to the deities of the Indigenous Religion were always maintained and was won-dering who the members of this religion were, since everyone claimed to be a Christian.

As my ministry in the village progressed, I asked my guide to lead me to a house that looked abandoned, but seemed to be inhabited. My guide refused and told me that an elderly priestess of the Indigenous Religion lived in the house. He called her a devil worshipper. My Christian nar-rative was not really different from that of my guide. In my opinion, this woman was the person I ought to be visiting so that I could introduce her to the salvific teachings of the Catholic faith. My guide told me that the Christians in the village had decided to have nothing to do with her because she insisted on worshipping the devil. The Christian community had equated the Indigenous Religion to devil worship.

I decided to visit the woman on my own, hoping that she would understand my attempt to speak the Igbo language, which I had learned somewhat while staying in the village. When I arrived at the house, I introduced myself as a Catholic missionary who was working in the village. The woman, in her seventies, welcomed me warmly and informed me that she had to welcome me before I could introduce my intention for the visit. She offered me a seat and a glass of water. Following the Igbo cultural custom, she prayed over a *kola* nut lobe and offered it to me. We both ate it. She then brought another one; put it in her mouth to show that there was no ill will between us. She gave it to me to take back home and share with the family I was staying in the village. She was happy to have somebody visit her and confirmed what my guide had previously told me: the Christians in the village had ostracized her from the community because she insisted on following the Indigenous Religion. She thanked me for going against the decision of the Christian community because no Christian had ever visited her home. In my mind, I was still determined to convert her to the Catholic faith.

After her welcome, she asked me why I was visiting her. I told her I was there to explain the Christian faith to her, as practiced by the Catholic Church. She told me she was already a believer in God and very happy. I could see the joy in her eyes. She was honest and very welcoming. She told me she was chosen by the deities to be their priestess at a very young age and thus had to live a celibate life. She spent her time ministering to believers who came to her at night. I was surprised because I had thought she was the only worshipper of the Indigenous Religion in the village. She told me that there were many worshippers who, due to restrictions placed on the religion by the Christians, could only identify with the religion secretly.

I asked her why she still worshipped these false gods and did not embrace Christianity. Her response was telling: she insisted that she worshipped the Supreme God who is true and just. As a priestess and a worshipper of the Indigenous Religion, she was obligated to be just, honest, kind, loving, hospitable, and respectful of everyone. She went on to educate me on her religion.

My hostess's hospitality had no end, even though this was a very poor woman who lived frugally and depended on the generosity of her fellow religionists to survive. She invited me to stay for dinner, and I gladly did. After my meal, I asked her if she would come and worship with us the next morning at the mission church. She gladly agreed to come and told me that she could not refuse to worship God wherever he/she was found. Those words were revelatory for me. Looking back now, I think those words became the springboard for my reflection on the relevance of religious pluralism. I kept asking myself if I had such courage to believe and pray truly in a non-Christian context. She taught me that it could be done.

The next morning, while I was conducting the morning service in the mission church, I saw the elderly priestess at the back of the church. She was sitting alone. No one would sit beside her. Even though she did not know the prayers, her demeanor was one of great reverence. I could see that she regarded the space as sacred and worthy of respect. After the service, I went to greet her. She told me that she was glad I invited her to our church. I asked her if I could visit her shrine. She said yes, and told me the times she would be at the shrine.

During my time in the village, I visited her shrine several times. Each time, she would invite me to pray aloud my intentions. At first, I politely declined. I was very confused. I had never prayed in the shrine of an Indigenous Religion. What was I going to say? I had no clue. Rather than pray as she expected me to, I took quick recourse to my Catholic faith as I understood it then, still believing that the priestess was worshipping a false god. In silence, I offered the following prayers: "Lord Jesus Christ, I do not know if what I am doing is right. I have always and continue to believe in you, and I know that you transcend my ability to comprehend you completely. If what I am doing is right, thank you for giving me the opportunity to pray with this woman in her own way. But if I have strayed, do forgive me."

Each time I visited the woman and her shrine, she made sure she prayed for the success of my ministry in the village; and this confused me more. How could my work be successful if I could not make a Catholic convert of her? She was as convinced of her religion's truth as I was of mine. However, a strange type of friendship developed between us. She could have been my grandmother, and was clearly wiser than I was. She saw in me a young man passionate about God. I saw in her a unique form of wisdom. She taught me about Indigenous Religion; she taught me about God.

As time went on, I summoned the courage to pray. I recall that the first prayer that I offered aloud was one of thanksgiving for having known the priestess. I thanked God for having given me the opportunity to know her. I thanked God for the work she and I were doing in the village. I prayed that peace might reign in our hearts. That was my first interfaith prayer. It was a prayer that freed my heart from doctrinal limitations. I also felt a little proud of myself; because I found out that I could go outside of my comfort zone and be less cerebral. My prayer came from the heart, and the words were truly not my own. They were those of the mysterious God who had led me into a situation where I was not in control.

When the time came for me to leave the mission and head back to the seminary, she was the last person I visited. I promised to always pray for her and she promised to do likewise for me. Her prayers have guided me to engage God in a different way; one different from the narrative I was introduced to when I became a Christian.

My Gradual Conversion

Listening to God's invitation to engage involves the entire life of a person. Even when we think we have figured it all out, God invites us to engage a new perspective in life that sometimes leaves us speechless. Both the Jewish and Christian Scriptures have many instances where those who think they know all that God wants them to know are invited to engage afresh their religious perceptions. The story of the Prophet Jonah is a clear example. The prophet of God is surprised to find that God's love extends even to the Ninevites whom he believed should face God's wrath.[2] In the New Testament, Jesus shocks the Jewish authorities by engaging people thought to be outside the economy of salvation. What does this tell us? God likes to surprise us when we think we have figured him/her out completely.

My encounter with the priestess raised many questions that have since helped me to engage my Christian faith critically. Let me list some of these questions. First, how do I know that worshippers of Indigenous Religions are devil worshippers? Second, how would Christ relate with the priestess? Would Jesus approve of what the Christian community in the village has done to her by ostracizing her from their midst, or would he embrace her as a worshipper of God? Third, are other religions capable of guiding the human person to live virtuously? And fourth, can non-Christians be truly committed to their religion, as a Christian is to Christianity? These questions helped shape my gradual conversion.

In what is present-day Nigeria, Christian missionary ventures occurred during different centuries. The first encounters with the Portuguese missionaries occurred in the fifteenth century in the Kingdom of Benin. Their missionary strategy was completely different from that utilized during the imperialistic adventures of the European powers in the nineteenth century. Accounts of the missionary encounters with the Benin Kingdom reveal a relationship of rational engagement on the validity of the Christian religion. It was never reduced to a negative presentation of the Indigenous Religion. Conversions did occur, but they were voluntary. Interestingly, remnants of the churches built during that fifteenth century still exist in the kingdom.[3] These churches are called "Aruosa"[4] and have their own clergy. The religious worship is a blend of the Indigenous Religious practices and the Christian religion. These churches serve as the official royal places of worship for the Oba of Benin and the Enogies (dukes and princes). The relationship with the Christian religion was so cordial that the Oba (King) of Benin and the entire nobility have dressed like the Catholic clergy since the fifteenth century.[5] They became the custodians of the Christian religion when the Portuguese left the kingdom at the advent of the Trans-Atlantic Slave Trade.

The dynamics of the Christian missionary presence during the nineteenth century changed dramatically. This was also the time of wars of territorial expansion in Africa by the British, French, German, Italian, Portuguese, and King Leopold II of Belgium, and later, by the Belgian state. The partitioning of Africa by the European powers at the Berlin Conference of 1884–1885 and the eventual scramble for more territories in Africa sealed the gains of these European countries and regulated the boundaries of their African possessions. It also intensified the "Scramble for Africa" by these European powers, who forced the African kingdoms and republics to sign false documents of their being protectorates without knowing they were giving up their independence. Those who refused to sign such treaties were conquered militarily, and their rulers were accused of continuing the already abolished slave trade. Leopold of Belgium even deceived his European counterparts by pretending to be a philanthropist with a desire to evangelize the African people.[6] His greed led to the death of more than ten million Africans living in the Congo Free State, which was essentially made his personal property by the European powers.

As a policy, the imperialists took along with them their fellow Christian compatriots to help "tame" the "savages" in Africa. As noted by Elizabeth Isichei, forced commerce and evangelization were the two realities brought to the African people by the European powers.[7] Psychologically, the relational engagement with the conquered Africans could not be based on one of equality. If it were based on equality, then the entire imperialistic and colonial agenda would have no legitimacy. At the heart of colonialism is the understanding of unequal relationships between the colonizer and the colonized. It emphasizes master-servant, civilized-uncivilized, true religion-false religion, white-black, and refined-unrefined dichotomies. These relationships were also the bases for the Christian evangelization of Africa. The evangelizers saw their African converts as children who were incapable of being engaged rationally. Even when they made converts of the Africans, the converts were not allowed to take up leadership roles in the faith communities. African Christians were not allowed to study for the priesthood because they were seen as incapable of withstanding the academic rigors that accompanied priestly formation.

An African was taught to reject everything that she was by the European missionaries. The sacred religions of the continent were simply considered evil and demonic. Unfortunately, even with the emergence of indigenous clergies in the respective Christian denominations, the European narrative endured. African Christians continue to see their religious heritage as unholy. However, while the Christian leaders continue to validate the colonial narrative, the average African Christian continues to have a crisis of identity. While she ostensibly professes the Christian religion, in times of crisis, she validates her indigenous religious heritage by secretly seeking help. Perhaps there is a positive note to this—the religious heritages of Africa defy human attempts to eradicate them, because they reveal God's enduring presence in the continent.

I came to see that my priestess friend professes a deep faith in God. For me to claim that I know God more than her, and that her worship of God is simply an attempt at devil worship, was spiritual pride on my part. I suddenly realized that I was the one worshipping a false god in my effort to reduce the priestess's religion to idolatry. I know some of my Christian readers may find this difficult to comprehend, but I do now believe that any time we try to make general conclusions on the religious other, and hence hide behind doctrinal statements on the sole validity of the Christian religion, we fall into idolatry and self-worship. God, in all religions, is always a God of transcendence. Even when he/she reveals himself/herself, the divine nature can never be fully comprehended by humans.

As the Sufi tradition teaches, God's revelation is always unique in each religion, thus validating the conclusion that divine revelation is never predicated by only one religion.[8] The Holy Qur'an and Jewish and Christian Scriptures teach us that it is God's prerogative to judge what and who is holy and righteous.[9] The Holy Qur'an teaches that God's presence is everywhere.[10] I ask myself and my fellow Christians: Can we say we truly believe this in the way we understand God? If we do, how do we justify such doctrinal statements that present God as a captive of the Christian religion? I use the word "captive" because each time we claim we know God completely, we attempt to make God our prisoner. There is so much of God we do not know and can never know.

I asked how Christ would relate to the priestess in the community. A false sense of religious triumphalism endures today in Nigeria and, perhaps, in other parts of the world. Christians see themselves as the chosen ones. The Catholic magisterium teaches that all religions derive their salvific validity from the merits of Jesus Christ and the Catholic Church. In all these teachings, we forget that God is a mystery. Even in his self-revelation in the Christian religion, God transcends finality in human comprehension. When I asked the catechist why the village decided to ostracize the woman, I was told that it was to deter Christians from abandoning their Christian faith. The freedom of worship, fundamental to authentic human life in community, was abandoned by this community. Indeed, as a general practice in most of the dioceses and archdioceses in the entire Eastern Nigeria, Catholics are prohibited from marrying non-Catholics, even if they are Christians. If one were to go against this norm, she would be prevented from participating fully in the life of the Catholic Church. She would even be refused a Catholic burial. These practices are a betrayal of the ideals of the Christian faith.

I asked if other religions could guide one to live virtuously. My encounter with the priestess has taught me that it is wrong to think that virtue is a sole attribute of the Christian religion. In fact, while the Christian community in the village was not at all virtuous in its treatment of my friend, it was the priestess who demonstrated virtue through the generous practice of hospitality. Through her determination to engage and live out the ideals of her religion in the midst of the hostility shown toward her by the Christian community, I began to see what was wrong with my own Christian community, and the error in our own narrative. The Christian community in the village took on an air of superiority without even realizing it. I was also guilty of this malaise until the priestess showed me how to be religious through her efforts to educate me on her faith, invite me to a meal, pray with me, come to my place of worship, invite me to her place of worship, and invite me to pray with her in her place of worship. Such actions demonstrated a great sense of trust and love on her part.

I asked myself if it was possible for non-Christians to be committed to their religions in the same way as a Christian ought to be. During the course of my reflections, I concluded that commitment to one's religion is a universal phenomenon and not unique to Christianity. God invites humans to engage him/her through diverse ways, and such an invitation does not logically lead to a denial of divine invitation of others. The priestess taught me this lesson through her example. While being very faithful to her religion, she was more than willing to pray with me in my own sacred space. Her response to me when I invited her to come to my own place of worship was truly telling. She said she could not refuse to worship God wherever he/she was found. I have always asked myself if Christians can say the same. The priestess's response demonstrates the spirit and attitude needed today in interreligious dialogue. If we are convinced of the progress being made in interreligious dialogue and ecumenism, we cannot but be willing to pray with our fellow Christians and people of other faith. What I am stating here is not the occasional display of pleasantries that mark ceremonies organized to show our respect for each other. It must go beyond that. We must be willing to embrace the religious other and make it a common practice to pray with each other. When we do this regularly, our fears will be dissipated, and gradually all polemics against the religious other will give way to reverence and love of one another. It will eventually reveal the glorious presence of God in our midst; that presence which constantly invites humanity to embrace itself as one large family that responds to God in diverse and yet authentic ways.

My encounter with the priestess eventually led me to start thinking of articulating a theological proposition that I call "collaborative worship." It involves the recognition of the religious other as a graced presence at the heart of one's own religious worship. It transcends the impulse to proselytize. It acknowledges and celebrates the presence of the religious other as a legitimate partner without any preconditions.

My friend invited me to pray aloud during the religious worship in her shrine; and although she prayed for the success of my work, I did not have the courage to return the prayer. Her approach is what collaborative worship is all about. At the heart of her worship, she not only created a sacred space for me to pray for my intentions but also prayed for the success of my work in the village. She showed me how to be truly courageous and demonstrated a maturity of faith that I am still hoping to eventually possess. Collaborative worship involves our willingness to pray with the religious other, confident that it is the will of God for us to pray with and for each other. We do not pray for the other's conversion; rather, we give thanksgiving to God for the presence of the other and pray for the success of the work and ministry engaged in by the religious other. Such bravery is needed today if interreligious friendship is to make any sense, and if we truly believe that our faith comes from the God that transcends our human comprehension.

I have come to see that Christianity is not very much different from Indigenous Religion. African scripture scholar, Israel Kadmuzandu, makes a similar observation:

> The world of the Bible and the world of African traditional religion over-
> lap and dovetail at many important points, yet Africa itself continues to
> grapple with issues of identity. Africa continues to wrestle with issues of
> demonization imposed on her by missionaries and colonialists. No con-
> tinent or nation has been associated with heathenism more than Africa;
> indeed most history books refer to Africa as a "Dark Continent" or as a
> continent behind God's face...Africa finds itself at a crossroad: searching
> and longing for a salvation that addresses not only the soul but also culture
> at its deepest level.[11]

The ignorance expressed by the Christian community in the village of Umudiala has become a global trend among Christians. Very few Christians in America today have any knowledge of other religions. Islamophobia is rampant in many American cities. Muslims are seen as terrorists. They are being told that they cannot erect places of worship for themselves. Some Christians openly declare that America is a Christian nation and must preserve its Christian roots. Such paranoia must be met with a determination to learn who and what the religious other stands for.

So far, I have reflected on how my encounter with the priestess in the village of Umudiala in the town of Ezinifite-Nnewi reshaped my sense of how to be a Christian, and how it also led me to embrace fully the vocation of being an agent of interreligious friendship. I now turn to lessons that can be learned by other Christian theologians as they attempt to engage other religious traditions.

A Lesson for Theologians

Let me repeat the words of hope of Martin Buber, words that predict how religions will relate with each other in the nearest future if people of faith take seriously their faith in God:

> A time of genuine religious conversations is beginning—not those so-called but fictitious conversations where none regarded and addressed his partner in reality, but genuine dialogues, speech from certainty to certainty, but also from one open-hearted person to another open-hearted person. Only then will genuine common life appear, not that of an identical content of faith which is alleged to be found in all religions, but that of the situation, of anguish and expectation.[12]

Buber highlights here the need for genuine encounter among people of different faith traditions. Indeed, many theologians have truly dedicated their academic careers to fostering dialogue among religions. They have written valuable books, shared their stories of encounters with members of other faiths, and, sometimes, they have even been censored by the leaders of their faith traditions for standing with their friends. These actions show courage and conviction that are necessary for interreligious dialogue.

Interreligious encounters are fruitless when theologians have preconceived perceptions of the religious other. Christianity has, over the centuries, shaped many false perceptions on Judaism and Islam. Jews were vilified, persecuted, and killed because they refused to convert to

Christianity. They were essentially made to live at the outskirts of society by their Christian neighbors. Sadly enough, this negative narrative perpetuated by Christians eventually led to the fiendish attack on, and the killing of, millions of innocent Jews by Nazi Germany. The history of Christian-Muslim relations has also not been exemplary. The antagonism between the two religions has existed for centuries and it is still the case in many parts of the world today.

If they are to make any positive contribution to the future of inter-religious relations among religions, theologians must begin by critically evaluating their own religious traditions and be courageous enough to speak truth about the problematic aspects of their traditions. For example, Muslim scholars must be willing to critique those hermeneutics that promote religious intolerance by drawing from the rich heritage of the Holy Qur'an that expressly approves of religious tolerance. They should also appreciate the wisdom of the holy Prophet Mohammad, who saw the need to live in peace with people of other faith. Recently, I read an article from the *Associated Press* titled "Dakar Mosque Lit up for Christmas in Senegal."[13] The article touched on the cordial relationship that exists between Christians and Muslims in Senegal. This is a country with 95 percent Muslims and 5 percent Christians. Everyone celebrates the religious feasts of Muslims and Christians in the country. This should be an example for people of faith in our world to emulate.

Christian theologians must challenge exclusivist theologies. At the height of Christendom, papal authority was confused with Christian identity. One begins to see a form of religious intolerance in such doctrinal proclamations made by Pope Boniface VIII and the Council of Florence. The former declared in the papal bull, *Unam Sanctam*, in 1302 CE that obedience to papal authority was a necessary condition for salvation.[14] The historical context for such a declaration must be part of the process of understanding why such an exclusivist position was being taught by the pope. The pope was more interested in consolidating papal power in the spiritual and secular spheres.

The Council of Florence, through *Cantate Domino* issued in 1442, declared that membership in the Catholic Church was a necessary condition for salvation for heretics, schismatics, pagans, and Jews.[15] Of course, context is important if one is to understand this teaching. The battle against the Hussites, who were considered heretics by the Catholic monarchs and supported by the papacy, occurred during this period. The threat of the Muslim Turks against the Eastern Roman Empire was also beginning. The unification between the Catholic Church and the Eastern Orthodox Churches was a constitutive part of the council's deliberations and needed to be affirmed by showing the universal significance of the

Catholic Church. Also, the refusal of Jews to convert to Christianity was seen as something that needed to be dealt with.

There has been a slow but gradual shift from the views held by Pope Boniface VIII and the Council of Florence as a result of real contacts made between Christians and non-Christians over the centuries.[16] In the twentieth century, increased contacts were made among people of different faiths. The events of wars, the process of globalization, and the concrete effort made by Catholic leaders living in non-Western societies, where religious pluralism was a common reality, helped to shape the conversation and guide the process of articulating a healthy theology on other religions.[17] The Second Vatican Council was the first official attempt at this movement and has led to more frequent dialogues between the Catholic Church and other religions.[18] However, there have also been regressions in this process, as is the case in the curial document released in 2000 by the Congregation for the Doctrine of the Faith. The document, *Dominus Iesus*, presents the claim of Christianity as being the plenitude of truth made possible by Jesus Christ and the Catholic Church.[19] Other religions are taught to have elements of truth that derive their efficacy from Jesus Christ and the Catholic Church. Theologians should have the courage to engage these teachings being taught by the Catholic Church today. One has to ask: Is this an attempt by the Catholic Church to preserve some form of relevance in a world that is fast becoming secular? Only time will tell, as historians and theologians continue to evaluate such teachings within the currents of history.

Openness of heart is necessary, if interreligious friendship is to be truly transformative. Openness of heart involves being able to trust God to guide one in the encounter with another. Christians need to learn to trust the religious other as an agent of God. In our desire to understand our respective religions, we must be careful that we not fall into the temptation of replacing God's wisdom with human foolishness. Let me repeat the words of Buber: "Meeting with God does not come to man [humanity] in order that he may concern himself with God, but in order that he may confirm that there is meaning in the world. All revelation is summons and sending."[20] In other words, faith in God does not mean we should reject others and focus solely on our doctrinal convictions; rather, faith in God means that we take seriously our relational engagement with others, because they, like us, are creatures of God.

Conclusion

I began this chapter telling my story about how an encounter with a priestess in a village in Southeastern Nigeria led me to a path of conversion. Even though my original intention was to expose the errors in her religion and move her to embrace the Catholic faith, I eventually came to appreciate the authenticity of her faith. In the process, she also helped me to appreciate more fully the authenticity of my Catholic faith. The type of conversion I was hoping for never occurred. A different conversion occurred instead: a conversion leading to greater understanding and appreciation of each other's faith. This is the type of conversion needed today in our world. If people of faith can learn to appreciate each other's faith traditions, the constant religious violence that has plagued our world will be greatly reduced or eradicated completely.

The era of isolation of religions is over. Globalization has redefined what community entails. Religions must now focus on engaging each other. Through such engagements, it is my hope that new perspectives will be formulated, those that acknowledge the complex presence of God in our world.

Notes

1. The Diocese of Nnewi, in Southeast Nigeria, was created on November 28, 2001, and Saint Michael's Parish falls within the jurisdiction of this newly erected diocese.
2. See Jonah 1:1–4:11.
3. There are three of these churches that still exist in the Kingdom of Benin, and they are Aruosa N'Akpakpava (Aruosa in Akpakpava), Aruosa N'Idunwuerie (Aruosa in Idunwuerie), and Aruosa N'Ogbelaka (Aruosa in Ogbelaka).
4. Aruosa, in the Bini language, means "the eye of God."
5. See "Benin Kingdom/Edo State Religions," accessed June 26, 2014, http://www.edoworld.net/EdotourismReligion.html.
6. See Thomas Pakenham, *The Scramble for Africa: White Man's Conquest of the Dark Continent from 1876 to 1912* (New York: Avon Books, 1991), 22.
7. Elizabeth Isichei, *A History of Christianity in Africa: From Antiquity to the Present* (Grand Rapids, MI: Eerdmans,,1995), 171.
8. William C. Chittick, *The Sufi Path of Knowledge: Ibn al-'Arabi's Metaphysics of Imagination* (Albany: State University of New York Press, 1989), 103.
9. Qur'an 16:125; John 3:10–4: 11; Matthew 8:11–12; Acts 10:28.
10. Qur'an 2:115.
11. Israel Kadmuzandu, "Biblical Interpretation and Criticism in Neocolonial Africa: Challenges, Conceptualizations, and Needs in the Twenty-First Century," in *The Future of the Biblical Past: Envisioning Biblical Studies on a Global Key*, ed. Roland Boer and Fernando F. Segovia (Atlanta, GA: Society of Biblical Literature, 2012), 4. See also John Wesley Z. Kurewa, *The Church in Mission: A Short History of the United Methodist Church in Zimbabwe, 1897-1997* (Nashville, TN: Abingdon, 1997), 37–50.

12. Martin Buber, *Between Man and Man*, with an Introduction by Maurice Friedman (New York: Macmillan, 1965), 7–8.

13. Krista Larson, "Dakar Mosque Lit Up for Christmas in Senegal," *Associated Press* (December 24, 2012), accessed June 26, 2014, http://news.yahoo.com /dakar-mosque-lit-christmas-senegal-111624409.html.

14. Boniface VIII, *Unam Sanctam* (November 18, 1302), accessed June 26, 2014, http://www.papalencyclicals.net/Bon08/B8unam.htm.

15. See Joseph Neuner and Jacques Dupuis, eds, *The Christian Faith in the Doctrinal Documents of the Catholic Church*, 7th ed. (Bangalore: Theological Publications in India, 2001), 309–310 (no. 810). See also Maurice Wiles, *Christian Theology and Inter-religious Dialogue* (Philadelphia, PA: Trinity Press International, 1992), 9.

16. See Ilaria Morali, "Salvation, Religions, and Dialogue in the Roman Magisterium: From Pius IX to Vatican II and Postconciliar Popes," in *Catholic Engagement with World Religions: A Comprehensive Study*, ed. Karl J. Becker and Ilaria Morali (Maryknoll: Orbis Books, 2010), 123–124.

17. See a summary of the conditions necessitating a shift in the Roman Catholic Church's perception of other religions and Christian denominations from Trent to Vatican II in Jeannine Hill Fletcher, "Responding to Religious Difference: Conciliar Perspectives," in *From Trent to Vatican II: Historical and Theological Investigations*, ed. Raymond F. Bulman and Frederick J. Parrella (Oxford: Oxford University Press, 2006), 267–281.

18. See *Nostra Aetate* (Vatican: October 28, 1965), 2, accessed June 26, 2014, http://www.vatican.va/archive/hist_councils/ii_vatican_council/documents /vat-ii_decl_19651028_nostra-aetate_en.html.

19. Congregation for the Doctrine of the Faith, *Dominus Iesus* (Vatican: August 6, 2000), 22, accessed June 26, 2014, http://www.vatican.va/roman_curia /congregations/cfaith/documents/rc_con_cfaith_doc_20000806_dominus -iesus_en.html.

20. Martin Buber, *I and Thou*, trans. Ronald Gregor Smith (New York: Charles Schibner, 1958), 115.

16

Interreligious Friendship: Symbiosis of Human Relationship vis-à-vis Religious Differences—A Christian Encounter with Two African Traditional Religionists

Marinus Chijioke Iwuchukwu

This article provides a reflection on the dialogic imperative of my encounter with two interlocutors from African Traditional Religious persuasion. One of the encounters happened in my early childhood, while the second took place when I was in my late twenties. The full import and lessons from those encounters were not appropriately unpacked and appreciated until decades after the encounters.

As a religious pluralist, my evolution in faith and theology has been richly influenced by encounters with people who profess faith beliefs different from mine. I consider the people that I have been privileged to interact with to be men and women of profound faith and spirituality.

My use and understanding of religious pluralism is both a worldview and pragmatic appreciation of the legitimacy and value of the religion of the other, which promotes healthy spiritual and social development in human society. My appreciation of religious pluralism stems from the understanding that religion is a human attempt to find ultimate meaning and fulfillment through faith. Religious faith is often bolstered and sustained by an aggregate of beliefs, virtues, and spiritually and emotionally therapeutic rituals and rites. Therefore, every religion is conditioned to engage its adherents in ongoing rituals, practices, beliefs, and teachings that are geared to making life and living more meaningful and purposeful. In light of the above understanding of religion, and from my Christian perspective, I completely assent to Jacques Dupuis's assertion that every religion is a human attempt to respond to the divine self-revelation (albeit knowing that some religions are non-theistic). Dupuis opines that every religion is a human attempt to respond to God who initiates the communication. This implies that humans are not the initiators of religion. They are, rather, responding to a divine initiative as human beings from different contexts, worldviews, and based on how best they understand the communication from the divine. Accordingly, Dupuis asserts, "if... religion and the religious originate in a self-manifestation of God to human beings, the primary foundation for the principle of multiplicity is the superabundant riches and variety of God's self-manifestation to humankind."[1] This conclusion profoundly enunciates the core of my theological assumption of religious pluralism and religious pluralism as a de jure of God's relationship with humankind.[2]

My focus in this chapter is on my encounters with two African traditional religionists: one is my maternal grandfather, Mazi Ihenachor Unachukwu, and the other is Mazi Nweke Ozieme, the maternal grandfather of my high school sweetheart. Both men are of Igbo ethnicity in Southeastern Nigeria. As I recount my interactions with these men of faith, I am convinced about how honest and enriching relationships are sustainable among friends, even if the friends are of different faith affiliations. These two African traditional religionists not only endeared themselves to me, but also elevated my eventual appreciation for religious diversity. Indeed, their hospitality and friendship, rooted in African traditional culture and faith, help us to think anew about dialogue and faith.

This reflective chapter will examine how the dialogic values of respect for the other, openness to the other, sufficient understanding of one's faith tradition, and normative worldview of religious pluralism are more effectively achieved through interreligious friendship between a Christian and an African traditional religionist; or rather, how an African traditional religionist's disposition to friendship models the values of dialogue to a Christian. Because the African traditional religionists I encountered demonstrated these dialogic values, I was drawn to them and their affable personalities. My conversations with them on faith development and religious diversity impacted me deeply and helped to substantiate today my understanding and appreciation for religious pluralism.

Many Christians treat African traditional religionists disrespectfully in Southeastern Nigeria. Typically, while many African traditional religionists tend to be older people, and often people with little or no Western education, Christians in different parts of Africa are often younger and more likely to have some levels of Western education. African Christians often regard African traditional religionists as ignorant, primitive, pagan, and uncivilized. They imply that something is wrong mentally or spiritually with the African traditional religionists, simply because they are not Christian or refused conversion to Christianity. Even so, many people publicly profess faith in Christianity while secretly believing and practicing their African traditional religious rituals and faith tradition.

A Summary of My Faith Development

Although I was baptized as an infant, my formal spiritual journey began when I was eight, with my First Holy Communion, and later, my Confirmation. The catechism of the Catholic Church provided for me and my peers our first organized doctrinal education. Its structure of questions and answers formed part of the pedagogy for memorization, which was also the format for much of my elementary school education. The first series of questions in the catechism (printed by Catholic Truth Society, a British publishing outfit) were: "Who made you?" and "Why did God make you?" The answer to the second question intrigued me because of its universal applicability. The answer goes, "God made me to know him, love him, serve him, and to be happy with him for ever in the next."

When I began to read the Bible in high school and listen to preachers' interpretations of the Bible, the universal applicability of the answer to the second question above that had appealed to me changed. In addition, Christian preachers' interpretation of authentic faith in God was more limited, and even exclusive. In the circle I found myself, it was clearly asserted that although heaven is the *telos* (end or goal) of every human being, the only guaranteed access to heaven is through Christianity. In essence, the answer to the question (Why did God make you?) changed to something like "although God created everyone, only Christians can successfully make it back to God in heaven." It was clearly underscored that Christianity was the only authentic and appropriate religion. All other religions were either false or quasi-religions. This is troubling to me now (not to mention problematic for effective interreligious dialogue), but this is what I learned.

As a Catholic, I was taught that the journey toward heaven is most effectively facilitated through the agency of the sacraments, especially Baptism, Confession, and Eucharist. In my childhood years and early teenage years, I was raised to appreciate the instructions of the Catholic catechism and church laws as the best and most comprehensive means to understand the principles and teaching of my faith tradition regarding eternal salvation. The search and desire for salvation underscored my interest and desire to become a more fervent Christian. But it also made me smug, to the point of feeling sorry for non-Christians.

As I became more mature intellectually and theologically, I was convinced of the need to reassess and even question some of the earlier ground rules and suggested prerequisites for eternal salvation. I began to rethink and reevaluate what really constituted an authentic religion. The more I understood the universal relevance of God and God's love for all God's creatures, a theological insight that really came from my understanding of Second Vatican Council (1962–1965), the more I appreciated and embraced the religious diversity around me.

In addition, my own relationships with many amazing people who were not Christians left no doubt in my mind that the exclusivist twist was inconsistent with my understanding of the universal relevance of God in the lives of all human beings. Moreover, no one, including Christians, have a monopoly of the God I read about in the Bible. And if any such monopoly or absolute understanding of the ways and activities of God by any human being is possible, then we are certainly not talking about the eternally omniscient, loving, and infinite God of the Jewish, Christian, and Muslim faith.

Grandpa Chacha

At this juncture, I would like to relate the encounters with two African traditionalist friends of mine: my maternal grandfather and the grandfather of my high school sweetheart. They were key to my affirmation of religious pluralism and my own development in interreligious dialogue.

The earliest memories of my maternal grandfather, Mazi Ihenachor Unachukwu, a man we all fondly called Chacha (short for Ihenachor) are filled with his warmth, friendship, and hospitality toward me as a child. The encounter with my high school sweetheart's grandfather, a man who was simply introduced to me as Mazi Nweke, occurred when I was a young adult religious leader. Nweke struck me particularly as a very warm and friendly person during our only one-on-one meeting—a meeting that turned out to be so meaningful because of what I learned about the deep spirituality and morality of African traditionalists. I later came to find out that Mazi Nweke was some kind of minister, priest, or acolyte for his African traditional religion.

Grandpa Chacha left me with memories of his outstanding friendship richly demonstrated in his amazing hospitality. While sharing with my mother my experience of friendship with Grandpa Chacha, she affirmed that her father was renowned for his outstanding friendship and generosity toward many people who interacted with him. He was the head of his polygamous home, but it was known that his friendship and hospitality extended far beyond his immediate family. He considered it his duty and responsibility to care for the family of his deceased brother. According to my mother, Chacha was truly a God-fearing man, whose affection, generosity, and friendship toward others was rooted in his traditional religious beliefs. My mother described how her father performed his rituals of prayer and blessings over all members of his household and invoked the protection of the Almighty over all.

Each time I visited my maternal home, my grandmother, Ezinne Egbediye Augustina Ihenachor, always lavished her love on me. Chacha, who had a long list of children and grandchildren, always appreciated my visits and offered me special treats. He often treated me with cooked eggs (which was a delicacy, especially to children); and at times he offered me chicken from his farm, which I brought to my grandmother to raise or cook for me. Chacha treated each one of us grandchildren and children with unique affection. One of my maternal cousins shared some of her own experiences of Chacha with me. She remembered his strong values of friendships and hospitality, as well as his genuine predisposition to peace, kindness, justice, and affection toward the people with whom he interacted. Another older cousin explained that Chacha was a highly disciplined person who was also pluralistic on matters of religion. According to this second cousin, Chacha considered the choice of religion a prerogative of every adult individual, even as he remained strongly convinced about the authenticity of his own faith tradition. Chacha was not just a strong believer in the absence of compulsion in religions; he actually appreciated the different choices of religion made by most members of his household. This second cousin remembered how Chacha, in his daily invocations, called on God to touch the hearts of evil people and heal society of the evil machinations of such men and women.

Each time I visited Chacha, even when he became frail due to age and illness, he made sure I was given a special treat and always invited me to sit on his lap or by his side. Because of his friendship, I was affectionately drawn to him. Later, I came to understand that almost everyone in his household had converted to Christianity, including my grandmother. He was literally alone in believing and practicing his traditional religious beliefs, yet his affection for all immediate and extended family members who had converted to Christianity never waned. In my mother's opinion, her father and one of her uncles, Mazi Iwuala, were the two most respectable, God-fearing, and altruistic elders she knew, despite their choice to remain African traditional religionists.

The distance from my village home to my maternal grandparents' home was less than two miles. It was a bit of a distant stretch of walk for a child my age, but it was a walk I was always excited to make. I enjoyed those visits with my maternal grandparents—first, because they were the only grandparents I knew (my paternal grandparents had both passed away before I was born), and second, because of the warmth and friendship I received when visiting my grandparents. Although my grandmother was so dear, loving, and friendly toward me, my grandfather's affection and friendship always struck me as unique, especially given the fact that he had many children my age running around his household.

While my grandmother converted to Christianity, Chacha remained a convinced and committed African traditional religion follower.[3] Outside his main house was a shrine, where he performed his daily rituals and prayers. According to my mother, Chacha was very committed not only to the rituals of his faith, but also to the virtues and values enjoined on him by his faith. My mom explained that it was customary for her dad to pray for and bless everyone in his household daily. She described her dad as a virtuous and upright man, whose life was worthy of emulation. My mother argued that although her dad expressly turned down the persuasions and pressures to convert to Christianity, both Christians and traditionalists respected him. According to my mother, my grandfather was baptized on his deathbed. My interpretation of that ceremony is that Grandpa Chacha's children, most of whom had converted to Christianity, performed the ritual more for their own religious satisfaction than meeting the need of a man whose consciousness was fading and who had no energy or desire to continue to fight his children on the question of conversion to Christianity. Therefore, it was a conversion ceremony and ritual conducted to appease Grandpa Chacha's children's exclusivistic Christian understanding of salvation.

For a man who was polygamous, it was indeed fascinating to know how kind, generous, and friendly he was to all his children and grandchildren, regardless of which wife the children and grandchildren came from. My grandfather's affection to his children and grandchildren was undergirded by his spirituality. In his religious practices and rituals, he devoted a good amount of time during his daily prayers toward the welfare of all his children and grandchildren. He was so generous toward his children and grandchildren that the older relations in the household had to ensure some adult member of the family was around him most of the time to prevent some of those children or grandchildren exploiting his generosity and asking for more than they needed.

Mazi Nweke

My other deep encounter with an African traditionalist was actually only a onetime event, but it was a rich and profound experience. It occurred when I traveled to celebrate one of the milestones of my friend, a onetime high school sweetheart, who had become a Catholic nun. Her family welcomed me and other guests. During the meet and greet, I was introduced to my friend's maternal grandfather, who was also present in a celebratory mood to mark the event. He was introduced to me as Mazi Nweke. After my long visit and conversation with Mazi Nweke, and given the friendly tone and atmosphere our conversation had, his daughter and granddaughter (my hosts) informed me that they were reluctant at first to have me meet with Mazi Nweke. According to them, Nweke was one of the very few in the village who strongly objected to every attempt to win him over to Christianity, even if it was only for ceremonial or cosmetic purposes.[4] Nweke would say that people who claimed publicly to be Christians, but still believed and practiced the rituals of traditional religion, were insincere toward both faith traditions or lacked the courage to be who they truly wished to be.

Nweke explained to me that while he did not object to what anyone chose as her or his faith, he did not see any material evidence to discredit the faith in which he was raised. According to him, the core of his faith beliefs and practices enjoined him to be honest, just, peace loving, kind, and friendly to all people, given that all human beings were created by the same Great Creator. He narrated how he had personally welcomed and warmly interacted with white missionaries who came to evangelize people in his community. He explained that his kind gestures and friendship to the missionaries were often misinterpreted to mean a predisposition toward conversion to Christianity, hence they (white missionaries) and their assistants were disappointed that he objected to become one of them. Nweke explained that he was satisfactorily and sufficiently mentored for his spiritual and religious needs by his African faith tradition. Therefore, he was not looking for an alternative religion.

I was deeply touched by the candor, genuineness, and commitment to faith of Nweke. More importantly, his attention to living a virtuous life and harboring no ill will toward anybody was outstanding to me. I was most definitely impressed by his openness to me, a stranger of a different faith tradition. He taught me a lot about honesty and fidelity to one's faith tradition that should be imperative for every religious person. He underscored unequivocally that his traditional religious faith taught him to honor every human person he came across, regardless of his or her differences, including choice of religion. According to him, a person's religious affiliation should not determine how he or she is treated or received in the community. He debunked the misconception that people who were African traditional religionists tended toward witchcraft and evil machinations against their neighbors. According to him, people who chose to be evil or malicious toward their neighbors did not need African traditional religion to do so. I felt welcomed and safe in his presence. His warmth and friendship were freely given in one conversation. Toward the end of our discussion, we exchanged blessings to each other, and he prayed for a safe return to my home and family.

Insights for Dialogue

Both of my interlocutors were men who commanded respect among their peers, friends, and relations. Both were men of distinctive faith in their African traditional religious affiliation and felt comfortable with their religious identity. Before my meeting with Mazi Nweke, his daughter and granddaughter had told me not to bother talking to him if my mission was to seek his conversion to Christianity, because he was stubbornly convinced about and set in his faith. My grandfather was equally very strong and convinced about his faith tradition, so convinced that the only way to make him a Christian was for his Christian children to baptize him on his deathbed, when he lacked the will, energy, and presence of mind to object.

The common thread I find between these two gentlemen is their warmth and friendship to me, regardless of my different religious identity. My experiences with both of them challenged my previous supersessionist attitude toward non-Christians and my lack of genuine friendship with people who were different from me in faith identity. My encounters were essential to clarifying and developing my inclusive religious pluralist stance.[5] They enriched my appreciation for the religious other, especially for African traditional faith followers.[6] In the words of *Nostra Aetate*, "The Catholic Church rejects nothing that is true and holy in these religions. She regards with sincere reverence those ways of conduct and of life, those precepts and teachings which, though differing in many aspects from the ones she holds and sets forth, nonetheless often reflect a ray of that Truth which enlightens all men."[7]

Although developments following the Second Vatican Council, and the World Council of Churches's openness to religious diversity, have been positive, many Christians are still quite resentful of, and indignant toward, non-Christians. African traditional religionists are still often maligned and even demonized by many Christians. In light of evolution of Christian theological understanding of other faith traditions, it has become imperative to seriously question Christian soteriological formulations (about salvation) that are hostile or negative toward people of other faith traditions, and especially toward people of the African traditional religious faith. It is therefore gratifying to heed the admonition of *Nostra Aetate*: "The Church, therefore, exhorts her sons, that through dialogue and collaboration with the followers of other religions, carried out with prudence and love and in witness to the Christian faith and life, they recognize, preserve and promote the good things, spiritual and moral, as well as the socio-cultural values found among these men."[8] Moreover, in a recent interview granted to an atheist (Eugenio Scalfari of *La Republica*) by Pope Francis, the dialogue-minded pope argued that the Church's primary role in the modern world is not proselytization, but addressing the needs of the world and restoring peace through dialogue.[9]

In fundamentalist Christian, and also conservative Christian, parlance, it is disappointing when upright men and women of other faith traditions fail to honor the invitation to convert to Christianity. These Christians are seriously concerned such upright people would end up in hell because they failed to become Christians when they had the opportunity to do so. It is instructive and dialogically exemplary to note that despite the condescending and disrespectful attitude of Christian friends, neighbors, and relatives toward my interlocutors, these African traditionalists conversely demonstrated profound respect toward their Christian relatives, friends, and neighbors. They must be commended as role models for dialogue, as they demonstrated essential elements for dialogue: respect toward the religious other, openness to learning, knowledge about and commitment to one's faith tradition.

Friendly disposition and hospitality are two major virtues and values of African traditional religions and African culture. Since the traditional African religion is borne out of African cultural values, it is often difficult to distinguish the two. They symmetrically dovetail into each other. These two, friendship and hospitality, are also major assets toward effective interreligious engagement. They are two manifest aspects of the functional approach to religion. The African cultural and religious practices of hospitality and friendship suggest a very practical openness and warmth toward a stranger or a guest, akin to the openness and warmth accorded to one's kith and kin. As Elochukwu Ezukwu asserts, "the minimum that the African expects from his kith and kin is hospitality."[10] The African cultural and religious philosophy of hospitality and friendship are inarguably responsible for the successful missionary establishment of Christianity in the Southeastern part of Nigeria.[11] Although many of these foreign missionaries took undue advantage of the African friendship and hospitality, African traditional religionists have continued to demonstrate genuine friendship to their other religious neighbors. John S. Pobee attests to the normative African religious pluralist landscape,[12] hence explaining why African traditional culture and religions welcome neighbors who are religiously different. Lamin Sanneh insightfully affirms Pobee's thoughts. He writes, "The fact is that Christian and Muslim Africa is for the most part enfolded within the larger setting of the old Africa, with its deep-rooted hospitality, tolerance, and generosity...and it cannot be stressed enough how much Christian and Muslim Africans owe to traditional Africa."[13]

The normative inclusive religious pluralism consistent with African pre-Islamic and pre-Christian societies is derived from the heterogeneity of religion in Africa, as well as the African worldview and accommodation of religious plurality. This phenomenon of inclusive religious pluralism is illustratively described by Jan G. Platvoet: "Traditional believers are known to have eagerly adopted, and adapted, the religious practices, ideas, and at times institutions, brought in from far and near by traders, hunters, pilgrims, and visitors, or members who had travelled, or those who had married into their society."[14] Platvoet persuasively argues, using historical data and anthropological findings, that African society is home to both the basic and advanced forms of religions among human beings and has continued to accommodate the major religions of the world from across the globe. But even before the advent of other world religions into Africa, African peoples had a diversity of religious practices and beliefs, which explains why many scholars use the term "African Traditional Religions," rather than "African Traditional Religion."[15]

The African inclusive religious pluralistic stance is in accord with an African philosophy of life that takes a "functionalistic approach" toward religion.[16] This approach to religion de-emphasizes the metaphysical in favor of the empirical realities of everyday life. Therefore, religion is meant to facilitate daily life and ensure that people successfully proceed from one day to the other. This approach assures that peace, security of life and property, and navigating the best model of human relationship with one's neighbors are primary concerns, rather than the obsessive desire for the fantasies of a paradise or heaven when the daily life experiences remain in shamble and disaster.

Conclusion

I have emphasized the manifest goodness, friendship, kindness, loving, and peaceful nature of the two African traditional religious people

I encountered many years ago. The objective of recalling my experiences with these two men is to demonstrate that many African traditional religionists have the required rudiments for effective interreligious dialogue as well as profound moral conscience and demonstrated virtuous life examples, in spite of being once and still maligned people by some Christians. African Traditional Religion has, and continues to be, a primary focus of Christian bashing and caricaturing in Southeastern Nigeria. The justification for desiring the conversion to Christianity of African religious traditionalists, is often contingent on the premises that they are ignorant of the God reflected and revealed by Jesus Christ, and that their lives are in the dark as people ruled by the agent of darkness. The pre-Vatican II exclusivism and concept of salvation for only Christians (or Catholics, to be more specific), was and continues to be (in some circumstances) another driving force behind the insensitive mission to convert African traditional religionists to Christianity. This second understanding of exclusive salvation was the major reason the Christian relatives of my grandfather ensured he was baptized prior to dying. When I, a convinced Christian, reflect on Matthew 25:31–46, I notice that Jesus does not make any particular mention of heaven being specially reserved for people based on their religious affiliations or associations. The primary standard used to determine each person's final destiny is how virtuous he or she lived on earth. This is not saying anything, negative or positive, about the content of the religious doctrine of any faith tradition. It simply emphasizes, as well as affirms, the value of the quality of life each person lives.

The core of my argument is that numerous African traditional religionists possess the ingredients required for living a good and honest life—so they may meet with God/Jesus Christ after their lives on earth are over. In addition, the hospitality, virtue, and friendship offered by traditionalists make them admirable agents for effective and lasting interreligious dialogue. African friendship is grounded in hospitality. The hospitality of both my grandfather, Chacha, and that of my friend's grandfather palpably demonstrates honest and true interreligious friendship. The question is not whether they can be friends with Christians, but whether Christians are able to extend similar gestures of hospitality and be true friends with them—friends that do not demand that these good men convert to Christianity or measure their moral and spiritual values based on an affiliation with Christianity.

Friendship is indispensable for effective interreligious dialogue among people of different religious identities; it is therefore imperative that Christians adopt and implement the spirit of friendship in their relationships with others, especially with those from African traditional religions.

Notes

1. Jacques Dupuis, *Christianity and the Religions: From Confrontation to Dialogue*, trans. Phillip Berryman (Maryknoll, NY: Orbis Books, 2002), 255.
2. This theological assumption does not and will not be dragged into the competitive and divisive debate of whose religion is better or more appropriate. I will leave that exercise to those whose preoccupation and focus may be comparative theology or missiology. As a pluralist and an interreligious dialogue theologian, my primary objective is to identify and appreciate the values and beauty of every religious manifestation in human society, and to decipher the most peaceful and respectful ways for these religions and their adherents to be involved in ongoing dialogue.
3. My mother informed me that her father (Grandpa Chacha) was baptized shortly before he passed on. It was a ritual that was performed more to please his children, especially his first-born son, who wanted his father to die a Christian. According to my mother, Chacha never attended any church service in his lifetime.
4. My hosts informed me that many of those who have embraced Christianity in that village did that mostly in response to public pressure and to be able to receive some of the material benefits and social advantages Christians were often bequeathed. Therefore, they are Christians on Sunday (in the public eyes), but continue to practice their traditional beliefs in the privacy of their homes during the week.
5. My inclusive religious pluralism assumption is anchored in classical Christological and Trinitarian beliefs. Jesus the Christ, second person of the Trinity, is inherently affirmed wherever God the Father and the Holy Spirit are recognized, affirmed, or appreciated. Therefore, you do not need to manifestly proclaim Christ as your savior to be both appreciated by Christ and redeemed by Christ. *Lumen Gentium* of the Second Vatican Council affirms the universal redemptive capacity of the Christ/God even for people who are outside the boundary of the physical Church and Christianity. For its part, *Nostra Aetate* acknowledges and respects the goodness in religions other than Christianity. See *Lumen Gentium* (Vatican: November 21, 1964), 16, accessed June 26, 2014, http://www.vatican.va/archive/hist_councils/ii _vatican_council/documents/vat-ii_const_19641121_lumen-gentium _en.html; *Nostra Aetate* (Vatican: October 28, 1965), 2–3, accessed June 26, 2014, http://www.vatican.va/archive/hist_councils/ii_vatican_council /documents/vat-ii_decl_19651028_nostra-aetate_en.html.
6. Many of us sub-Saharan African Christians have been brainwashed to think and assume the worst of the traditional religion of our ancestors and people. Such brainwashing primarily came from the Western Christian missionaries' approach to African traditional religion from the earliest days of colonialism. Elochukwu Uzukwu confirms this brainwashing and denigrative understanding of African traditional religions in his work, *God, Spirit, and Human Wholeness* (Eugene, OR: Pickwick, 2012), 52–55.

7. See *Nostra Aetate*, 2.
8. Ibid.
9. For more details on this, see Michael Sean Winters, "Pope Francis' Latest Bombshell Interview," *National Catholic Reporter* (October 1, 2013), accessed June 24, 2014, http://ncronline.org/blogs/distinctly-catholic/pope-francis -latest-bombshell-interview.
10. Elochukwu E. Uzukwu, "Missiology Today: The African Situation," in *Religion and African Culture: Inculturation—A Nigerian Perspective*, ed. Elochukwu E. Uzukwu (Enugu: SNAAP Press, 1988), 146.
11. Uzukwu underscores the preeminent value of hospitality obtainable in different African cultural social milieu. See Uzukwu, "Missiology Today," 146–173. Chinua Achebe alludes to the normative friendship and hospitality of an African social and religious philosophy in his epic work, *Things Fall Apart* (New York: Anchor Books, 1994). According to Achebe, the local people accommodated the white man and his religion even when his ways were different from that of the natives. The natives had never contemplated fighting on behalf of their gods, albeit each person had the right to choose or decline the offer of new religious identity the white man was promoting.
12. John S. Pobee, *Toward an African Theology* (Nashville, TN: Abingdon Press, 1979), 43–44.
13. Lamin Sanneh, *Piety and Power: Muslims and Christians in West Africa* (Maryknoll: Orbis Books, 1996), 24.
14. Jan Platvoet, "The Religions of Africa in their Historical Order," in *Study of Religions in Africa: Past, Present and Prospects*, ed. Jan Platvoet, James Cox, and Jacob Olupona (Cambridge: Roots and Branches, 1996), 52. Many other scholars also make the argument that the African-inclusive pluralistic worldview is the reason many world religions have found themselves comfortable in their adopted homes in Africa—a phenomenon that has led to some scholars like Jan G. Platvoet to describe the religious landscape in Africa as "Africa's rainbow of religions." See Platvoet, "The Religions of Africa in Their Historical Order," 46–102. Or other scholars, such as Jacob Olupona, concede the authenticity of nomenclatures like "African Independent Churches," "African Pentecostal," and "African Islam" in his article "Thinking Globally about African Religion." See Jacob Olupona, "Thinking Globally about African Religion," in *Global Religions*, ed. Mark Juergensmeyer (Oxford and New York: Oxford University Press, 2006), 527–535. Using the illustration of Ifa divination among his native Yoruba religious culture and theology, Olupona underscores the inclusive pluralistic paradigm obtainable in African religious worldview. See Olupona, "Religious Pluralism in Africa: Insights from Ifa Divination Poetry," in *Ethics That Matters: African, Caribbean, and African American Sources*, ed. Marcia Y. Riggs and James Samuel Logan (Minneapolis, MN: Fortress Press, 2012), 51–58.
15. Platvoet, "The Religions of Africa in their Historical Order," 46–102. Laurenti Magesa argues, however, that the essence and fundamental beliefs among Africans is identical, albeit with different rituals and practices. He is

therefore of the opinion that the religion of Africans should be considered in the same vein as Christianity or Islam, both of which encompass certain level of diversity in the same religion. See Laurenti Magesa, *African Religion: The Moral Traditions of Abundant Life* (Maryknoll: Orbis Books, 1997), 15–18.

16. Martien E. Brinkman, *Non-Western Jesus: Jesus as Bodhisattva, Avatara, Guru, Prophet, Ancestor, or Healer?* (London: Equinox, 2009), 210–223. Brinkman, while affirming the "functionalist approach" to religion of African traditional religions, goes on to argue that even though African traditional religions significantly emphasize an immanent God, they do not deny the transcendence of God. He makes the case that African traditional religions hold both views in harmony as composite understanding of God and life. Therefore, African traditional religions do not deny the existence of life after life, but requires a balance of focus on both the life now and the life hereafter. Uzukwu confirms this fundamental philosophy and religious view of life. See Uzukwu, "Missiology Today," 151–152.

Conclusion

Mary Margaret Funk, OSB

There are many aspects of this sacrament we call Church, and one is the side of human experience that has already become what has been promised through grace. This charism in the Church is quick to recognize the treasure—and grace—of friendship, and can testify to the divine promise that has already been fulfilled in our lifetime. The "we" of each one and one another becomes a part of our personal experience and of our experience of the divine. The chapters in this book both celebrate *Nostra Aetate*'s invitation to dialogue and proclaim its fulfillment. Friendship happens when we open our hearts to extend and receive. Exponential hospitality emerges.

These chapters are brief reports of how Catholics have become friends with Jews, Muslims, Hindus, Buddhists, and African indigenous believers. Each chapter lifts up a particular experience; and while there is no comparison to one another, a reader can find satisfying brush strokes of similar encounters in one's own life. These carefully crafted reflections are like pearls. Taken as a whole we can string these beads into a fine necklace. These precious stones circle round and are held together with the clasp of friendship.

The essays do not presume a common understanding of friendship. And yet similar themes emerge. Friends are teachers, colleagues, family, and partners in the spiritual quest. Friends can be with us for brief—though powerful—periods of time, or journey with us for years. Friends are present to us even in their absence. Friends change us in large and small ways.

David Burrell and Francis X. Clooney provide us with rich narratives of lives dedicated to interreligious work. Burrell shares his immersion in the triadic study of Judaism, Christianity, and Islam. He shows how both philosophy and the actualities of living together in the same physical space (and holy land) bond human souls. Burrell promotes friendship over dialogue: two face each other across a table in dialogue, but in friendship the two walk side by side. Clooney takes the reader through his journeys in Nepal, Oxford (UK), and Cambridge (USA). Although some of his closest interfaith friends have been books, he honors the many Hindu scholars and gurus who have been an important part of his life. Like Burrell, Clooney discusses the role of friendship in conflict. If Burrell points to the healing nature of friendship, Clooney describes the delicate balancing act that friendship sometimes requires.

Mary Boys, Elena Procario-Foley, and Rosemary Radford Reuther discuss friendship among those whose work bridges formal dialogue and shared lives. Boys shares her friendship with her Jewish colleague and collaborator, Sara Lee. The story of their collaboration involves trips to Auschwitz and Birkenau and academic encounters where both showed up together after months of careful planning and personal research. Two scholars, two women rooted in differing religions, reveal to the rest of us that going deeper in our own tradition is our best lever for mutuality and a loving friendship. Ruether writes of her long-term friendship with Rita Gross. Both have been deeply involved in Buddhist-Christian Dialogue, growing close as the few feminist scholars in their dialogue. Ruether calls her friend a soul mate who is united to her at a deeper level than words could ever express. If Ruether and Boys describe scholarly friends in dialogue, Procario-Foley demonstrates the power of dialogue for the classroom. She gives readers a front row seat to her Jewish-Christian Studies Course, with insight and intimacy through her friend Bill Donat, a survivor of the Holocaust (Shoah). The story unfolds over ten years. This friendship had the power to hold together two religions such that love became strong enough to face not only life, but also death.

John Cavadini, Marianne Farina, Masarrat Khan, Peter Phan, and Simon Mary Aihiokhai describe friendships that blossom through work. Cavadini was a colleague of the late Rabbi Michael Singer. Cavadini describes two professors who shared texts at such a depth that truth yielded fresh meaning and particular substance beyond their original studies as scholars. No words needed parsing: meaning was shared. Their friendship evolved beyond content of theology into the content of personal cost of truth between two seekers. Farina and Khan have been friends for 30 years. They first met at Holy Cross High School in Dhaka, Bangladesh. Their paths separated only to converge once again in Boston. Together, they discuss rich resources for dialogue from their Muslim and Christian ways of life. Phan writes of Nguyen Tu Cuong, a friend first "met" through a book. His friend inspired and supported him deeply, offering him courage in a dark time. For Phan, there is salvific and liberative power in friendship. Aihiokhai was powerfully transformed though his missionary work. Ironically, although he was sent to convert and catechize, it was a traditional African Indigenous priestess who "converted" him. Moved by the power of her hospitality, Aihiokhai learned that to convert the other was not respectful, helpful, or needed. With his ongoing conversion, he came to see a whole new possibility: absolute openness to encounter.

Rita George-Tvrtković, Bradley J. Malkovsky, Mugdha Yeolekar, Tracy Tiemeier, and Marinus Iwuchukwu all describe dialogue in the context of family and family connections. George-Tvrtković takes us inside her household and writes of her Bosnian Muslim mother-in-law, Izeta. She and Izeta grew from a simple kinship into a friendship that is precious and life giving. For George-Tvrtković, the notion of interfaith kinship can be helpful for its ability to spark dialogue between people otherwise unlikely to speak across religious borders and to sustain dialogue over the long haul—even and especially when the conversation gets difficult. It was Malkovsky's wife, Mariam, who introduced him to a Shiite Muslim from Iran, Rasoul Rasoulipour. Their friendship is family-to-family. Their lesson is deeper than any course on interfaith dialogue: in the hearts of two men is a felt-presence of a shared God. Although Tracy Sayuki Tiemeier and Mughda Yeolekar were colleagues, it was their toddler daughters who really sparked conversation and friendship. In the end, they let the lessons of their daughters instruct them in their professional and theological work. Marinus Iwuchukwu focuses on his friendships and encounters with two African traditional religionists: Mazi Ihenachor Unachukwu, his maternal grandfather, and Mazi Nweke Ozieme, the grandfather of his high school girlfriend. These African elders did not try to convert him. They offered pure friendship and hospitality. This gives Iwuchukwu a profound appreciation of religious pluralism.

Finally, Reid Locklin, Karen Enriquez, and James L. Fredericks show us how teachers become friends. Locklin offers in-depth access to his teacher/guru, Swami Paramarthananda. The friendship involved personal interaction, a challenge when encountering the absolute freedom of a liberated being. The relationship then continued in physical absence, as Locklin reviewed the cassette tape recordings of Swamiji's lectures and classes. Enriquez details her relationship with mentor, John Makransky. As a teacher-student relationship, the friendship was expressed with reserve and reverence. His capacity for silence to receive each student not only captured her own experience of being heard, but she also continues to this day the technique of slowly responding to students and taking each question, then pausing to give them that same reverence. And so the dialogue gets deeper and deeper. This is not scholastic talk and abstract theory, but taking the fabric of our lived experience of good and evil and making sense of our options in this current world of ours. Fredericks reflects on his friendship with the late Masao Abe. This complex and deep relationship leads him to a profound insight: if this is friendship, it is profoundly one of difference. It is the other and the distinctiveness of the other that allow for shared space and dialogue. This is the very point: a friend cannot define the other.

These essays are precious pearls of wisdom, strung together into a beautiful necklace. Each pearl is beautiful on its own; we come to know each person better, deeper. Together, we come to know each other and grow together as a diverse, yet united, "we." Many readers of this book can add their own encounters that will continue to deepen their own faith and provide a spaciousness opening them up to this transformative interfaith "we" experience. Not everyone has the opportunity for interfaith friendships like the ones described here, but we all have friends that, with some effort, we can call on together toward spiritual depth and mutual transformation. We need not waste any opportunity to call each other for "more."

My own story of "we" involves nuns and monks from a variety of religious traditions. Monastic interfaith dialogue is unique, for while the differences of religious thought and practice are real, the similar lifestyles bring us together in deep ways. But it requires particular discretion, in order to protect and respect our friends' vowed membership in community. Our dialogues are intensely personal and often confidential. Our stories are often too sacred, too close to report in public forums or books. I cannot yet share my own stories of interreligious friendship. To do so would be to violate friendship's bonds and possibly harm the people I love.

Indeed, all friendships are defined as much by what we cannot say about them as what we can say about them. Here, the monastic value of silence offers us an important caveat for a discussion on friendship. Friendship requires prudent and respectful silence, a silence that has to come from the deep quiet within ourselves. Silence awakens our spiritual senses and provides reverent space for receiving the holy in ourselves, others, and the world. Silence attracts us to holiness wherever it may be found, and leads us, perhaps ironically, to dialogue. Silence listens attentively to the other. Silence offers trust that we are safe together. Silence bends the knee, bows the head, clasps the hand, and strikes the heart.

According to the great monk, Thomas Merton, there's a natural progression to be at home with others who differ and to find great satisfaction in paradox, mystery, and the unknowable.[1] Differences do not divide, but instead allow for an experience of solidarity, and even communion. And thus, we are different and the same, one and many, entirely our own and part of a cosmic whole. We apprehend our life fully and wholly from an inner ground that is at once more universal than the empirical ego and yet entirely our own. In a similar way, all of these authors came to feel at home with persons from very different traditions. Whether the friendship was entirely egalitarian or somewhat asymmetrical, brief or long, familial or academic, the world was forever changed for the authors when they came to know and be known by their friends. These friends report a graced way of living in love and solidarity. If *Nostra Aetate* has changed the Church, then the interreligious friendships that have come from *Nostra Aetate* are changing the world.

Note

1. See Thomas Merton, "Final Integration: Toward a Monastic Therapy," in *Merton and Sufism: The Untold Story: A Complete Compendium*, ed. Rob Baker and Gray Henry (Louisville, KY: Fons Vitae, 1999), 266–277.

Contributors

SimonMary Asese Aihiokhai, PhD, is lecturer of Theological Studies at Loyola Marymount University (Los Angeles, CA). His research and publications engage religion and identity in Islam, Christianity, and African Traditional Religions; African approaches to virtue ethics; philosophy, culture, and theology; theology and economics; religion and violence; theological, cultural, philosophical, and sociological issues facing Catholicism in Africa; and interreligious dialogue in the global South.

Mary C. Boys, SNJM, PhD, is dean of Academic Affairs and Skinner and McAlpin Professor of Practical Theology at Union Theological Seminary (New York). Boys has received honorary doctorates from Hebrew College-Jewish Institute of Religion (2004), The Catholic Theological Union (2007), The Jewish Theological Seminary of America (2011), and Gratz College (2012). She was the recipient of the Sternberg Award from the International Council of Christians and Jews in 2005. Her books include *Jewish-Christian Dialogue: One Woman's Experience* (Paulist, 1997), *Has God Only One Blessing? Judaism as a Source of Christian Self-Understanding* (Paulist, 2000), *Christians and Jews in Dialogue: Learning in the Presence of the Other* (SkyLight Paths, 2006; co-authored with Sara S. Lee), and *Redeeming Our Sacred Story: The Death of Jesus and Relations between Jews and Christians* (Paulist, 2013).

David B. Burrell, CSC, PhD, is Theodore Hesburgh Professor emeritus in Philosophy and Theology at the University of Notre Dame (Notre Dame, IN), and is currently serving the Holy Cross congregation in Bangladesh. His service as rector of the Tantur Ecumenical Institute in Jerusalem (1980) has spurred sustained inquiry into comparative theology, including: *Knowing the Unknowable God: Ibn-Sina, Maimonides, Aquinas* (University of Notre Dame Press, 1986), *Freedom and Creation in Three Traditions* (University of Notre Dame Press, 1993), *Original Peace: Restoring God's Creation* (Paulist, 1998; co-authored with Elena Malits), *Friendship and Ways to Truth* (University of Notre Dame Press,

2000), *Faith and Freedom: An Interfaith Perspective* (Wiley-Blackwell, 2004), *Learning to Trust in Freedom: Signs from Jewish, Christian, and Muslim Traditions* (University of Scranton Press, 2010), and *Towards a Jewish-Christian-Muslim Theology* (Wiley-Blackwell, 2011).

John C. Cavadini, PhD, is professor of Theology at the University of Notre Dame (Notre Dame, IN), where he served as chair of the Department from 1997–2010. At Notre Dame, he also serves as the McGrath-Cavadini Director of the Institute for Church Life. His areas of scholarly specialization include the theology of the early Church, with special focus on St. Augustine and Origen, and on patristic exegesis of the Bible.

Francis X. Clooney, SJ, PhD, is Parkman Professor of Divinity and professor of Comparative Theology at Harvard Divinity School, Harvard University (Cambridge, MA), and, since 2010, director of the Center for the Study of World Religions. In July 2010, he was elected a Fellow of the British Academy, and he has received two honorary doctorates. Clooney's books include: *Beyond Compare: St. Francis de Sales and Sri Vedanta Desika on Loving Surrender to God* (Georgetown University Press, 2008), *The Truth, the Way, the Life: Christian Commentary on the Three Holy Mantras of the Srivaisnava Hindus* (Peeters Publishing, 2008), *Comparative Theology: Deep Learning across Religious Borders* (Wiley-Blackwell, 2010), and *His Hiding Place Is Darkness: A Hindu-Catholic Theopoetics of Divine Absence* (Stanford University Press, 2013).

Karen B. Enriquez, PhD, is assistant professor in Comparative Theology at Xavier University (Cincinnati, OH). She received her PhD from Boston College, where she focused on the comparison of Buddhism and Christianity. Her research interests include the comparison of spiritual practices in Buddhism and Christianity and the transformation of the self and society, dialogue among religions, and Filipino and other contextual theologies.

Marianne Farina, CSC, PhD, is a religious sister of the Congregation of the Sisters of the Holy Cross (Notre Dame, IN) and associate professor at the Dominican School of Philosophy and Theology (Berkeley, CA). She teaches courses in social ethics, virtue, sexual ethics, philosophical ethics, Islamic philosophy, human rights, and Muslim-Christian dialogue. She worked for 11 years in Bangladesh as a teacher, pastoral assistant, and school supervisor, and ministered with Muslim, Christian, Hindu, Buddhist, and Tribal communities. With more than 35 years of experience in education and pastoral ministry, Farina seeks to promote social justice and interfaith dialogue in the United States, Africa, and Asia.

James L. Fredericks, PhD, is a Roman Catholic priest of the Archdiocese of San Francisco and professor of Theological Studies at Loyola Marymount University (Los Angeles, CA). He specializes in interreligious dialogue and comparative theology, particularly with Buddhism and Christianity. He is the author of *Faith among Faiths: Christian Theology and the Non-Christian Religions* (Paulist, 1999) and *Buddhists and Christians: Through Comparative Theology to a New Solidarity* (Orbis, 2004).

Mary Margaret Funk, OSB, MA, MS, is a Benedictine nun of Our Lady of Grace Monastery (Beech Grove, IN). From 1994 through 2004, she served as executive director of Monastic Interreligious Dialogue, which fosters dialogue among monastics of the world's religions. She spoke at the World's Parliament of Religions in 1993. She traveled to India and Tibet on the Sixth Spiritual Exchange Program in 1995 and 1999, and has been in formal dialogue with Hindu, Zen Buddhist, Islam, Confucius, Taoist traditions. She holds graduate degrees from Catholic University (1973) and Indiana University (1979), and is a graduate of Epiphany Certification Program of Formative Spirituality (2002).

Rita George-Tvrtković, PhD, is assistant professor of Theology at Benedictine University (Lisle, IL), where she specializes in historical theology and medieval Christian-Muslim relations. She is the author of *A Christian Pilgrim in Medieval Iraq: Riccoldo da Montecroce's Encounter with Islam* (Brepols, 2012).

Marinus Chijioke Iwuchukwu, PhD, is associate professor of Theology at Duquesne University (Pittsburgh, PA). He specializes in interreligious dialogue, religious pluralism, and media and religion. Among his publications are *Media Ecology and Religious Pluralism: Engaging Walter Ong and Jacques Dupuis toward Effective Interreligious Dialogue* (Lambert Academic Publishing, 2010), *Muslim-Christian Dialogue in Post-Colonial Northern Nigeria and the Challenges of Inclusive Cultural and Religious Pluralism* (Palgrave Macmillan, 2013), and a coedited volume, *Can Muslims and Christians Resolve their Religious and Social Conflicts? Cases from Africa and the United States* (Edwin Mellen, 2013). He is also the current chair of the Duquesne University Christian-Muslim Dialogue committee.

Masarrat Khan, MA, started her career as a teacher at Rotary School (Khulna, Bangladesh), after graduating from Holy Cross College (Dhaka, Bangladesh) in 1967. Khan took a break from teaching and was admitted to Dhaka University, completing a master's degree in English literature in 1976. She then joined the faculty of Holy Cross School (Dhaka,

Bangladesh) and taught English language and literature to the upper division classes. In 1996, Khan, with a few associates, set up a school that focused on children with learning disabilities and special needs. She retired in 2012.

Reid B. Locklin, PhD, is associate professor of Christianity and the Intellectual Tradition at the University of Toronto, a joint appointment with St. Michael's College and the Department for the Study of Religion. He is the author of *Spiritual but Not Religious?* (Liturgical Press, 2005) and *Liturgy of Liberation* (Peeters, 2011), as well as various essays and articles in comparative theology and Hindu-Christian studies.

Bradley J. Malkovsky, PhD, is associate professor of Comparative Theology at the University of Notre Dame (Notre Dame, IN). His most recent book, *God's Other Children: Personal Encounters with Faith, Love, and Holiness in Sacred India* (HarperOne, 2013), won the Huston Smith Publishing Prize from HarperOne publishers. He is editor of the *Journal of Hindu-Christian Studies.*

Peter C. Phan, PhD, is a Roman Catholic priest of the Diocese of Dallas and Ignacio Ellacuría chair of Catholic Social Thought at Georgetown University (Washington, DC). Phan was president of the Catholic Theological Society of America (CTSA) in 2001–2002 and has won the John Courtney Murray Award (2010), the highest honor of the CTSA. His books include *Culture and Eschatology: The Iconographical Vision of Paul Evdokimmov* (Peter Lang, 1985), *Eternity in Time: A Study of Karl Rahner's Eschatology* (Susquehanna University Press, 1988), *Mission and Catechesis: Alexandre de Rhodes and Inculturation in Seventeenth-Century Vietnam* (Orbis, 1998), *Christianity with an Asian Face: Asian American Theology in the Making* (Orbis, 2003), *In Our Own Tongues: Perspectives from Asia on Mission and Inculturation* (Orbis, 2003), and *Being Religious Interreligiously: Asian Perspectives on Interfaith Dialogue* (Orbis, 2004).

Elena Procario-Foley, PhD, is Brother John G. Driscoll Professor of Jewish-Catholic Studies and associate professor of Religious Studies at Iona College (New Rochelle, NY), where she has chaired the Religious Studies Department since 2008. She is immediate past chair of the Council of Centers on Jewish-Catholic Relations, and has previously served on the boards of the College Theology Society and the Catholic Theological Society of America. She currently serves on the board of directors for the Stimulus Foundation of Paulist Press, which fosters publications in Jewish-Christian Studies, as well as on the board of the Manhattan College Holocaust, Genocide, and Interfaith Center.

Rosemary Radford Ruether, PhD, is a senior scholar at the Claremont School of Theology and the Claremont Graduate University (Claremont, CA). She is the Carpenter Professor of Feminist Theology emerita at the Graduate Theological Union (Berkeley, CA). She taught for 27 years at the Garrett Theological Seminary and Northwestern University (Evanston, IL). She is the author or editor of 48 books, among them a three-volume *Encyclopedia of Women and Religion in North America* (Indiana University Press, 2006). Her most recent books include *America, Amerikkka: Elect Nation and Imperial Violence* (Equinox, 2007) and *Many Forms of Madness: A Family's Struggle with Mental Illness and the Mental Health System* (Fortress, 2010).

Tracy Sayuki Tiemeier, PhD, is associate professor of Theological Studies at Loyola Marymount University (Los Angeles, CA). She teaches and researches in the areas of Hinduism, comparative theology, interreligious dialogue, feminist theology, Asian and Asian American theology, and religion and popular culture. She also cochairs the Los Angeles Hindu-Catholic Dialogue.

Mugdha Yeolekar, PhD, is lecturer of Theological Studies at Loyola Marymount University (Los Angeles, CA). She received her doctorate in religious studies from Arizona State University. Her research interests include agency, gender and religion, materiality and religion, and ritual reading of Hindu scriptures. In particular, her work focuses on religion in Maharashtra, India, with reference to the above topics.

Index

Printed in the USA
CPSIA information can be obtained
at www.ICGtesting.com
LVHW051523010823
754048LV00003B/71

9 781349 501120